Optimal Human Being

An Integrated Multi-Level Perspective

Optimal Human Being

An Integrated Multi-Level Perspective

Kennon M. Sheldon
University of Missouri–Columbia

2004

LAWRENCE ERLBAUM ASSOCIATES, PUBLISHERS
Mahwah, New Jersey London

Lawrence Erlbaum Associates, Inc., Publishers
10 Industrial Avenue
Mahwah, New Jersey 07430

Cover photo taken by author Kennon M. Sheldon
Cover design by Kathryn Houghtaling Lacey

Library of Congress Cataloging-in-Publication Data

Sheldon, Kennon M. (Kennon Marshall)
    Optimal human being : an integrated approach / Kennon M. Sheldon
        p. cm.
Includes bibliographical references and index.
ISBN 0-8058-4188-1 (cloth : alk. Paper)
ISBN 0-8058-4189-x (pbk. : alk. Paper)
    1. Self-actualization (Psychology) 2. Personality.   I. Title.

BF637.S4S517 2004
155.2'5—dc22   2004046924
                                                        CIP

Books published by Lawrence Erlbaum Associates are printed on acid-free paper, and their bindings are chosen for strength and durability.

Printed in the United States of America
10 9 8 7 6 5 4 3 2

Contents

Preface

Given the perennial salience of human misery, failure, intolerance, and brutality, it may be naïve to write a book dealing with the concept of *optimal human being*. Sometimes it seems that there is precious little optimal functioning going on. Indeed, given my own faults and failings (just ask my children), I have to wonder whether I could possibly be justified in undertaking such a task. What makes me think I have the requisite wisdom and authority, or that I am personally evolved enough to write about such a topic?

Obviously, I persisted. I was motivated to continue not by a desire to become a savant or talk show guru, but rather by a desire to share some fascinating new ideas about the nature of human nature. These ideas suggest that an optimistic and appreciative view of human nature is warranted. People are, literally, amazing—we already have all of the abilities we need to solve our problems, we simply need to learn to use these abilities more effectively. I hope to convince my readers that optimal human being is not so mysterious or far from our grasp as we might think—in fact, many people have already achieved it. Of course, one can always improve no matter how well one is doing—but many of us are doing quite well already, better than we think.

I was also motivated to communicate the emerging scientific data that supports these positive ideas concerning human nature. Of course, many self-help books are written on these topics every year; books extolling the virtues of the transcendental self, the inner child, right-brain wisdom, the seven habits, and so forth. These books provide elaborated and sometimes ingenious theories about optimal human functioning, make no mistake about it. However, few of these tomes rest their case on empirical research, nor do they tie their advice into the evolving paradigms of mainstream science. Thus, unfortunately, they fail to advance their arguments beyond the uncertain status of mere opinion. In such cases the game (or the sale) goes to the one who can communicate best, whether his or her message is accurate and legitimate. Although the ability to communicate hope and stimulate new thinking within readers is certainly important and can do much good, "the message is more than the medium." In this book I attempt to deliver a scientifically supported message, one that is consistent with much that is found in the self-help books, but that rests on a strong foundation of empirical research.

Thus, although the book is intended primarily for research psychologists and other biological and social scientists, I believe any educated reader will find it interesting and useful. Indeed, one important goal of the book is to provide readers with concrete tools they can use to effect personal growth. In addition, the book also serves as a useful supplemental text for graduate or undergraduate courses in personality psychology; one aim of the book is to canvass and integrate contemporary personality theory (as described next). Finally, the book served as a text or supplement for courses in motivation, positive psychology, well-being, personal growth, or positive adaptation.

Scientific Goals and Structure of the Book

My first goal is to provide an integrative framework within which to locate all the human sciences. This is necessary because, as described in chapter 1, to properly consider optimal human being we must consider all the different levels, or facets, of a person—that is, the biochemical, neuronal, cognitive, personality, social, and cultural factors that each make unique contributions to human behavior. Few frameworks exist for considering all such factors at once and in combination, and thus in chapter 2, I propose a comprehensive conceptual hierarchy of levels of influence on human behavior, ranging from biological, to cognitive, personality, social, and cultural. I show that one can locate all of the various human sciences within the framework, giving each a secure place within the whole. In addition, the framework can be used to consider all the major factors that can help cause any particular behavior, and also to consider the contingencies and interactions between factors at different levels of analysis. After presenting this framework, I use it to briefly consider some important philosophical questions such as free will versus determinism, reductionism versus holism, scientific consilience versus scientific pluralism, and the potential utility of the framework for the social sciences.

Chapter 3 focuses in detail on one of the levels of analysis discussed in chapter 2, namely, personality. I consider several overarching models of personality, before settling on a hierarchy consisting of species-typical organismic characteristics, on which rest personality traits, goals and intentions, and selves and life stories. I show that this 4-level hierarchy can be substituted seamlessly into the more general hierarchy of potential causes of human behavior developed in chapter 2, helping to make personality theory more consilient with other natural and human sciences.

Chapters 4 through 7 focus in depth on each subsequent level of the personality hierarchy, examining the state of the art in each area. After introducing the major relevant concepts at each level, I consider their implications for the question of optimal human being. What prescriptions or recommendations for optimal human being might be derived at each level of analysis? Specifically, chapter 4 considers evolved human nature in terms of species-typical physiological needs, psychological needs, sociocognitive mechanisms, and sociocultural practices. Chapter 5 considers personality trait theory, and the question of whether traits have legitimate causal status in and of themselves, or whether they are instead merely effects of lower-level genetic or biological factors. Chapter 6 considers goals and intentions, making use of both "systemic" and "organismic" theoretical perspectives to consider the nature of optimal goal-striving. Finally, chapter 7 considers the nature and functions of the self, arguing that the concept of a "psychological homunculus" is worth reviving, and may supply the best way of thinking about the self and optimal selfhood.

Chapters 8 and 9 consider two even higher levels of analysis within the larger picture, which are relevant to but which go beyond personality: social interactions and culture. Chapter 8 uses evolutionary game theory and social role theory to analyze the nature of positive social interactions and make prescriptions for optimal human being at this level of analysis. Chapter 9 considers the relation between cultural and genetic evolution, the causal status of the cultural level of analysis, and the implications of different cultural types for the optimal functioning of their members.

Finally, chapter 10 collects all the earlier recommendations together into a set of 28 "prescriptions" for optimal human being. Chapter 10 also explores the question of whether there can be content- or value-free conceptualizations of optimal human being, perhaps involving consistency between the different levels of the person, no matter what content occupies those levels. In the context of this discussion, five "meta-prescriptions" for optimal human being are suggested that move beyond consideration of optimal human being from within each level of analysis, to consider it in terms of the functioning of the system as a whole. Finally, chapter 10 considers the question of the optimal relations between the different human sciences. I advocate a form of hierarchical pluralism where each level of analysis has its own legitimate place and effects, depending on the behavioral phenomenon being studied. However, I also advocate giving the greatest attention to the foundational level of personality, because only by understanding basic human nature (i.e., how all human beings are the same) can we hope to understand the meaning of human differences.

In summary, this book tackles two large and perennially debated questions: How can research scientists best integrate the different levels of analysis within the human sciences to create a complete picture? And how can individual persons best integrate the different levels or facets of themselves to achieve optimal being? I describe how these two questions complement each other and converge in important ways.

ACKNOWLEDGMENTS

I would like to acknowledge the positive influences of John Donaldson, my stepfather and a dedicated determinist, who has continually challenged me concerning many of the issues in this book. I also thank Tim Kasser, my long-term collaborator, who gave me detailed feedback on an earlier draft of this manuscript; Andrew Elliot, another frequent collaborator, for his help in elaborating the self-concordance construct; Robert Emmons, my graduate mentor, who taught me the importance of understanding positive goal-striving; Edward Deci and Richard Ryan, my postdoctoral mentors, who taught me that humanistic issues can be studied with empirical rigor; and Melanie Sheldon, my wife, who provided an invaluable sounding board throughout this project. Finally, I would like to thank David Myers, Richard Koestner, Jack Bauer, Eunkook Suh, and Shige Oishi, who reviewed earlier versions of the manuscript, as well as an anonymous reviewer. Their comments were invaluable in focusing the final product that you now hold in your hands.

1

What Is Optimal Human Being?

Can you to bring to mind a person who seems to have achieved a state of harmony, both between the different parts of herself and between herself and the world? Someone who is actively involved in life, who is successful, who seems to be unusually happy and satisfied, and who also enhances and make happier those around him? Hopefully we can all think of at least one such person, who seems to have reached some "optimal" way of functioning and being. What is different about this person, compared to those more entangled in the ordinary? Can his or her quality of living be measured and quantified? Could his or her mode of being have been predicted in advance, knowing everything about that person's constitution and history? Is there a theory out there that can explain this person, and perhaps tell us how to be more like him or her? Obviously these are very pressing questions, whose answers might tell us much about how to improve both individual lives, and human life as a whole. In this book I hope to begin to provide some answers to them.

SCOPE AND GOALS OF THE BOOK

My first task is to outline the overall goals of the book, so that the reader may grasp the scope of the journey I propose. In this chapter, I begin by discussing the term *optimal human being,* showing the difficulty of defining it. The primary difficulty may be this: Human beings are extremely complex systems, whose activities, interactions, and outcomes can be examined from very many different perspectives. Reflecting this fact is the broad suite of human sciences, ranging from evolutionary psychology to biological psychology to cognitive psychology to personality psychology to social psychology to sociology to cultural psychology. As discussed in chapter 2, each of these can be said to occupy a different "level of analy-

1

sis" in a hierarchy of possible causes of human behavior. Assuming that each perspective or level of analysis is equally important and legitimate, then presumably each can provide unique information concerning human being and human nature, and also concerning the nature of optimal human being.

Thus, in order to understand optimal human being as inclusively as possible, I consider the question from a wide variety of different perspectives. As an organizing framework for this inquiry, I consider these perspectives in hierarchical order, moving from lower and more biologically based levels of analysis, to higher and more socially based levels. Specifically, there will be chapters drawing from evolutionary psychology, personality psychology, social psychology, and cultural psychology. Within each chapter I first present and compare the predominant issues and theories within that field, in order to understand each level's depiction of basic human nature. Then, toward the end of each chapter, I consider what each field or level of analysis might have to say about optimal human being.

A second major theme for the book, implied by its title, is that of the relations between the different fields and levels of analysis. For example, how does social personality relate to personality psychology, and how does evolutionary psychology relate to cultural psychology? Are the effects observed by scientists within any particular fields reducible to the effects observed within a lower level field, such that the first field's theoretical perspective is non-parsimonious and perhaps unnecessary for understanding human behavior? For example, might culture-level effects be reducible to sociobiology, or personality-level effects be reducible to cognitive psychology? If so, then perhaps culture-level or personality-level effects and concepts do not need to be considered in a "final" model of human behavior.

One reason for exploring this second theme is that integration between the different perspectives and levels of analysis on human behavior is sorely needed. There is too little cross-talk and cross-theorizing between the different human sciences, and too much chest thumping and turf defending. I hope to propose some novel ideas about how to think about the different disciplines in relation to each other. But the second and more important reason for considering positive relations between the different human sciences is that this inquiry may provide substantial leverage for understanding the first theme of the book, that is, the nature of optimal human being. As discussed later, optimal human being may involve having harmonious relations between the different levels within one's personal existence (i.e., between one's evolved nature, one's personality, one's social relationships, and one's culture). By better understanding the connections between these different levels of scientific analysis, we may gain tools and analogies for better understanding positive connections between the corresponding aspects of a person. In other words, there may be a potentially important convergence between the task of integrating or optimizing the human sciences, and the task of understanding the integrated or optimized human being.

Because my training is in personality psychology, and because I believe that the personality level of analysis may be particularly important for understanding optimal human being, the book will devote particular attention to this level. Specifically, I propose four different levels of analysis contained *within* the level of personality, namely, organismic foundations, personality traits, goals/intentions, and selves/self-concepts. Each personality topic will receive its own chapter, and of course, the boundary relations between the four topics will also be considered. During these four chapters I hope to provide an inclusive framework that can help integrate contemporary personality theory, as well as provide better understanding of the integrated human personality.

In sum, then, this book has three major goals. The first goal is to consider the nature of optimal human being, with the aim of arriving at a reasonably comprehensive understanding of the phrase by the end of the book. This question is focal in chapters 1 and 10, and is discussed primarily in the latter part of the other eight chapters. A second goal, which will occupy much of the book, is to canvass and in some cases criticize the state of the art in a wide variety of human sciences (personality theory being just one exemplar), while also examining some possible linkages between these different perspectives. In addition, we consider the ontological basis for each level of analysis, asking whether each in turn might be reducible to lower levels of analysis, such that that level need not be considered in a "final" model of human behavior. The premise is that we need to do such an evaluation before we can make informed speculations about the multilevel nature of optimal human being. The third goal of the book is to propose a novel conceptual framework for the field of personality psychology, in which the major domains of personality theory and research can be located, and also, to illuminate the ways in which personality psychology can be considered in relation to the other human sciences, such as evolutionary biology, anthropology, and cognitive psychology. These issues are addressed primarily in chapters 3 through 7.

These may be overly ambitious objectives. However, as E. O. Wilson (1998) argued in his noteworthy book, *Consilience: The Unity of Knowledge,* the sciences *should* fit together—after all, it's all one self-consistent universe. If so, then the task of mapping out the basic relations between the different human sciences, and also between the different aspects of the person, may be tractable after all. It is my hope that the quest to understand optimal human being will provide a useful lens for studying these relations, and vice versa.

DEFINING OPTIMAL HUMAN BEING

Political Considerations in Studying Optimal Human Being

In beginning to talk about "optimal human being," we immediately run into a problem: that in so doing we might be forced to make subjective and potentially invalid value judgments about what is optimal. Given the wide differences between individuals and between cultures, who is to say what is optimal, or that the optimal is the same for every person? Perhaps it is necessarily a question of cultural preference or personal choice, and should not be the subject of scientific study. Indeed, the idea that there is an optimal way to be is to some extent a politically incorrect perspective—many psychologists would instead subscribe to an eclectic point of view, in which there are many possible life paths, none of which are any better than any other. Some have suggested that to believe the opposite may be to fall into a self-aggrandizing or culturally insensitive trap, as well as into scientific error (Kendler, 1999). Thus, those interested in human potential may inevitably have to walk a difficult line between subjective values and objective science. Can a scientist both believe in and hope to promote a set of values, and be an objective investigator concerning those values? Maybe not (but see Sheldon, Schmuck, & Kasser, 2000, for a counterargument).

A related issue is whether it is even safe to study optimal human being, given the difficult moral and ethical implications that come along with acquiring such knowledge. For example, if we are able to say that a particular way of being is "best," does this mean we should try to "make" people be that way? That is, should optimal ways of being be legislated or even mandated? This is an uncomfortable notion, which intuition suggests, if implemented, would be doomed to backfire. Again, there is a danger here—that scientists working in the area of optimal human being may become zealots and inadvisedly try to cross the treacherous bridge leading from "is" to "ought" (Kendler, 1999). The examples of Timothy Leary and Richard Alpert, the LSD advocates of the late 1960s, suggest that it is perhaps a shorter step than we realize from scientific neutrality to sociospiritual crusader! And of course, religious crusaders, convinced that their version of the good life ought to be adopted by all, have been guilty of many horrendous crimes throughout history.

Still, the obvious fact remains that some people get more out of life and contribute more to society than others. They thrive and flourish, whereas others do not. Again, what is different about these people? This is an ancient question, reaching back to Greek philosophers' inquiries into the nature of virtue, continuing through the Renaissance and Enlightenment philosophers' strivings for tolerance and reason, and into the 20th century through the humanists' inquiries into self-actualization and the nature of the fully functioning person (as is elaborated in the next section, which is a historical review). Indeed, the question of the ideal life has once again come to the fore in the contemporary scene, as "positive psychologists" attempt to list core human strengths and virtues, redressing empirical psychology's predominant focus on human malaise and deficiencies (Seligman & Csikszentmihalyi, 2000; Sheldon & King, 2001). One supplemental aim for this book is to help provide more solid theoretical foundations for positive psychology (Lazarus, 2003).

Choice of the Phrase "Optimal Human Being"

Before beginning to consider theoretical perspectives, I should first clarify what I mean by the phrase "optimal human being," as well as by each of the three words within the phrase. In using the overall phrase, I do not mean to refer to any particular human being, nor to any particular "optimal" human being (i.e., Mother Theresa). Instead, I mean to refer to the empirically documented features that tend to characterize high-quality human functioning. "Optimal human being" is a profile that we try to develop within the book, by consulting what contemporary theorizing at many different levels of analysis might have to say about what causes optimal functioning. Notably, this profile might be construed either as a set of consequences and outcomes resultant from optimal human functioning, or as a set of paths and prescriptions leading to optimal human functioning. In most of the literatures we survey, it is still too soon to make a clear distinction between pathways and outcomes.

Turning to the three words in the phrase: First, I do not mean to refer to *optimal* as unattainable or as involving perfection. Instead, optimal means to have attained a reasonably successful and rewarding means of functioning, in the face of whatever circumstances one encounters. It means to be at least in the top third of the distribution formed by those people with circumstances similar to oneself, on variables or processes known to be predictive or indicative of health, growth, and happiness. As this implies, optimal personality functioning is not defined in terms of any particular constructs (i.e., via high self-esteem, self-regulation, self-actualization, subjective well-being, ego development, etc.), but rather is understood to be inclusive of a wide variety of such constructs. Although there are certainly important differences between these various conceptions of human thriving (Keyes, Shmotkin, & Ryff, 2002), I believe there is also a latent commonality underlying them, such that people who manifest any one such characteristic are also more likely to manifest many if not most of the others (Compton, Smith, Cornish, & Qualls, 1996). A major goal of this book is to try to understand this latent factor.

Turning to the second word in the phrase, *human:* This may need no explanation, but it is perhaps worth stating that what is optimal for a human being is likely to be different from what is optimal for other animals or entities—human beings have a distinctive way of being, which is optimized in its own way. Thus, I assume that there is a core human nature (Pinker, 2002) that we need to understand before we can understand optimal human being. To illustrate, consider that we would not expect to be able to understand why a particular automobile performs so well without first understanding the basic principles underlying the prototypical automobile. Chapter 4 considers prototypical human nature in detail.

Turning to the third word in the phrase: I do not mean to refer to *being* as a passive state or condition. Instead, I would like to define it as a verb, denoting a person's "way" of being (Maslow, 1962). In other words, the act of living requires people to project an intentional attitude into the world, in which they literally choose their way of being and living (consciously or not), as they go along. As this activist conception implies, optimal human being may be in part something that people do, rather than something they are. Thus, it may also be something that we can create, and re-create, for ourselves; we are not simply fated by our genes, history, or circumstances to maintain suboptimal states of being. Chapter 5 explores the latter issue in depth, in a discussion of the heritability versus changeability of happiness and subjective well-being.

HISTORICAL AND CONTEMPORARY PERSPECTIVES
ON OPTIMAL HUMAN BEING

Before presenting my own working definition of optimal human being, it is first useful to consider where the field has been already. Thus, in this section of the chapter I consider the history of Western thought on the topic of optimal human being (notably, I omit discussion of Eastern thought, because most of it does not fit easily into the hierarchy of levels of analysis in which I wish to ground the book). Of course, the history of Western thought and research concerning human potential and thriving could easily form the subject for an entire book (Tarnas, 1991). However, I try to boil it down to a few pages, beginning with the ancient Hebrews and Greeks, continuing on through the Middle and Renaissance ages, and on up to the present day.

The development of Western thought regarding optimal human being is usefully summarized in terms of a cycling between hedonistic and eudaemonist philosophical perspectives (Ryan & Deci, 2000; Waterman, 1993). This distinction is worth employing in this historical review, because it foreshadows several other important issues that are explored in the book. Hedonism views the "good" in terms of maximizing the pleasure–pain balance, and tends to assume that narrow self-interest is the driving force behind human behavior. In other words, this perspective views humans as relatively selfish, pleasure-seeking animals. In contrast, eudaemonism regards optimal human being in terms of the actualization of ideal potentials, visions, or quests. It tends to assume that there are inherent meanings or truths, contained or embedded in reality, that the virtuous human can learn to access and express. Thus, this perspective views human beings as relatively noble, meaning-seeking creatures, who are perhaps even on their way to perfection. The hedonism/eudaemonia dichotomy is very basic, and can also be seen reflected in the contrast between analytic versus intuitive, reductionistic versus holistic, and "disenchanted" versus "enchanted" theoretical perspectives (Kendler, 1999). Is the theorist an optimist and even an idealist regarding human nature, or rather a realist and even a cynic?

The ancient Greeks helped to found both types of perspective. Some schools of Greek philosophical thought were hedonistic in their conception of optimal human being, viewing it as arising when sensory pleasures are maximized (epicurianism) or when the sting of displeasure is minimized (stoicism). Similarly, the skeptics and the sophists disavowed the possibility of grander or deeper meaning, recommending that the road to the "good life" requires giving up such quests, in favor of relativism, comfort, and moderation. In this view, the idea that it is possible to know reality and find truth is a false belief, which should be dispensed with forthwith.

However, the roots of eudaemonia can also be found in Greek thought. For example, Socrates emphasized that virtue involves transcending pleasure seeking to develop deeper knowledge of "the good." From his perspective, the road to the good life involves careful self-examination ("know thyself"); although this may reveal unpleasant truths, the important thing is that truth is indeed approached.

Plato developed these ideas further in his cave parable, suggesting that virtue involves waking to the world of ideal forms and abstract meanings. Optimal human being, in this view, occurs when we can directly apprehend beauty, truth, and goodness. These exist on a transcendent level of pure ideas, which must be approached if one is to escape delusion.

Although Aristotle is typically contrasted with Plato because of his orientation toward empiricism and classification, he also emphasized a eudamonist view: According to Aristotle, virtuous living involves finding the "golden mean," leading to moral perfection and a balanced and harmonious mode of life. Although they shared an emphasis on using the powers of the mind to penetrate to a meaningful reality, Plato and Aristotle differed in that Aristotle leaned toward logical clarity, and Plato leaned towards intuitive insights. Thus, Aristotle endorsed a more skeptical version of eudaemonia than Plato (Tarnas, 1991).

In medieval times Christian theology dominated the consideration of optimal human being, defining it in terms of adherence to various conceptions of God's law, a tradition that began even earlier with the Hebrews. Real happiness would not come until after death, and then only if one had been sufficiently pious. This perspective was not hedonistic. However, given its emphasis on self-abnegation and unquestioning adherence to scriptural dictates, it was not eudaemonist either, in that meaning, self-expression, and personal growth were beside the point or were even viewed as sinful. Not surprisingly, this view of optimal human being has become increasingly unpopular over the centuries, lingering most conspicuously in certain Islamic societies.

Although the ideal of self-abnegation has been rejected by most world societies, it is worth pointing out that many medieval or scholastic conceptions of religious virtue, including justice, prudence, fortitude, temperance, faith, hope, and charity, still find resonance in some contemporary formulations of the good life. These formulations assume, probably quite rightly, that some degree or forms of self-denial (i.e., prudence and temperance) may be beneficial for optimal human being (Tarnas, 1991).

In the early renaissance, hedonism again came to the fore, as Bacon, Hobbes, Locke, and Hume renounced religious and idealistic conceptions of the good, instead endorsing skepticism and assuming that the rational pursuit of self-interest defines the good. Utilitarianism, functionalism, and Adam Smith's economics all assumed that people were essentially motivated by the desire for personal gain, and that the role of philosophy was to clearly face this fact. However, in the Romantic era the pendulum swung back the other way, toward a vision of self-realization and self-as-quest (Baumeister, 1986). According to Shelly, Byron, Goethe, and Coleridge, we must seek to fulfill our destinies and experience the richest possible emotional life. Obviously, this is a very eudaemonist perspective. But then once again the pendulum swung back, when the romanticist bubble was thoroughly punctured by Nietzsche and Freud. Because Freud may be said to define the start of the modern era, I consider his vision of optimal human being in somewhat more detail next.

Freud's most notable achievement was to point out the unconscious animal lurking behind the veneer of civilization. Freud's was a singularly hedonistic and unflattering vision of humans, one that split the mind into several parts, each with different criteria for success. Optimal human being for the id is unlimited pleasure and gratification, whereas optimal human being for the superego is to achieve control and restraint of immoral impulses. Accordingly, optimal human being for the ego is merely to "stay afloat," in the midst of this profound conflict. That is, the best that man can do, from Freud's perspective, is to strike an uneasy compromise between the hedonistic id, the hapless ego, and the hectoring superego.

Freud's analysis, which paints the conscious ego as a defensive captive of unconscious forces, set the tone for much of the intellectual discourse of the 20th century, in fields as diverse as art history, anthropology, sociology, and comparative literature. Although it was probably a useful counterpoint to the overblown hyperbole of the Romantic era, Freud's vision of optimal human being falls something short of inspirational—meaning and self-expression (eudaemonia) have little place within his theory, except to be dismissed as probable illusions.

Another major theory of human nature in the early and mid 20th century was operant behaviorism. It too endorsed a hedonistic perspective, in that biological needs and pleasures were viewed as the ultimate or primary sources of reinforcement potential (Reeve, 1992). Optimal human being, in B. F. Skinner's (1948) *Walden Two*, arises when reward structures are clear and satisfying, so that biological needs are met, and harmful or antisocial behaviors are never acquired. However, behaviorism offered no real vision of the "good," beyond attaining regular external rewards and minimizing social conflict. Thus, it also fails to address eudaemonist perspectives on optimal human being.

An additional limitation of both operant behaviorism and Freudianism lay in their denial of agency to the conscious individual. In both views the self is a pawn, of one's history of reinforcement on the one hand, and of one's animalistic impulses and psychological defenses on the other. Furthermore, both theories proclaimed, as a matter of principle, that free will is an illusion. It is hard to imagine how people could achieve eudaemonia and a meaningful life starting from this set of assumptions, and indeed, this fact may account for much of the rejection of Freudian and behaviorist theories that occurred at mid-century.

The late 1950s and early 1960s ushered in a very different zeitgeist, as the pendulum swung back toward the intuitive and the subjective. The 1960s, a decade of liberalization and societal upheaval, saw the emergence of "third force" psychology, the human potential movement, and a reclamation of the eudamonist agenda. Not only was the self now to be allowed into the scientific arena, it was to become the very focus of study! Carl Rogers and Abraham Maslow were probably the two most prominent proponents of third force psychology, and thus their views of optimal human being are worth considering in more detail.

Rogers (1961) outlined a coherent and thoughtful vision of optimal human being, or the fully functioning person, as he called it. In his view optimal human being is not a place, but rather a process and, ideally, a lifelong journey. The fully functioning person is one who seeks increasing openness to experience, enhanced awareness of his or her feelings, and reduced defensiveness, over time. She is in touch with herself, and in touch with her "organismic valuing process," so that she is able to make healthy and growth-supportive decisions. Full functioning involves living in the moment, with few preconceptions—taking what is, as it evolves. It also involves developing increasing trust in one's own organism and increasing ability to integrate across social/internal demands, so that the person is able to compute, and then enact, the "most economical vector of need satisfaction" (Rogers, 1961). Notably, need satisfaction in Rogers's perspective does not just involve individual pleasure, but also involves connectivity with important others, and with society as a whole. It is also noteworthy that although Rogers's ideas have received surprisingly little attention in the arena of experimental psychology, Rogers was in favor of empirical research and pioneered some important techniques.

Maslow (1971) defined optimal human being in a somewhat similar way, specifically focusing on the self-actualization process. Self-actualizers evidence eight characteristics:

1. They experience fully, becoming absorbed in the moment.
2. They make the difficult choices, risking pain in the hopes of new growth and integration.
3. They accept themselves, allowing even the negative parts of themselves self-expression.
4. They are honest, taking responsibility for their choices.
5. They attend carefully to their own reactions and experiences, as important life information.
6. They are concerned with developing their strengths and potentials.
7. They have peak experiences, or moments of transcendent insight and vision.
8. They seek to identify, and give up, their psychological defenses.

Maslow's vision of optimal human being is an eloquent one, and his descriptive studies of self-actualized individuals were invaluable to the field, overfocused as it was on human malaise. Notably, however, Maslow resisted empirical study of the question of self-actualization, claiming that large-sample studies miss or even violate the uniqueness and individuality of persons. This insistence helps make Maslow's approach somewhat unpalatable to those who believe that any claims regarding "the good" must be defended with impeccable empirical data. In addition, Maslow claimed that fewer than one person in a thousand achieved self-actualization. This is a decidedly pessimistic view for a theorist so well known for supplying a positive perspective upon human nature! As discussed earlier, I view optimal human being as much more widely accessible than that—arguably, the top third of the population is functioning reasonably optimally.

In parallel with the humanist movement, a related tradition in philosophy also emphasized the struggle of self to attain greater control and integrity: existentialism. Rejecting determinism, existentialist perspectives emphasized the fact that freedom is a defining characteristic of human nature. Humans have no essence, and thus have to make their own, hopefully through their carefully considered choices (Sartre, 1965). In this view, the central struggle for people is coming to terms with their radical freedom, rather than radical determinism. How do we cope with the fact that although we find ourselves already "thrown" into the world, we nevertheless have the next move in the game? Optimal human being is to live fully in the present, with the knowledge that, like it or not, one is necessarily the author of oneself and one's life, in the face of the gaping, undetermined future.

Other mid-century psychological traditions also began to view optimal human being in more meaning-based terms. Within the psychoanalytic tradition, the conscious ego was granted more and more power as the decades went by. Hartmann said that the ego has its own "conflict-free" energy independent of the id, Heinz Kohut championed the primacy of the self and self-processes, and Otto Kernberg discussed the processes of psychic integration. Erich Fromm bridged psychoanalytic and humanistic theory, focusing on the dialectic between "having" (nonoptimal human being) and "being" (optimal human being). Erik Erikson also contributed to this synthesis, supplying a lifespan developmental perspective on optimal human being. In his model, optimal human being involves consolidating and finally transcending one's identity, at the same time that one expands one's range of concerns beyond oneself, taking responsibility for younger people and for the culture as a whole. The "increasingly enlightened ego" conception of optimal human being continued in the latter half of the 20th century, finding expression in Loevinger's work on ego autonomy, Block's work on ego resilience, and Waterman's work on identity as personal expressiveness.

In contemporary social-personality psychology, the trend toward defining optimal human being in terms of eudaemonia is perhaps best represented by Deci and Ryan's self-determination theory (SDT) (1985, 1991, 2000; but see Csikszentmihalyi, 1993, 1997, or Seligman, 2002, for related views). As discussed in greater detail in chapters 4, 6, 7, and 8, SDT emphasizes the struggle of the self to gain greater self-regulatory control over its own behavior, and highlights both the interpersonal (i.e., controlling authorities, nonsupportive environments) and intrapersonal (i.e., ego involvements and nonmastered drives) factors that can detract from optimal human being. As people develop greater self-determination and authorship regarding their lives, they also maximally develop their skills and interests, satisfy psychological needs, and build meaningful relationships with others.

Again, SDT is a decidedly eudaemonist theory of motivation. However, there are also more mechanistic and hedonistic perspectives on human motivation available in the current scene. For example, cybernetic control theory (Carver & Scheier, 1981, 1998) defines optimal human being in terms of the coherent and effective functioning of a hierarchically organized action system. In essence, humans are viewed in terms of a robot metaphor, in which the robot is more or less successful in taking action to move itself toward its programmed ends. Assuming the robot is moving fast enough, positive feelings result. This is a decidedly hedonist perspective, because it does not really matter what the robot is moving toward (love, or money? growth, or image?), or why it is moving (guilt, or conviction? interest, or pressure?). Chapters 2, 3, and 6 discuss control theory in more detail, and chapter 6 discusses some recommended emendations to control theory, based on SDT.

Finally, the hedonistic versus eudaemonia dichotomy is still alive and well in contemporary subjective well-being (SWB) research (Kahneman, Diener, & Schwartz, 1999). Diener and colleagues define SWB in terms of high positive and low negative affect, as well as in terms of feelings of global satisfaction with one's life (Diener, 1994). In their hedonic approach to happiness, SWB is largely a question of experiencing pleasant rather than unpleasant moods, along with achieving a sense of contentment in life. Diener and colleagues are reluctant to accept eudaemonist-type theories of SWB, in part because they are wary of the science/values dichotomy, and also in part because of their concerns regarding the cross-cultural generalizability of any particular perspective on optimal human being (Diener & Suh, 2000). For example, they argue that SDT's emphasis on the universal importance of agency and authenticity may founder because of large cultural differences in autonomy and autonomy-support (Oishi & Diener, 2001; see chap. 4, concerning psychological needs, and chap. 9, concerning cultural processes and optimal human being, for more information on these issues).

In contrast, Ryff and her colleagues (Ryff & Keyes, 1995; Ryff & Singer, 1998) insist that issues of purpose, personal growth, meaning, and social connectedness are essential to understanding SWB; that is, merely having "many positive moods and few negative ones" is not an adequate conception of human thriving. Obviously, this is a much more eudaemonist perspective on well-being than that of the Diener group. Indeed, like SDT, Ryff's view is grounded in the ego, psychosocial, organismic, and humanistic perspectives, discussed earlier, which again tend to focus on the self's quest for enhanced self-development and greater social connectedness.

A MULTILEVEL CONCEPTION OF OPTIMAL HUMAN BEING

As can be seen, there is a wide variety of existing ways of defining and understanding optimal human being. Some of these ways focus on a person's emotional life and experience, others on cognitive growth and the creation of meaning, others on the development of identity, others on positive relations between the person and his or her intimates and community, others on positive functioning or efficient action, and others on the attainment of rewards and reinforcements. Obviously, these different perspectives might lead to widely different prescriptions for how to attain optimal human being. This very fact suggests that a broader view is needed, one that is potentially inclusive with respect to all of the different scientific perspectives that one might bring to bear on the problem.

Ideally, this broader perspective would also provide a *content-free* way of conceptualizing optimal human being. By this I mean a conceptualization that avoids endorsing any particular philosophy, set of values, or behavioral practices, as optimal—one that instead focuses on the structure or configuration of elements within the person's system, in some abstract sense. In this way, our conceptualization might avoid the trap of merely reflecting the style of the times, the norms of the culture, or the vagaries of the theorist's personality, as was undoubtedly true for many of the historical definitions discussed earlier. One aim of this book is to consider whether there can be content-free criteria for defining optimal human being (a question most fully discussed in chap. 10).

For now, let us take leave of the historical perspectives, and also take leave of the hedonism/eudaemonia dichotomy. Instead, let us consider this potentially content-free definition: that *optimal human being is indexed by the degree of integration between the many different levels of analysis that constitute a human being, ranging from neurobiological to cognitive to personal to social to cultural.* That is, there should be health-promoting internal consistencies and coherent functional linkages between all of the levels of a person. Empirically, optimal human being might be indicated by the sum of the measured coherences existing across the different levels within the person's total system. To what extent does each level function optimally in its own internal processes, and to what extent does each level help or support each other level's optimization? Much of this book is devoted to providing the background knowledge to begin answering these questions.

Although my general approach concentrates on the question of how to enhance integration between the different levels of the person, I expect that this approach will at least be consistent with many of the historical prescriptions for optimal human being raised earlier. For example, Aristotle's conception of virtue, as involving finding the "golden mean" or balance between different forces, has a similar systemic view. My general approach to defining optimal human being should also be consistent with the specific definitions of optimal human being derived in each chapter with respect to each particular level of analysis, because many of these definitions refer implicitly to interlevel integration. Finally, the approach should also be consistent with the phenomenological perspective on optimal human functioning discussed earlier, in which optimal human being involves living in a certain mature and intentional way.

In addition to considering optimal integration between the many levels of an individual person, I also consider the nature of optimal integration between the human sciences. To use E. O. Wilson's terminology, how might the different theoretical perspectives on human nature be made consilient, so that they all fit into a single self-consistent whole? Borrowing from the multilevel conceptualization of optimal human being outlined earlier, I suggest that optimal scientific functioning involves seeking internal consistencies and coherent linkages between all of the different perspectives on human nature, located at all of the different levels of analysis (i.e., evolutionary, personality, social, cultural). According to this hierarchical pluralist approach, no level's effects can be reduced to, or subsumed by, any other level's effects; instead, each science's piece of the picture should be respected, and incorporated into the final paradigm. The question of how to do this is a major subtext within this book, and receives the most attention at the end of the book.

LOOKING AHEAD

Chapter 2 turns away from the question of optimal human being, to focus on the question of the interrelation of the different human sciences. Specifically, I attempt to delineate all of the major possible influences on a person's behavior, locate them within a comprehensive conceptual framework that also hierarchically organizes the major human sciences, and show how the different levels of analysis interact to determine behavior. Chapter 2 also tackles the difficult issues of reductionism versus holism, free will versus determinism, and mechanism versus emergentism. These issues must be addressed if human intentionality is considered to be part of the causal equation, with regards to optimal human being, or to anything else.

Chapter 3 considers in detail just one of these levels of analysis, which I believe is very important for understanding optimal human being—namely, personality. After reviewing several global models of personality, I postulate a novel hierarchical organization within the field of personality, and also within the person. This organization consists of four levels, ranging from organismic foundations, to personality traits, to goals and intentions, to selves and life stories. I also try to show that these four levels of analysis can be inserted directly into the comprehensive conceptual framework that was developed in chapter 2, as potential causes of human behavior.

Chapters 4–7 focus separately on each of these four levels of personality. First, they consider the nature of each level and what we know about the functioning of that level. Then, each of chapters 4–7 considers how the most important processes identified at each level of personality relate to the question of optimal human being.

Chapters 8 and 9 then consider two higher levels of analysis that are also very relevant to personality, namely, social interaction and culture. Similarly to chapters 4–7, at the end of chapters 8 and 9 I return to address the optimal human being question, as viewed from each level.

Finally, chapter 10 attempts to bring it all together and provide a reasonably comprehensive profile of the nature of optimal human being, both by reviewing each chapter's specific recommendations for thriving, and by further developing the multilevel definition of optimal human being offered earlier, based on integration between the many levels of functioning. In addition, chapter 10 also offers concluding speculations on the nature of optimal human science.

2

Hierarchies and Levels of Analysis: Locating Behavior in the Physical World and Seeking Integration Between the Human Sciences

In this chapter I leave aside the question of optimal human being, to consider a host of difficult issues in the philosophy of science, in particular, human science. In the process, we carefully consider "the nature of the person." What are the different spheres or levels that both constitute and encompass a person, and how are they related to each other? Although the discussion is quite abstract in places, hopefully the inclusion of a salient running example ("Why did the killer do it?") will help to ground the material and enhance its relevance. But first, let's talk about some problems in the field of psychology.

E. O. Wilson's noteworthy 1998 book, *Consilience: The Unity of Knowledge,* argues that all of the sciences should be integratable into one large picture. As discussed in chapter 1, they are all describing the same singular self-consistent universe—thus they should be consistent with each other. Much of Wilson's book is devoted to drawing out the connections and increasing convergences between different physical sciences—for example, ways in which the boundaries are becoming ever more fluid between physics, chemistry, physiology, and evolutionary biology.

However, Wilson has a somewhat different view regarding the social sciences, which he views as profoundly "out of touch" with the physical sciences. Wilson also views the social sciences as failing in their natural tasks of reducing ethnopolitical conflict, optimizing world trade, minimizing individual suffering, and so on.

To illustrate, he compares progress in the social and medical sciences. In the latter arena knowledge advances steadily, as medical researchers, informed by the latest science in physics, genetics and biochemistry, and evolutionary biology, develop increasingly efficacious treatments for formerly intractable diseases. In contrast, the social sciences' concrete achievements are much more difficult to identify—certainly, the social sciences have yielded few panaceas for society's ills.

Granting that the problems faced by social science are likely much more difficult than those faced by medical science, Wilson still asks, "What's the difference
between the two disciplines?" He argues that the medical sciences have a *foundation,* grounded in the physical sciences but also reaching across multiple levels of
organization and analysis, whereas the social sciences do not. Instead, each social
science has tended to consider its own level of analysis alone, in isolation from
other levels and sciences. Thus, psychologists, sociologists, economists, and anthropologists know little about each other's approaches and about the important
concepts in each other's fields; instead, each field has its own language and vocabulary, which defines, defends, and to some extent cloaks the field. They also little
consider the biological foundations of human nature.

Why has such dispersal and fragmentation occurred within the social sciences?
Doubtless, the phenomenon can be traced in part to each social science's attempt to
secure an identity for itself as a discipline, a goal that required, at least at first, severing the ties with the physical sciences, and later severing the ties with the other
social sciences. In other words, psychology, sociology, anthropology, and economics each had to secure its content area for itself, as a legitimate domain of inquiry not addressed by prior or existing sciences. By definition this meant moving
away from, rather than toward, the other sciences.

Still, this is a historical factor. Why is the division between the social and the
physical sciences maintained today? Wilson argues that one important factor is the
social sciences' resistance to genetic determinism, the idea that human behavior is
hard-wired and preprogrammed. Although few medical or physical scientists
would fully embrace genetic determinism, the social sciences have, by and large,
rejected out of hand the possibility of such biological influence. This is perhaps
understandable, especially when one considers the battles against racism and sexism that social scientists have helped spearhead—if human behavior is
hard-wired, then how is it possible to bring about a more just and humane society?
Also, doesn't such a perspective give bigots and racists precisely the rationale they
need for maintaining social inequalities? Again, however, few physical scientists
would espouse such a hard-line reductionist view, instead believing that some
combination of physical and psychological factors determines outcomes (more is
said on reductionism later in the chapter).

Another important factor maintaining the split between physical and social sciences, according to Wilson, is the standard social science model (SSSM). This is
the idea that humans are largely blank slates and all-purpose learners, whose
minds are created by culture, and who thus are, in an important sense, cut off from
biology. In other words, the SSSM (Tooby & Cosmides, 1992) assumes a nearly
infinitely malleable human nature. Unfortunately, this assumption can cause social scientists to overlook or ignore biological and evolutionary constraints that
have shaped, and continue to shape, the contours of the phenomena they study
(Pinker, 2002). Yet another important factor maintaining the split is cultural relativism (Brown, 1991), according to which there are no absolutes in human nature,
and no real criteria for identifying personal and cultural success; each path and

way of being is "just as good as" the next. Although cultural relativism can also be viewed as a reaction against racism, determinism, and elitism, it can also be viewed as part of the intellectual norms that maintain the split of the social sciences from the physical sciences. Also, it can have the effect of discouraging the search for optimal functioning, that is, understanding how organisms best solve adaptive life problems. If all paths are equally valid, why seek the better or best ones?

Thus, Wilson concludes that although social scientists have uncovered many important phenomena, "they have not yet crafted a web of causal explanation that successfully cuts down through the levels of organization from society to mind and brain. Failing to probe this far, they lack what can be called a true scientific theory" (p. 189).

Although I am a psychologist, I have considerable sympathy for Wilson's view. In other words, I agree that it is necessary to acknowledge and include biological and evolutionary foundations within our models of human behavior, certainly more so than psychologists have done in the past. However, I would emphasize that it is necessary to give equal attention and causal weight to all levels of the hierarchy. Although Wilson pays lip service to this idea, it is clear that he views the physical and biological as perhaps the most important perspective for scientists to take. In contrast to the reductionism endorsed by Wilson, I argue that holistic perspectives have much to supply, especially if their practitioners maintain their ties to biology and other lower level processes. More specifically, I suggest that a hierarchical pluralist approach, in which all sciences and levels of analysis play their unique role, is likely to be best. This book is organized in such a manner. Although the book does not (of course) succeed in achieving scientific consilience, hopefully it provides some useful new directions and ways of thinking about the question.

A GUIDING CONCEPTUAL FRAMEWORK

Figure 2.1 presents an overarching framework for viewing the different kinds of forces or factors that can influence human behavior, which I believe is the primary phenomenon to be explained by the human sciences. The general idea for the framework is not new (e.g., see Rose, 1998, p. 9, or Barlow, 1998, p. 153, for figures similar to Fig. 2.1), although the specific configuration proposed here may be novel, and may provide the most accurate picture of the true underlying structure. In addition to illustrating the different kinds of causal accounts we might invoke to explain a particular person's behavior, the framework can also help to illustrate the relations between the different branches of science, at least, as they intersect in their consideration of human behavior. Drawing all of the sciences into one conceptual framework might accelerate the process of achieving consilience between them. In addition, the model can give a clear picture of the location of psychology, and also the human self, in relation to the rest of the sciences. Finally, as I hope to show later in the book, the model can provide some new ways of thinking about optimal human being.

Prior to discussing the framework in detail, it is useful to consider a running example. The example is this: An American black man murders an American white

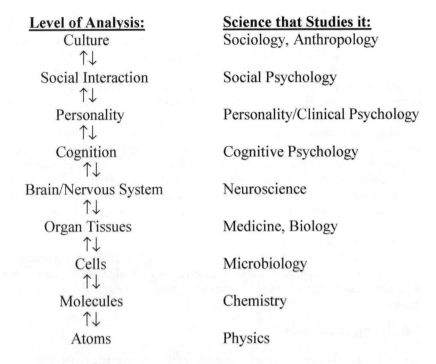

FIG. 2.1. Potential influences on human behavior.

man. The question to consider is, *why did the killer do it?* In other words, what kinds of causal explanations might we suggest, to try to understand what forces or processes brought about one man's act of killing another man? In principle, the type of analysis undertaken next should apply for explaining any human behavior, not just highly significant, extreme, or violent behaviors. Thus it should also apply to "positive" behaviors, such as a person's decision to help another, or even to sacrifice his or her life for another. I have chosen this somewhat negative (and perhaps politically incorrect) example not to arouse anger or to create a sensation, but rather because it is easy to identify possible explanations at many levels of analysis for this event, including considerations of racism in America.

Let's consider just a few of the possible answers to the question of "why did the killer do it?" Moving from the bottom toward the top of Fig. 2.1, the act might be said to have been caused (at least in part) by disruptions in endogenous brain chemistry, hormonal imbalances, arousal-regulation needs, a brain tumor, Tourette's syndrome, drug intake, evolved jealousy responses, maladaptive thinking patterns or cognitive styles, pathological personality organization, poor self-esteem or self-concept, uncontrollable frustration, exaggerated narcissism or sense of entitlement, distorted interpersonal relations or contradictory messages from important others, nonnurturing developmental environments, negative role models in past or present environment, the American culture of violence and/or sexism with attendant media exposures, American culture's history of racism and the pressures this places on black men, and even the world as a whole's long history of condoning slavery and unequal power relations between the races. In addition to being simultaneously influenced to varying degrees by the additive combination of each of these factors, the behavior might also be caused by many possible interactions or synergies, between any or all of these factors.

Obviously, this is a bewildering range of conceptual entities and candidates for causality, located within many different disciplines, no doubt leading to many turf wars and disagreements between disciplines. One purpose of Fig. 2.1 is to try to bring order to this complexity.

Describing Each Level

Let's start at the bottom of Figure 2.1, at the level where particle physicists focus: atomic and subatomic processes. Obviously, humans are composed of atoms, and are sustained by interactions within and among atoms. Although some neurobiological theories of behavior might make implicit reference to this level of analysis, no theories would rely on atomic and subatomic processes as the focal causative factor explaining human behavior. Therefore I do not talk further about this level of analysis. However, this does not mean that the atomic level of analysis is irrelevant for human behavior; of course, everything else is founded on atomic structure and processes. Rather, as explained shortly, this is likely not the most fruitful place to focus in order to explain human behavior.

The next level up in the hierarchy is the *molecular* one, at which combinations of atoms (molecules) occur. Here, atoms are organized together, as the constituent "building blocks" of some larger or more complex unit of analysis. This is the domain of chemistry, and its attempts to understand the nature of material compounds, both organic and inorganic. Although the molecular level of analysis might at first seem to have little to do with answering the question "why did the killer do it," in fact, it has much potential relevance. Several theories of individual dysfunction or misregulation focus on deficiencies or surpluses of chemical substances such as hormones, drugs, neurotransmitters, medications, and the like. Perhaps the killer had a surfeit of anabolic steroids in his system, or was suffering from severe serotonin deficiencies. Indeed, as discussed later, some types of insanity defense arguments focus at this level of analysis.

The next level in the hierarchy has been labeled *cellular*. Here, a threshold has been crossed, from the organization of physical substances (molecular) to the organization of physical substances within a living thing. Once again, the higher level in some ways exists and acts "on top of" the level below. Of course, cellular functioning is the province of molecular biology, in its quest to understand basic life processes. One might propose many causal explanations of the killer's act at this level; for example, the killing might have resulted from rage or debilitation brought on by the misregulation of cellular glucose, or from deficiencies in the functioning of brain cells (neurons).

As should be apparent by now, a key idea being illustrated by Fig. 2.1 is that each new level is more than the "sum of its parts." Although processes at a given level of analysis rely or are built on processes at lower levels, each level has its own dynamics and regularities that are often nonreducible to their constituent elements. In other words, Fig. 2.1 assumes that the phenomenon of *emergence* occurs and is an important fact of the physical universe: There are many phenomena and processes that cannot be explained solely by reference to processes lower in the hierarchy (Sperry, 1988). For example, the properties of water (H_2O; liquid at room temperature) are not in principle derivable from knowledge of the properties of hydrogen and oxygen alone (which are gaseous at room temperature)—the whole is more than the sum of the parts.

For another perspective on the issue, consider Gould's (1984) claim that

> The principles of physics and chemistry are not sufficient to explain complex biological objects because new properties emerge as a result of organization and interaction. These properties can only be understood by the direct study of the whole, living systems in their normal state. The insufficiency of physics and chemistry to encompass life records no mystical addition, no contradiction to the basic sciences, but only reflects the hierarchy of natural objects and the principle of emergent properties at higher levels of organization. (quoted in Barlow, 1991, p. 103)

In other words, Gould suggests that we will never be able to fully understand life processes by referring only to physics and chemistry—there is more to it than that.

The next level of analysis in Fig. 2.1 is labeled *organ tissues,* and represents the fact that cells of different types are aggregated and organized together into structures within the body, which fulfill specific functions for the organism. Such tissues include bone tissue, skin tissue, liver tissue, and so on. As denoted in the figure, this is the province of medical and physiological researchers. It is possible to adduce potential causal explanations for the killer's behavior at this level of analysis, also; for example, drive theories of motivation have long assumed that deficiencies within the organ tissues are the biological source of the psychological impetus to act. Secondary drives, including fear responses, are acquired via association with the satisfaction of primary biological drives; perhaps the killer was acting due to an anger response ultimately rooted in biological needs or deprivations, or in accordance with learned fear-reducing behavior.

The next level in Fig. 2.1 has been labeled *brain/nervous system,* the province of neuroscience and neurobiology. The nervous system may be viewed as the organizer and regulator of the body. It is of course built on and enabled by the organ systems, but it is also more than them, in that its function is to regulate and coordinate the various organ systems for the good of the whole. One might also adduce explanations for the killer's act at this level of analysis. For example, some theories focus on the search for optimal brain arousal as a powerful motivational source; perhaps the killer was seeking a cure for understimulation. Other theories focus on brain reward systems, and their influence on behavior; perhaps the killer was seeking to obtain pleasurable discharges in certain brain regions.

The next level up in Fig. 2.1 is that of *cognition,* the focus of cognitive psychology. Here another threshold is crossed, between the neural "hardware" that enables cognitive activity, and the cognitive activity itself, the "software" that makes use of the neural hardware. Continuing the theme, cognitive activity may be viewed as that which organizes the functioning of the nervous system, an emergent level or unit of analysis that has its own rules and principles that can be "more than" the rules that guide the functioning of the nervous system more generally. Here, explanations for the killer's act might refer to the killer's expectancies regarding the act, his attributions regarding the victim's behavior immediately preceding the act, and the goals that guided his behavior in that moment.

Notably, at this level of analysis a second type of threshold is apparently crossed: between "brain" and "mind," or between "objectivity" and "subjectivity." But aren't mind and matter the same thing, really, such that thoughts could, in principle, be shown to be nothing more than specific brain events or patterns of neuronal firing? My own perspective, based on emergentism, is that thoughts are more than neural activity, just as water is more than hydrogen and oxygen. Cognitions can have effects that are (at least sometimes) irreducible to the neural substrate that supports cognition. Here, it is instructive to consider in detail Roger Sperry's (1988, 1993) ideas, as he has studied and thought most directly about the issues at or near this level of analysis.

Sperry was a Nobel prize-winning neurophysiologist, known for his research into split-brain processes, who focused later in his career on providing a new ontology for the physical and social sciences. In his own words, he was attempting to "replace reductive micro-deterministic views of personhood and physical world" with a "more holistic, top-down view in which the higher, more evolved entities throughout nature, including the mental, vital, social, and other higher-order forces, gain their due recognition along with physics and chemistry" (1993, p. 879). Concerning the emergent causal effects of cognition and conscious experiences, he wrote: "The contents of conscious experience, with their subjective qualities, long banned as being mere acausal epiphenomena or as just identical to brain activity … have now made a dramatic comeback. Reconceived in the new outlook, subjective mental states become functionally interactive and essential for a full explanation of behavior" (p. 879). Sperry coined the term *monist interactionism* to describe his view that there is just one material universe, that is, no dualistic mind/body split. Although the mental is constituted from physical processes, still, there is "interaction," such that emergent cognitive activity can gain control of global fate of the system. This means that mental processes, even though they could not exist without neural activity, could still have causal efficacy by interacting with and influencing the temporal destiny of the neural substrates on which they rest (Juarrero, 1999).

To return to our example, from Sperry's perspective, the killer's cognitions (i.e., his intentions, expectations, and attributions) may be said to have had *direct* effects on the killer's behavior, effects irreducible to the neurological processes that underlie and support those cognitions. Of course, such cognitions are far from the whole story, and indeed, they may not have had as much influence as the killer himself believed; people can be deceived about their own degree of agency or self-control (Wegner, 2002). More is said later in the chapter on the important question of free will, and on the potential legitimacy of the self's belief that it is the author of its own behavior.

The next level of analysis in Fig. 2.1 is labeled *personality*. It is the province of clinical and personality research psychologists, as well as psychiatrists. One very reasonable way to define personality is in terms of stable patterns of thinking and feeling that characterize a person over time (Allport, 1961). In other words, personality may be viewed as an emergent organization of the cognitive activity occurring within the organism's brain, an organization that both exerts some degree of higher level control over these lower level processes, and that also has some degree of stability or persistence over time. The concept of personality crosses yet another threshold, from the realm of momentary cognition and subjectivity, to the realm of a person, actively living and constructing his or her life over time. Again, this realm can be viewed as more than the sum of the particular thoughts and feelings that compose it—personhood has its own patterns and effects, which are not necessarily reducible to the laws that govern lower level processes (Allport, 1961).

Of course, there are many ways of conceptualizing personality, for example, in terms of underlying needs and motives, manifest behavioral traits or dispositions, or particular self-beliefs and feelings. In fact, the personality level represents the predominant focus of this book. Thus, in chapter 3, I introduce a "hierarchy *within* the hierarchy," that is, a scheme for identifying different levels of analysis within personality, which magnifies this one level of the overall scheme presented in Fig. 2.1. For now, let us content ourselves by pointing out how readily personality-level factors supply potential explanations for the killer's act: One might say that he was motivated by unmet psychological needs, by antisocial traits or tendencies, by inadequate self-regulatory abilities, by unconscious conflicts, by a maladaptive self-concept, and so on.

The next level up in Fig. 2.1 is that of *social interaction,* the phenomenon that social psychologists and communication scholars study. In terms of the concept of emergent patterns, we might say that the patterns and processes of social discourse represent an organization of personalities, in which two or more personalities interface with each other in various ways. Here another threshold is crossed, as the principle of higher level organization extends beyond the body of the particular person, into a network that includes two or more different persons. Once again, I argue that these patterns are often not explainable simply in terms of the constituent parts, but require consideration of the synergy between personalities, as well as consideration of social forces and contingencies that have their own logic and ways of changing, and that to some extent condition and constrain those patterns.

For example, the phenomenon of deindividuation, in social psychology, concerns the conditions under which groups of individuals "run amok"; members of groups sharing collective identities, whose identities have been violated and whose individual responses to this violation are likely to be anonymous, will sometimes forget their individual identities and engage in atrocious crimes. This phenomenon emerges from group dynamics and the sociohistorical context, rather than being predictable from the characteristics of the particular individuals who compose the group. In terms of explaining the killer's act, at the social interaction level one might refer to negative patterns of communication between the killer and victim, such as a persistent inability or unwillingness to grant legitimacy to each other's point of view. Or, one might refer to a downward spiral occurring during the interaction prior to the killing, in which threats and counterthreats finally got out of control.

The final level of analysis depicted in Fig. 2.1 is that of *culture,* the province of sociologists, anthropologists, and social critics. In terms of the emergence concept, culture represents the relatively enduring organization of social norms, traditions, beliefs, and practices that emerge within a geographical, national, or linguistic sphere, that help to shape and constrain the social interactions that occur between cultural members. Again, I would argue that the forces and processes active at this level cannot be reduced to the workings of the personalities or interaction styles of those within the culture: There are historically based laws and regularities operative here, which, of course, are contingent on the presence of persons, but which are more than the sum of those persons taken singly (Kincaid, 1997). In terms of explaining the killer's act, one might say that the killing was in part caused by the "culture of violence" found within the United States (Nisbett & Cohen, 1996); one might also refer to the racial prejudices that exist within U.S. culture, breeding resentment and anger (Swim, Cohen, & Hyers, 1998); or one might refer to the killer's exposure to many movies and dramas in which a dominant male, wronged by another, takes justice into his own hands (Perse, 2001).

FURTHER EXPLICATION OF FIG. 2.1

In the section that follows I point out some other important facts and implications concerning the Fig. 2.1 model, which will hopefully serve to further illustrate its usefulness. Before doing so, let's acknowledge that the issues I touch on next are daunting and complex—for example, questions of free will, determinism, reductionism, holism, mechanism, and the like have occupied philosophers of science and philosophers of mind for centuries, and will doubtless continue to do so, in ways far beyond the scope of this book. My intention for the rest of this chapter is simply to chart a reasonably simple course through this thicket, stating my basic assumptions, so that we can move on to other issues.

Time Scales at Each Level of Analysis

One thing to notice about Fig. 2.1 is that processes tend to happen more slowly at higher levels of analysis, and more swiftly at lower levels of analysis. Literally millions of events occur every second at the atomic level, with radical changes possible within an instant. As one moves up the hierarchy, however, the structures and processes have greater stability and enduringness. Reaching the level of personality, one finds elements and patterns that can remain stable for decades, and at the level of culture can be found norms and traditions that span centuries. It also tends to be more difficult to change or alter patterns and regularities at higher levels, compared to lower levels. For example, organ tissues and their functioning can be affected by short-term changes, such as glucose availability or alcohol levels; thoughts and feelings are less readily altered, and personalities less alterable still; and cultures can be extremely resistant to change, as illustrated by the continuing conflict between Israel and Palestine.

Equivalent Causal Status of Each Level of Analysis

Another aspect of the model is that it "plays no favorites" in terms of which level is predominant, or most important. They all have a piece of the pie, doubtless to a greater or lesser extent as a function of the particular behavioral phenomenon being studied. In addition, lower and higher level phenomena are treated equally in terms of their potential influence on each other—as can be seen in Fig. 2.1, there can be both up and down arrows linking each level of analysis, to represent both top-down and bottom-up causation. Indeed, one might also include arrows linking levels to other levels that are more than one level away from each other.

In terms of the "killer" example, a top-down flow of causation might explain the behavior if the victim delivered an insult (social interaction level), which triggered insecurities in the killer (personality level), which triggered thoughts and feelings of rage (cognition level), which influenced autonomic arousal levels (nervous system level), which influenced hormonal secretions (cellular level), which caused disinhibition of the limbic system, leading to the behavior. A bottom-up flow of causation might occur if a genetic flaw (cellular level) produced a chronic tendency to misregulate a particular neurotransmitter (nervous system level), which led to recurring negative thoughts and feelings (cognition level), which led to maladaptive personality styles and defenses (personality level), which led to the disposition to antagonize social partners (social interaction level), leading to the behavior. Doubtless, in many cases, both ascending and descending directions of causality are occurring simultaneously.

Reductionism and Holism

A third issue that is readily addressable in terms of Fig. 2.1 is the distinction between reductionism and holism. Although this issue has been alluded to already, it is worthy of more direct consideration here. *Reductionism* can be defined as "the process whereby concepts or statements that apply to one type of entity are redefined in terms of concepts, or analyzed in terms of statements, of another kind, normally regarded as more elementary" (Bullock & Stallybrass, 1978; *Harper Dictionary of Modern Thought,* p. 530). Reductionism has provided huge benefits in the sciences, as much new understanding and control of physical phenomena have been gained by considering the constituent parts of phenomena. In particular, reductionism is consistent with the principal of *parsimony,* in which events are to be explained in terms of simpler or more basic facts, constituents, or principles.

In terms of Fig. 2.1, reduction occurs when a phenomenon at a particular level of analysis is explained in terms of simpler or more elemental processes at a lower level of analysis. Thus, one might explain the properties of molecules in terms of the atoms that compose them (i.e., in terms of which orbitals are filled or empty within which atom), or one might explain cognition in terms of the brain areas being activated at that time, or one might explain a personality factor such as the person's susceptibility to helplessness in terms of the cognitive attributions the person makes for events (i.e., unstable and uncontrollable; Weiner, 1992).

How far down the hierarchy should a reductionist go? Although some take a "strong reductionist" stance, according to which everything should be reducible to the very bottom level of the hierarchy (Brandon, 1996), there are probably limits to the usefulness of reductionism. For example, Richard Dawkins, the prominent evolutionary theorist, wrote, in *The Blind Watchmaker* (1986):

> For any given level of complex organization, satisfying explanations may normally be attained if we peel the hierarchy down one or two layers from our starting layer, but not more. The behavior of a motorcar is explained in terms of cylinders, carburetors, and sparking plugs. It is true that each one of these components rests atop a pyramid of explanations at lower levels. But if you asked me how a motorcar worked you would think me somewhat pompous if I answered in terms of Newton's laws and the laws of thermodynamics, and downright obscurantist if I answered in terms of fundamental particles. It is doubtless true that at bottom the behavior of a motorcar is to be explained in terms of interactions between fundamental particles. But it is much more useful to explain it in terms of interactions between pistons, cylinders and sparking plugs. (quoted in Barlow, 1991, p. 12)

In short, Dawkins advocates a more modest form of reductionism, in which explanations should occur at levels not too far below the phenomenon, for efficiency's sake if nothing else.

In contrast to reductionism, *holism* can be defined as "the thesis that wholes, or some wholes, are more than the sum of their parts in the sense that the wholes in question have characteristics that cannot be explained in terms of the properties and relations to one another of their constituents" (*Harper Dictionary of Modern Thought,* 1978, p. 288). Thus, as alluded to earlier, a holistic perspective would say that contextual factors within an entity's larger environmental matrix have influences that cannot be understood purely in terms of the entity. The case of stem cells turning into different kinds of tissue as a function of their location within the embryo supplies one good example of a holistically determined process. As another example, living in a culture that permits and even encourages citizens to carry handguns might provide part of the causal explanation for a particular shooting occurring in the world.

While we are considering reductionism versus holism, let us pause to make another interesting observation. Although psychologists decry the tendency of the "harder" sciences to try to reduce human behavior to physical or biological processes, the tendency does not stop at chemists and biologists. Anthropologists and sociologists sometimes decry the tendency of psychologists to reduce all behavior to characteristics of the individual! For example, Kincaid's (1997) book is dedicated to the proposition that behavior cannot be understood solely at the level of the individual (the assumption of "methodological individualism"; Popper 1961), but must take into account the social systems in which individuals are embedded ("sociological holism"; Durkheim, 1938). Similarly, in the last decade cross-cultural psychologists have been urging the field as a whole to move away from its focus on the individual and the psychological self, to gain a greater awareness of the diversity of different kinds of selves that can emerge within different cultural matrices (Markus, Kitayama, & Heiman, 1996). Perhaps, in the search for both "turf" and parsimony, it is inevitable that each level of analysis should try to reduce and subsume the ones above it. Again, my perspective is that this is unnecessary and unfortunate, because it impedes scientific progress.

THE FREE WILL QUESTION

Given the proposal that optimal human being to some extent results from the intentional attitude a person takes toward the world (i.e., his or her "way" of being, as discussed in chap. 1), the question of whether people have free will or not becomes an important one. Thus, it is useful to consider, in some detail, the meaning and nature of free will. The Fig. 2.1 model admits the possibility of free will. It does this by defining cognition and conscious selfhood as emergent processes that have a somewhat independent status within the material universe, in the same way that social and cultural forces, above them, are also designated as having somewhat independent reality.

Free Will and Determinism

To defend my assertion that humans have some degree of free will, it is necessary to briefly talk about the concept of determinism. Simply put, I take the position that all events (behavioral and otherwise) are determined. That is, they result from some combination of prior conditions, conditions that might be found and measured at any or all levels of the Fig. 2.1 hierarchy. Indeed, without the assumption of determination, science could not proceed.

Despite being determined by antecedent events, not all events are predictable—that is, they are not all predetermined. In part this is because of the nature of dynamical system processes, such as sensitive dependence on initial conditions and the potential for nonlinear change (Vallacher & Nowak, 1994). As is now well known, these facts entail that systems can enter new and unanticipatable functional states in an instant. However in part it is due to emergence, especially at the middle levels of the hierarchy, where the autonomous human being processes information and makes choices. In other words, one characteristic of emergent processes, particularly within the human brain, is that they can achieve spontaneous new integrations or organizations of prior facts and feelings that could not have been predicted in advance.

Here is an example that emphasizes the surprising properties of emergent human cognitions. I believe that nobody could have predicted in advance Einstein's conceptual breakthrough in creating the theory of relativity: Only his or a very similar human brain, assembling all the evidence for itself, could have arrived at this realization, in the same painstaking way that Einstein did. This is not to say that somebody else wouldn't have had his insights eventually; rather, it is to say that no natural or social scientist could have predicted in advance what Einstein was about to discover, no matter how much they knew about Einstein and his brain. The vocabulary, the conceptual order, simply did not exist as yet. Again, this does not mean that the event was magical or uncaused; one might readily identify, in retrospect, the mechanisms and processes that indeed determined the realization (Juarrero, 1999). It just means that the event was not predetermined. One might argue that "God," if God exists, might have known in advance of Einstein's achievement; however, there is reason to believe that even such an all-powerful entity might not be able to predict in advance the results of such iterative, recursive processes (Sigmund, 1993). Perhaps this is one reason why "God" bothered to create the universe: curiosity.

One implication of the rejection of predetermination is that complete predictability, at least regarding naturally occurring human behavior, is probably impossible. Still, one can presumably achieve better predictability (i.e., a lower error rate) than one had before, in part by further studying the antecedent conditions to particular events. Because events are in fact determined (at least at the moment of their occurrence, if not before), it is possible to derive increasing information about how particular events, or types of events, were actually caused.

Free Will and the Self

In order to more thoroughly consider the question of free will, it is necessary to focus on the "personality" level of analysis, particularly on individual phenomenology and experience. In a deep sense, what is the free will question but the personality's search to affirm its intuition that it has some degree of reality and influence upon the world? Although chapter 7 addresses the question of selfhood in more detail, for now we can define self as "personality from the inside," that is, as the sense of conscious presence and agency that we feel as we express our personalities within daily life. The question is, do these feelings of agency and choice have any objective reality?

My own position, consistent with Sperry's ideas and the emergentist position, is that they do: Feelings of agency represent special brain processes in which the feelings of agency or choice themselves, contained within or "folded into" the brain events, are partially or potentially determinative of the organism's subsequent behavior. The fact that internal conscious events can be *causal* (just as they seem to be, in our experience) does not mean that they are not *lawful,* and cannot be understood and to some extent predicted, for example, via knowledge of the narrative rules through which selves or this self constructs itself, or through knowledge of regularities in the person's past history and responses. Also, the self's belief that it has caused a particular behavior is not necessarily accurate; again, people can be deceived regarding the real influence of their own choices and experience. Still, the self and its conscious choices are one of the more potent causal influences operative on human behavior (but see Wegner, 2002, for a somewhat contrasting view).

Free Will and Teleology

Still, there are significant difficulties here. By allowing a subjective factor into the causal account of human behavior one opens the door to *teleology,* anathema to the reductionist. Teleology is the idea that events are guided by (necessarily subjective) purposes, rather than being driven aimlessly by lower level mechanisms. For example, Dawkins's question of "how does an automobile work," discussed earlier, referred only to factors below the level of the car (i.e., basic chemistry and physics, or pistons and spark plugs). The question was, how far down the hierarchy should one go for an explanation of the automobile's functioning?

Dawkins did not consider perhaps the most obvious answer to the question, namely, "because a human designed it to work that way"—what Aristotle referred to as the "final" cause. In part, this reflects reductionists' desire to focus on the "how" of things more so than the "why" of them. But in part, it also reflects many scientists' suspicions concerning admitting human intentions into the causal equation. In arguing that the mental intentions and the experienced self have some legitimacy and causal status within the material universe, one is forced admit the "why" of things into the account, that is, to open the door to teleology. Indeed, the entire point of the book from which Dawkins's quote was taken, *The Blind Watchmaker,* is to argue against the necessity of positing a designer (i.e., supreme being), operative within the material universe. In other words, Dawkins's book is an attack on divine teleology, and the idea that the universe is here for a reason.

Although it raises perilous issues, I believe it is necessary to open the door to teleology, at least at the human level. As is shown in chapters 3 and 6, this approach can offer rich explanatory dividends.

Different Sciences' Differing Perspectives on Free Will

A further feature of Fig. 2.1 is that it can help us to understand the differing positions on free will found by scientists focusing on differing levels of analysis. Physical scientists and biologically oriented psychologists tend to deny free will, because their focus is on levels of causality "beneath" the level of self/personality. When a neurological researcher finds that a certain part of the brain lights up as a person makes a decision, that researcher is prone to say, "The brain event was causal, and the sense of agency that accompanied it had nothing to do with the person's subsequent behavior" (Shweder, 2001). Analogously, saying that a person's genetic code or hormones caused the person's behavior also doesn't allow much role for conscious choice.

However, as one moves up the hierarchy, one finds greater consideration of the possibility of free will. Many cognitive scientists, especially those focusing on higher order processes such as decision making and meta-cognition, would perforce grant causal status to the person's computations. Personality and clinical psychologists focus even more on the self and its functions and capabilities; indeed, the very premise of many forms of psychotherapy is that the person must decide for him- or herself to seek a change, if positive change is to occur. As is discussed in detail in chapters 5 and 6, self-determination theory, within social-personality psychology, focuses in much detail on the self's efforts to "find itself" and assume control over its own destiny, a phenomenological struggle with great practical import (Deci & Ryan, 2000).

Ironically, emphasis on the causal efficacy of the self is sometimes reduced as one continues up the hierarchy of sciences above the personality level. For example, some sociologists and anthropologists take the position that the self is conditioned and caused by cultural forces, social role expectations, and demographic/historical facts, rather than being a causal factor in and of itself. Thus, we see that holistic theories can be just as assertive as reductionist theories, in insisting that their perspective completely accounts for a particular event! Again, my own position is that rarely can a particular phenomenon be completely explained via consideration of just one other factor, higher level or lower level.

Assumptions Regarding Free Will in Human Society

Putting aside the scientific debate concerning the potential causal efficacy of the conscious self or personality, what is assumed in "real life," in society at large? Obviously, most of us (excepting the most fatalistic or psychologically helpless among us) believe we have some choice over what we do! Furthermore, our legal institutions rest on this assumption: We assume that criminals could stop themselves from committing crimes, should they so choose. Thus, laws are designed, in part, to specify penalties that will be imposed should people choose to break the law—hopefully, these penalties are sufficient to serve as a deterrent to lawbreaking.

However, there are conditions under which the assumption of self-choice is put aside: People are sometimes exculpated from crimes, on the basis of their "temporary insanity," typically defined as a state in which the person could not have chosen not to do something, even if there had been a "policeman at their elbow." Insanity pleas are greatly bolstered when the person can point to a medical, physiological, or psychiatric condition that overwhelmed their capacity to choose, such as disordered brain chemistry, disordered, delusional thought patterns, and the like (Rose, 1997). In other words, the law allows for instances in which a person's behavior is reducible to (and completely determined by) the influence of lower level factors, such that the self had no real power to choose.

Interestingly, another condition under which conventional proscriptions (such as "thou shalt not kill") are sometimes put aside comes from higher level factors. For example, when the person's culture as a whole condones participation in a war, then a person might be expected to kill as often and as effectively as possible! Indeed, those who resist such higher level influences ("conscientious objectors") may face substantial penalties—how dare they choose to act apart from the influence of the community?

Utility of Fig. 2.1 for Psychologists

Finally, it is worth discussing the model's potential utility for psychologists. One application is that it can be used to clarify what is being focused on, and what is being left out, by a particular research program. For example, the field of social cognition traditionally bridges the cognitive and the social interaction levels of analysis, largely bypassing the personality level of analysis that lies between these two foci. In addition to typically ignoring individual differences, social-cognitive research has been accused of ignoring culture-level influences on the processes it studies. Some contemporary research is rectifying this gap, showing, for example, that "the fundamental attribution error" is not as fundamental in non-Western cultures (Norenzayan & Nisbett, 2000). Ideally, future research effort in the field of social cognition will simultaneously consider all four of the top levels in the Fig. 2.1 hierarchy.

A second possible use of the model for psychologists is to classify the different kinds of explanations that might be offered to account for a particular behavior. For example, as was illustrated earlier in the chapter, some potential explanations for a killing might focus on cognitive factors, others on personality factors, and still others on social or cultural factors. Of course, each discipline focuses on its own unique piece of a particular phenomenon—in terms of the well-known "blind men and the elephant" parable, each discipline has something unique to contribute to the totality of the phenomenon in question, because the phenomenon exists at each level of analysis simultaneously. Clearly recognizing this might help to reduce turf wars, in which each discipline insists that its own level of analysis is the best and most proper focus of research attention.

To illustrate the nature of such turf wars, consider how styles of explanation change over time within psychology, as perspectives at varying levels of analysis emerge to dominant the current causal accounts. For example, the "double-bind" theory was a prominent account of the etiology of schizophrenia in the 1960s; the idea was that schizophrenia results when the individual receives mixed or contradictory messages from important others (at the level of social interaction). Now biochemical theories largely dominate contemporary accounts of the etiology of schizophrenia. My own view is that the pendulum will doubtless swing back toward interpersonal perspectives (Joiner, 2002), as we move closer to the multifactorial truth of the matter.

RETURNING TO CONSILIENCE

Scientific Consilience as a Threat to the Higher Levels of Analysis?

At this point it is worth returning to the issue that began this chapter, namely, the concept of consilience—the possibility of unifying knowledge across every scientific discipline, including the natural and social sciences. Although E. O. Wilson is optimistic about the prospects, many scientists are not. For example, in a very cogent analysis, Richard Shweder, the cultural anthropologist, objected rather strenuously to the idea. He argued that the world of human meanings is simply not amenable to characterization in terms of physical processes (Shweder, 2001). Wilson stated that self and meanings do not exist in an "astral plane," independent of the physical world, and thus that they should obviously be amenable (in principal) to analysis in natural science terms, whereas Shweder suggests that self and meanings do exist in a different "place" altogether, and thus that the connection is not so obvious. In this context, he cited Karl Popper's notion that there are three "worlds": World I, the realm of the physical, World II, the realm of the subjective, and World III, the realm of collective meanings (Popper & Eccles, 1977). Each world, according to Popper, is separate and distinct from the others. Here is a truly startling idea—perhaps the most respected and cited philosopher of science, Karl Popper, advocated not just dualism, but a trichotomy!

What Schweder (2001) really seemed to be objecting to was the reductionist program that he perceived lurking at the heart of Wilson's (1998) position. In other words, Shweder believed that what Wilson wanted to be able to say, for example, is that the experience of "justice" is nothing more than a particular pattern of neuronal activity, perhaps programmed into the human brain by natural selection. Shweder made a persuasive argument for the misleading nature of such an approach. People's conceptions of justice are influenced not just by their endogenous brain chemistries and by the evolutionary history of the species but, in addition, by seemingly endless and exquisite variations on cultural norms, practices, and histories, as well as by peoples' personal foibles, dispositions, and developmental histories.

However, once we acknowledge the limitations of reductionism, then consilience may be possible after all (Pinker, 2002). The higher levels of analysis cannot be made obsolete by advances in lower levels of analysis; they carry information that cannot be gotten anywhere else. However, the essential dependence of higher level phenomena on lower level processes and supports must be recognized. Thus, I agree with Wilson that culture, meanings, and subjectivity are certainly of the physical world—that is, they have to be underlain and supported by physical processes. Selves are not astral projections, and there is no use in taking a dualist perspective, with the attendant problems of explaining how the mental and the physical worlds manage to interact, what happens to the mental when the physical perishes, and so on. Again, I subscribe to Sperry's (1993) notion of "monist interactionism," in which mental processes are partially independent of their neural substrates, operating via laws and processes "at their own level." Thus, they can have top-down influences that are more than neural activity. Returning to Popper's conception of three worlds, World I would be located at the bottom of the Fig. 2.1 hierarchy, World II would be located at the middle of the hierarchy, and World III would be located at the top of the hierarchy. Yes, the worlds are independent, in that they are not scientifically reducible to each other. Yet they all fit into the same unitary reality, helping to determine events via the actions within and interactions between them.

From this perspective, then, the task for those seeking the big picture is to understand the interactions between levels, involving both top-down and bottom-up causal chains. For example, a person's thought that "an injustice has been done here!" and violent behavioral response might simultaneously be determined by processes at every level of analysis, from the molecular and cognitive (perhaps via an innate sensitivity to unfairness, hard-wired into the human brain by evolution) up to the personal (perhaps via the individual's emotional and interpretive dispositions) up to the cultural (perhaps via particular norms or traditions, which help determine which acts count as unjust within a particular society). In principle, the differing contributions of each level of analysis to a particular event or type of event should be discernable, as well as the moderating influence of different levels upon each other's effects.

Multilevel Models and Fig. 2.1

In this light, it is useful to consider the nature of multilevel statistical models (Bryk & Raudenbush, 1992). Such models take account of the fact that the units of study are often nested inside of larger units. For example, in predicting reading outcomes for a particular schoolchild, it might be necessary to study the larger context in which the data were collected, that is, the particular classroom in which the child did the learning. Such two-level models can be applied in many ways, for example, to examine repeated observations nested within a particular person, to examine a person's behavior nested within a particular group of people, or to examine a particular group's behavior, nested within a group of groups. Typically, the lower level unit is the primary object of study, and the aim is to predict some outcome associated with that unit while also taking into account variables at the higher level. For example, we might try to predict the schoolchild's reading score (a lower level variable) from a different lower level variable (i.e., his or her intelligence), and also from a higher level variable (i.e., whether the child is in a classroom that uses cooperative learning strategies, or not). One can potentially find main effects of variables at each level (i.e., intelligence is a positive predictor, and cooperative classroom is a positive predictor), and can also find cross-level interactions in which the upper level variable moderates the effect of a lower level variable (i.e., less intelligent children may gain extra benefits from being in a cooperative classroom). In addition one can simultaneously model more than two levels: n-level models are possible, given a large enough and comprehensive enough data base with which to work.

I propose that Fig. 2.1 could, in principle at least, be viewed as a nine-level model in which any given outcome might be best predicted from some combination of main effects at each level, and cross-level interactions in which higher levels moderate lower level effects. In other words, reality is potentially a nine-way interaction, on top of eight-way interactions, on top of seven-way interactions, and so on, down to the simple main effects of each level. Of course, for any particular phenomenon or outcome, the appropriate constructs and measures to use at each level of analysis would have to be identified. Also, the exact pattern of effects would doubtless vary depending on the particular phenomenon or outcome in question; as noted earlier, lower levels might be better for explaining some phenomena (i.e., a person's physiological condition may best explain his or her trip to the refrigerator), whereas higher levels might be better for explaining other phenomena (i.e., cultural conditions may best explain a suicide bombing in Iraq); ultimately, these are empirical questions. Although creating and testing models drawing from all of the levels in Fig. 2.1 remains beyond us, hopefully, this will become more practical as our theoretical, methodological, and statistical expertise grows. I believe that this type of modeling approach will be necessary, in order for the true complexity of reality to be approximated scientifically.

Locating the Person

Where is the person in Fig. 2.1; and in the scheme I have outlined, more generally? In one sense, the person is everywhere, because people exist at all levels of analysis simultaneously, and cannot be removed from the basic matrix. This defines the person more broadly than is typical, to include both others and the society in which the person is embedded, as well as including elementary brain processes, as well as genetic dispositions and propensities embedded within the person. Again referring to the "elephant and the blind men" parable, the person exists simultaneously within all of these frames of reference.

However, in another sense, the person exists primarily at the *middle* levels of analysis (cognition, personality, and social interactions), because these are the levels at which the experiencing person can hope to have the most potential influence upon his/her own outcomes. In other words, people can best influence and guide their lives and outcomes via their expectations, judgments, decisions, and calculations (cognitions), via the expression of their characteristic traits, identities, and goals (personality), and via their communications and commitments to others (social interactions). Via these online processes, circumstances may be modified and events channeled so that the "most optimal" individual outcomes may potentially occur (Nozick, 1993). Again, this does not preclude the possibility that factors at lower levels of analysis also play a causal role.

Thus, in the next five chapters I focus in more depth at the personality level of analysis, which, as I argued earlier, may be most important for understanding optimal human being. Hopefully, however, the location of personality and personality theory with respect to the other sciences and the other levels of analysis is now clear.

3

Focusing on the Personality Level: Comprehensive Models of Personality

This chapter focuses in more detail on the personality level of analysis, specifically considering some of the broadest conceptual frameworks currently available for encompassing personality. In the process, I consider several ways of viewing personality in hierarchical terms, in the same way that Fig. 2.1 provided a way of viewing human behavior in hierarchical terms. In other words, we focus on one particular level within Fig. 2.1, personality, and attempt to identify some useful hierarchical organizations nested within that level of analysis. The goal is to derive a unitary framework that both includes and integrates the major schools of personality theory, and, links these schools to Fig. 2.1 more generally.

I begin by further considering Carver and Scheier's (1981, 1998) control-theory model of human behavior, which attempts to simultaneously incorporate multiple levels of analysis to understand both the momentary and the long-term organization of human action. Implications of the model for questions of reductionism, holism, and teleology are considered, so that the vital role of human intentionality for any model of optimal human being can be appreciated. Then, I consider some other global models of personality theory, starting with McAdams's (1996) proposition that there are three primary tiers within personality (traits, goals, and selves). Next, I consider McCrae and Costa's (1995) comprehensive model of these three aspects of personality. After showing the overly reductionist implications of McCrae and Costa's model, I propose an emendation to McAdams's model, such that personality consists of four major levels of analysis: organismic foundations, personality traits, goals and intentions, and self and self-concepts. Chapters 4–7 consider each level of analysis within this hierarchy separately, and also, the perspectives on optimal human being that might be supplied by that level.

CARVER AND SCHEIER'S CONTROL
THEORY MODEL OF ACTION

The Basic Model

Perhaps the most ambitious attempt to place all of human behavior into a single organizational hierarchy has been supplied by Carver and Scheier, in their "control theory" model of behavior (1981, 1990, 1998). This model, which is based on cybernetic principles of nested feedback loops, attempts to completely account for human action—not only how it occurs, but why it occurs. Notably, Carver and Scheier's model does not concern levels of personality and personality theory; instead, it focuses on providing a global context for understanding complex behavior. Given the Fig. 2.1's emphasis on explaining behavior, and also the philosophical issues raised in chapter 2, this seems an appropriate starting place. However, as we show later in this chapter, there are other hierarchical models available that focus on understanding levels of personality, rather than levels of behavior.

Figure 3.1 presents Carver and Scheiers' basic hierarchical model of the human action system, which is built on many earlier theoretical innovations including those by Powers, Pribram, Miller, Ford, and Bandura, and which is also built on well-known engineering principles. The model proposes multiple levels of control within the human action system, ranging from very low-level and molecular (even down to the twitchings of individual nerve fibers) up to very high-level and molar (the person's broadest ambitions and dreamed-of selves). The mental structures residing at these different levels of control, and the functional interactions between them, are responsible for much if not most human behavior, according to Carver and Scheier.

Rather than explicate their control theory model in the abstract, I instead start with an example, as did Carver and Scheier in their 1982 exposition (i.e., "one is returning notes to a friend"). However, I employ a slightly different example than they, which will allow me to illustrate, later, some issues not addressed by the control theory model. Here is the example: "One is driving across town, to get a book from the Health Sciences Library." What is happening, and how do we explain this event?

According to Carver and Scheier's model, the event can be understood as the output of the functioning of the human action system. The action system functions by setting or accepting goals or standards for behavior. These subsequently motivate attempts to enact or achieve those standards (i.e., behavior occurs). Cognitive control processes continually compare actual states (i.e., what's happening now) to the standards, attempting to detect discrepancies. When discrepancies are detected, further action is initiated, or ongoing action is revised or redirected, or perhaps standards themselves are revised, in order to better approach the standard. In this way, people manage to adequately maintain themselves, and hopefully to make at least some forward progress toward desired new skills and circumstances. In essence, then, the control theory model explains behavior by saying that it occurs in the service of discrepancy reduction.

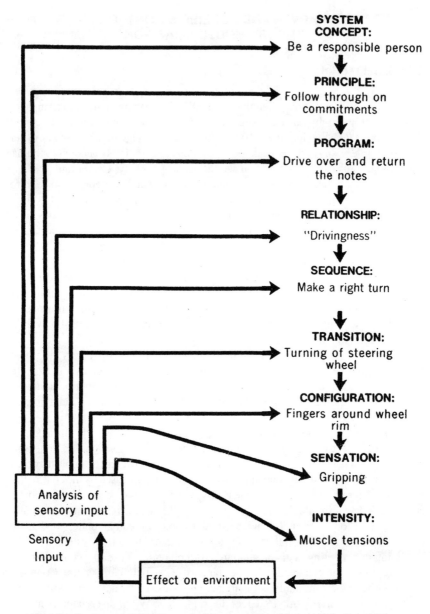

FIG. 3.1. Carver and Scheier's control theory model of action. *From* Control theory: A useful conceptual framework for personality—social, clinical, and health psychology, printed in *Psychological Bulletin, 92,* p. 115, by Carver, C. S. & Scheier, M. F. © 1982 by Springer-Verlag. Reprinted with permission.

Control tends to flow down from the top in Carver and Scheier's model. For example, the person driving to the Health Sciences Library may be going there because that was what was necessary for getting a book needed for a course. In control language terms, the person is acting to reduce the discrepancy between a desired future state ("having the book") and a current state ("not having the book"). The image of the book is the higher level goal or standard that is controlling the behavior. A negative feedback loop is created, in which the image remains salient or active until the current state finally matches the desired state, after which the loop is terminated.

Thus, perhaps, the answer to the question "Why is this behavior occurring?" is, "Because the person is going to get a book." However, this quickly leads to the next question: "Why does the person want to retrieve the book?" Perhaps because retrieving the book will help reduce the discrepancy between a higher level or more abstract goal standard ("turn the completed paper in next Monday") and a broader construal of the current state ("the paper has not yet been completed"). One can continue on up the hierarchy in this manner: For example, the person may be turning in the paper in order to get an A in the course, in order to get a high GPA in medical school, in order to get a surgical residence following medical school, in order to get the intended surgical career, and so on.

Carver and Scheier suggest names for each level of the hierarchy, based on the types of standards and the degree of abstraction existing at each level (see Fig. 3.1). These range from "sensation" to "configuration" to "sequence" to "program" to "principle" levels of control. Finally, at the top of the hierarchy, at the "system" level of control, are the person's guiding "possible self images" (Markus & Ruvolo, 1989). These are the person's broadest construals of "myself-in-the-future," which, according to Carver and Scheier's theory, supply the most global reference standards for the system's functioning. Because of this, they also exert potentially the longest term and most stable influence upon the system's functioning. Note that, just as in the Fig. 2.1 hierarchy, higher levels within Carver and Scheier's hierarchy are more stable and change more slowly, whereas processes and change occur much more rapidly at lower levels within the hierarchy (although the Fig. 3.1 hierarchy is also different from the Fig. 2.1 hierarchy, as it focuses on action regulation, rather than on multiple levels of causal influence).

In short, one might explain "the book-retrieving behavior" as occurring, ultimately, because this was the next step in a sequential path or plan leading toward the possible self-image of "me as a surgeon." Indeed, much of the person's behavior, reaching back perhaps many years, might potentially be explainable in terms of this highest level goal.

Of course, not all of the levels or processes in Carver and Scheier's model are active within the conscious mind at once. In particular, people may not often pause to think about the higher level goals and purposes of their action system. Instead, according to Carver and Scheier, people primarily direct their attention where it is most needed—that is, they focus on solving problems at "middle" levels of control (i.e., at the "program" level, in Fig. 3.1). Here lies the domain of yes–no decisions, as people strategize their way through the day, continually deciding between distinct modes or means of enacting their guiding principles.

Still, the higher level purposes are implicit in ongoing functioning even when they are not within awareness, and people can usually report on them when asked (Emmons, 1989). At some earlier point in time the purposes were selected and invested, and now they persist, like puppet masters, at the top of the action system. And indeed, if they were not there, our behavior would be largely chaotic, as we bounced reactively from one event to the next. Again, Carver and Scheier's model nicely explains how humans may proactively shape their own destiny, efficiently linking together serial programs of activity over time (Murray, 1938). Notably, there are many more specific details within the model, which I cannot go into here; see Carver and Scheier (1998) for a more complete exposition.

Action Systems and Entropy

Let us make the discussion more abstract for a minute. The action system can be viewed as a "negentropy producer." Entropy is the tendency for matter and energy to become less organized over time. It is the predominant "force" (or anti-force) operative in the universe, which will inevitably win in the end, as the universe moves toward final heat death. In contrast, negentropy is the process by which new organization arises in the universe. Negentropy represents the temporary victory of structure and order, making use of energy in order to act against the predominant tendency toward disorder and disintegration (Seife, 2003).

Life is the prototypical negentropy producer. Living things are highly organized and highly improbable phenomena, seen from an information-theory or stochastic perspective. The number of different types and compounds of matter that can be found assembled together inside of a living organism is remarkable; just as "one hundred monkeys typing forever will never produce Shakespeare," a living thing would never happen by random chance. Even more remarkable is the ability of this matter and organization to keep itself together over time, resisting the natural tendency toward entropy. Indeed, one of the best definitions of a living system is "a system that maintains itself via dynamic processes at a level of energy and order far from equilibrium" (Glansdorff & Prigogine, 1971; Kauffman, 1995). Living systems are able to go against the predominant trend toward entropy because they are open to the environment—that is, they can incorporate energy and information from the environment into themselves.

Species each have their own characteristic adaptations for staying alive, and arguably, humans' most characteristic adaptation is the ability to create and manage an action system (Carver & Scheier, 1998; MacDonald, 1991). Action systems allow people to flexibly adjust to environmental problems, counteracting present potential entropy, and also to proactively mold the environment to avoid problems, reducing entropy in the future (Sheldon & Vansteenkiste, in press). Not only that, action systems enable people to create new environments and opportunities never dreamed of before, which can permanently reduce or forestall entropy for everyone (i.e., the steam engine). Thus, action systems allow humans to survive and thrive in an amazing variety of locations and situations. Of course, individual action systems differ in the amount of organization they produce, ranging from just enough to stay alive, to enough to potentially transform a whole culture or a whole science (as in the case of Einstein, discussed in chap. 2).

FURTHER IMPLICATIONS OF CARVER AND SCHEIER'S MODEL

Action Systems Are Teleological

One fascinating feature of Carver and Scheier's framework is that it is inherently teleological (which, again, many physical scientists would resist). In other words, what moves the human organism and causes its behavior, according to control theory? The organism's own goals and purposes! Thus, in this framework, people are self-movers and self-causers. Although this would be ridiculous to say with respect to a motorcar, to use Richard Dawkins's example ("Why did the car turn left? Because it made itself do so!"), it is entirely natural to say with reference to living control systems. There is no other way to make sense of them except to say that internal processes are making use of information to direct energy, in order to bring about highly organized outcomes that would never occur otherwise. Again, Carver and Scheier's endorsement of the potential for purposive cognition to gain new control over behavior, implying the existence of free will, is typical for theorists at the middle levels of the Fig. 2.1 hierarchy.

Action Systems Are Holistic

Another important feature of Carver and Scheier's model is that it is holistic. How does one explain a person's behavior? By going up in the action hierarchy, continually asking, "But why is he doing that? Okay, why is he doing that? Okay, why is he doing that?" In other words, although Dawkins explained the workings of a motorcar by reducing it to the workings of pistons and cylinders (going down in the hierarchy, to the "how" of action), Carver and Scheier explained it by going up, to the "why" of action—toward purposive cognition and teleology.

As noted earlier, a higher level in the control hierarchy does not have to be conscious or activated in mind at a particular moment, in order to guide action—higher level standards implicitly influence the functioning of all of the levels below them, because each level "passes the goal down" through the system, directing or at least constraining lower level processes. Thus, the student seeking the book is not necessarily thinking about the "me as surgeon" goal; nevertheless, it is an important part of the context causally shaping his/her behavior at that moment. Also, the higher level does not have to be effective; as is discussed in chapter 6, there are many reasons why people might fail to achieve goals and standards, and thus fail to arrive at otherwise unlikely "possible futures" (Sheldon & Vansteenkiste, in press). Thus, although control theory is teleological in allowing purpose into the scientific theory as an explanatory construct, it does not equate conscious purpose with effective behavior. Again, conscious intentions are only one of many potential influences on behavior, and they may not even have as much control as their owners think they do.

To more vividly illustrate the difference between Carver and Scheier's holistic and teleological model and the standard model of explanation in science, consider this question: What would it mean to apply Dawkins's reductionistic explanatory strategy (i.e., explaining the functioning of the automobile in terms of the functioning of its parts), within the context of Carver and Scheier's model? Let's try it, again considering the example of driving to the library. Dawkins's strategy would reverse everything: Control would originate at the bottom (at the neurobiological or sensory level), and then move up the hierarchy from there. Goals, awareness, and purpose would be nothing more than the functioning of lower levels, each of which determined outcomes at the level above itself, and ultimately determined the goals themselves. So, why did the muscle squeeze? Not because a motion was sought, but rather, because the nerve cells within the muscle were firing. Why did the person think he was seeking a book? Not because he had an assignment in mind, but rather, because he found himself driving to the library. Why did the person think he wanted to get good grades in medical school? Not because this was instrumental to a long-time ambition of his, but rather, because he found himself concerned about getting the paper in on time. Of course, Dawkins argued that we should only go "one or two levels down" in our reductionism. Thus, in terms of Carver and Scheier's model, Dawkins might say that the person is driving to the library (program-level control) because the physical musculature of his body happens to be carrying out actions that will bring him there (sequence-level control).

Hopefully, the contrariness of this example is apparent (although one can find some theories in social psychology, such as self-perception theory, that rely on this kind of approach). The example permits me to emphasize something important: When we get up to the cognitive level of analysis, and also when we begin considering human functionality and adaptation more generally, letting teleology into our explanations is almost inevitable. Indeed, teleological assumptions are commonplace in many applied realms, including artificial intelligence, robotics, and expert systems analysis—again, the purposes or control standards contained within such physical systems' internal software are assumed to guide the functioning of those systems within the material world (Juarrero, 1999). Although the "rest" of the universe may be buffeted about by lower level forces, intelligent organisms or mechanisms containing hierarchical cognitive control systems are irreducibly different—they "give back," shaping and organizing the world to their own purposes (within constraints, of course), reducing the entropy in their lives and the universe in their own unique ways.

Action Systems Are Mechanistic

Although Carver and Scheier's model is holistic and teleological, it is important to point out that it is also mechanistic: Action is viewed as the output of specifiable mental structures and control processes, much in the same manner that a robot, ultimately, functions very mechanistically. This illustrates that one does not have to abandon mechanism, a foundational assumption of science, in order to be a holist (Brandon, 1996). For example, one can posit specific causal mechanisms by which higher level cultural factors (in the Fig. 2.1 model) or higher level goal principles (in Carver and Scheier's Fig. 3.1 model) influence more molecular behaviors.

Finally, let us note that the assumption of mechanism (i.e., of causal regularities and linkages) does not necessarily require the assumption that "man is a machine," despite the robotic implications of Carver and Scheier's model. In chapters 6 and 7 I argue that to the extent people have control over their mechanisms rather than the mechanisms having control of them, they themselves are not machines. As this suggests, the struggle of the human self to achieve greater awareness and to overcome feelings of being mechanically determined by external forces is a very important issue (Deci & Ryan, 2000).

Control Theory and Consilience

One of the most remarkable things about the Carver and Scheier model is that it manages to simultaneously consider many different levels of processing occurring within the brain. Thus, it potentially links the domains of social, personality, cognitive, behavioral, and physiological psychology into one totality. To again use E. O. Wilson's term, this is no small feat of consilience! To illustrate this consilience more concretely, consider an example. As one executes a left-turn in traffic, one is simultaneously: (a) firing a particular set of nerve fibers, (b) coordinating muscles in one's hand, (c) turning the wheel, (d) approaching the library, (e) approaching the paper's completion, (f) approaching the A in the class, (g) approaching the high medical-school GPA, and (h) approaching the image of self-as-surgeon. It seems apparent that such multifinality is the true state of affairs underlying most behaviors, and it is encouraging to find a theoretical perspective that can encompass it. Further consistent with the principle of consilience, the levels all tend to be consistent with another: At a particular moment there is typically "vertical coherence" (Sheldon & Kasser, 1995), such that each process is acting in the service of the same basic goal or set of compatible goals. Muscle contractions to serve the goal of executing a right term are at the same time serving the self-as-surgeon goal, by way of the turn-the-wheel goal, the drive-to-the-library goal, the get-the-book goal, and the get-an-A goal.

Of course, the effectiveness and "interlevel consilience" of the action system are far from given: Action systems can be misregulated, misaligned, or misdirected, as for example when people try to pursue standards without the appropriate skills, pursue standards that are too abstract and ill-specified, or cannot disengage from standards that may no longer be appropriate (see chap. 6 for more detailed consideration of these processes). Thus, the control-theory model can readily address the adaptive and functional outcomes of behavior—the proper focus of biological and social scientists, said Wilson (1998).

Control Theory Suggests Definitions of Optimal Human Being

Finally, another important feature of Carver and Scheier's control-theory model is that it offers a clear potential definition of optimal human being, and clear prescriptions for how to improve human being. Simply put, control theory implies that the more teleological and holistic is an organism's behavior (i.e., the better guided by higher-level purposes), the better off it is. Effectively functioning action systems are those in which longer term goals and purposes are being consistently enacted, via reliable linkages between higher level principles and purposes and the lower level action units that can be entrained to carry out steps toward those purposes. In this manner people can move forward into the future, toward functional states at higher levels of negentropy. The more efficiently they do so (relative to their own standards for rate of forward progress), the more frequently they feel positive emotions (Carver & Scheier, 1990), and the happier they are. Thus, from this perspective, the key for promoting thriving is to promote effective forward motion toward goals.

LIMITATIONS OF CONTROL THEORY

Despite its strengths, Carver and Scheier's approach is not without its critics. For one, few if any of these "nested control loops" have been located within the brain, that is, within the neural architecture (Carver & Scheier, 1998). Rather, the loops' existence is inferred from a logical analysis of the patterning of planned activity. Thus, as with many psychological theories, consilience has not yet been achieved between the physical sciences (working up from the bottom) and the top-down mental processes proposed within the control-theory model (however, see Carver and Scheier, 1998, p. 37, for a discussion of emerging neuroscience data linking frontal lobe activation with self-regulatory cognition).

A more important potential criticism of the control theory model is that the source of the goals or standards within the action system remains unclear (Ryan & Deci, 1999). For example, where did the medical student's goal of "becoming a surgeon" come from? Did it emerge spontaneously within the action system, or was it implanted by the social environment? Surprisingly, Carver and Scheier (1998) said nothing at all about this question in their 350-page book—their discussion only begins after a goal somehow appears within the action system. Presumably, in line with conventional social psychological theory, Carver and Scheier would talk about social norms, role modeling, cognitive dissonance reduction, mere-exposure effects, and the like, in their explanation of how goals appear in the action system. Consistent with this speculation, Carver and Scheier suggested that there are external origins for people's standards for how rapidly they should be moving toward goals—for example, a person in medical school would feel that the proper rate of progress through medical school is the rate expected by the program and faculty (p. 112). Extrapolating from this idea, perhaps the possible self-images themselves, such as the one of "me as a surgeon," also come directly from some source in the environment.

Notice that this picture paints the individual as a relatively passive recipient of system- or self-level standards and implantations; the implication is that we do what we are programmed or told to do. To date, Carver and Scheier have not addressed the issue of how action systems might come to be self-programmed, rather than programmed by the environment. Again, this is a critical issue for optimal human being as seen from the existentialist perspective, and is an important issue in many other theories of personality development.

In short, I believe that Carver and Scheier's model is somewhat incomplete, in that it fails to discuss the source or process of goal engagement (although it does discuss the question of how and when people disengage from goals). With consideration of goal engagement come difficult but also potentially crucial issues, such as: How does people's attention get attracted to particular goals or motives in the first place? How does the nature of their interaction with authorities influence which goals they select? How can people be encouraged to enact important goals and behaviors they don't want to do, such as voting, paying taxes, and serving on committees? Can goals be mis-selected, such that a person squanders time and energy working toward purposes that, somehow, won't be worth it? How can people avoid being controlled by their own control systems—instead, making choices and exerting control over them? These issues occupy much of our attention in chapters 6 and 7.

Despite its limitations, control theory is an impressive achievement, which offers many tools for deriving an integrative understanding of the functional organization of human behavior. However, there are other aspects of the person that are also important to personality researchers, such as biological temperament, foundational traits, evolved predispositions, beliefs and schemas about the world, and self-narratives. It is not clear how to get these constructs into Carver and Scheier's model, as most of them are not explicitly purposive constructs. To try to address these, I now turn to another integrative conception of personality and personality theory, recently proposed by Dan McAdams.

MCADAMS'S HIERARCHICAL MODEL OF PERSONALITY

The Basic Model

Figure 3.2 illustrates McAdams's (1995, 1996, 1998) well-received conceptual integration of the diverse conceptual terrain of personality theory. The model proposes three levels or "tiers" of personality theory. Each tier represents an important branch or area of personality theory, areas that have traditionally been investigated in isolation from each other. McAdams argues that in order to know a person, we must have information about not only the person's dispositional or habitual traits (Level 1), but also his or her conscious goals and purposes (Level 2), and unfolding identities and self-stories (Level 3). I briefly consider each level next, and then consider each level in more detail in later chapters.

Level 1 is the realm of personality traits and dispositions. Here can be located many conceptions and investigations, including those of the California–Berkeley school, the Eysenckian school, the Cattelian school, and the current Big Five school. In these approaches personality is construed as a set of

$$\text{Personality} = \begin{array}{c} \text{Self/Life-Story} \\ + \\ \text{Motives/Goals/Intentions} \\ + \\ \text{Traits/Individual Differences} \end{array}$$

FIG. 3.2.   McAdams's "three tiers" of personality theory.

habits or predispositions, which shape individuals' behaviors in predictable ways. There is typically little focus on intentionality, adaptive functioning, or subjectivity, that is, the "active" individual; as befits a lower level of analysis, the emphasis is not on free will and intentionality. As illustrated in greater detail in chapter 5, the primary controversies in this area have involved reaching agreement on the correct number of, and definition of, foundational human traits—for example, are there three or five fundamental traits? In addition, attention has been focused on cross-cultural generalizability. Do the same personality factors emerge in other types of cultures? Also, how should traits be named—should the creativity trait be labeled openness, intellect, absorption, or cultivation?

Level 2, according to McAdams's model, concerns goals, intentions, and plans. This domain of research focuses on the intentional world. Here can be located the investigations of the early German action theorists (Asch, Lewin), as well as the current contingent of European action theorists (Kuhl, Baltes, Heckhausen); the motive disposition theorists, including McClelland, Atkinson, Stewart, and Winter; the personal goal theorists, including Emmons, Little, Klinger, Cantor, and myself; and, to some extent, the social-cognitive camp, led by Mischel, Cervone, and Shoda. These "middle" perspectives focus directly on people's motivational and intentional lives, typically from a first-person perspective. In addition, such middle-level perspectives typically assume some degree of free will and self-determination of behavior, as discussed earlier.

Notably, Carver and Scheier's control theory could possibly be located at Level 2 in Fig. 3.2, as the most comprehensive available account of the functioning of the intentional system. However, I believe that Carver and Scheier's model is more than just a theory at the "goals and intentions" level of personality; this is because the model addresses every aspect of the behaving individual, potentially at every level of analysis found in Fig. 2.1. In contrast, McAdams's hierarchy does not explicitly concern the organization of behavior, but rather, the organization of personality theory. Thus, the models have somewhat different objectives.

Finally, Level 3, according to McAdams, is the domain of the self, or the constructed set of self-beliefs and narratives. Self and self-processes are a huge area of inquiry in contemporary social-personality psychology. Some researchers seek to identify universal self-processes or patterns, typically using experimental methods. Other researchers focus on personality and individual differences in self, typically using qualitative and correlational methods. Because McAdams discusses the self primarily in individual difference terms, I do so also.

Potentially the most interesting perspective on the self-as-individual, for the question of defining and understanding optimal human being, is individual differences in the "stories people tell" about themselves and their lives, that is, the ongoing personal narratives being constructed and updated over the person's life. The assumption is that the self is, literally, the narrative that it tells about itself. Understanding these phenomenologically rich and cognitively complex mental structures can lend deep thematic unity to our understanding of personality, says McAdams, unity that we cannot derive merely by considering the expression of personality traits (Level 1) and the workings of the action system (Level 2). I agree with him, noting also that self-as-story is the level of analysis that receives the least attention in Carver and Scheier's model.

Does McAdams's Model Depict a Functional Hierarchy?

One important question that arises concerning McAdams's model is this: Do the levels in his model depict a functional arrangement, in the same way that different levels within Carver and Scheier's model function together? That is, do a person's traits, goals, and selves interact or combine in some way? Taking the functional perspective further, might one say that a person is somehow "better off," or has reached a more optimal state of being, if the three different levels posited by McAdams's model are more effectively linked or intercoordinated within that person?

McAdams (1996) disavowed (or at least deemphasized) possible connections between the levels, in part to discourage reductionism. Again, he views each of the three levels within his model as necessary and complementary accounts of personhood, such that no level can be reduced to another level. Thus, goals are more than just "traits working themselves out," and selves are more than just the end products of trait and motivational processes. Also, McAdams asserted that "the levels do not need to exist in meaningful relation to each other in order to exist as meaningful levels" (McAdams, 1995, p. 386).

Still, I believe that it may be useful to consider the linkages between the different levels in McAdams's model, especially as one attempts to define optimal human being for a particular person. Do a person's traits, goals, and self-stories cohere with one another, or do inconsistencies between them introduce conflicts into his or her personality system? For example, it seems logical to say that a person is more integrated and is more likely to be happy and successful, to the extent that (a) his or her personality traits match or even serve his/her goals and intentions, or to the extent that (b) his or her personality traits match or even serve his or her sense of self and life story, and (c) his or her goals and intentions match or even serve his or her sense of self and life story. These three suggestions exemplify chapter 1's working definition of optimal human being, namely, that optimality in part involves functional coherence between the different levels of the person. Accordingly, they each receive considerable attention later in the book.

A Proposed Extension of McAdams's Model

Although I believe McAdams's model represents a breakthrough for achieving consilience within personality theory, here I would like to propose that one more level be added to his model. Figure 3.3 contains this proposed addition. In brief, I suggest that it will also be fruitful to consider a fourth level, namely, the organismic foundations of personality on which individual differences rest. In other words, it is useful to consider basic personality processes, needs, and characteristics built into the psychology of all people, which are inherent to the human organism. By understanding what is common to and necessary for all people, we will be better able to understand why some individual differences or unique ways of being are successful, and others not so successful. Thus, we may gain some important new criteria for evaluating optimal human being (in the same way that understanding a prototypical automobile's functioning may help to understand optimal automotive functioning). Also, by positing an underlying "organismic nature" level, we gain a framework for considering the evolved (or species-typical) characteristics and tendencies existing within human beings. Thus, it may help personality theory to achieve consilience with evolutionary and biological theory. I further discuss these possibilities in chapter 4, as the universal features of human nature are considered in detail.

MCCRAE AND COSTA'S MODEL OF PERSONALITY

The Basic Model

Figure 3.4 presents yet another comprehensive attempt to organize the different domains of personality theory into a single picture. The model was created by two prominent trait theorists, Robert McCrae and Paul Costa (1995). Similarly to McAdams's model, the framework focuses on three major aspects of personality: traits, goals, and selves. However, McCrae and Costa's model differs from the models presented earlier, which focused on the hierarchical relations between dif-

Self/Life-Story

+

Personality =   Motives/Goals/Intentions

+

Traits/Individual Differences

+

Universal Characteristics

FIG. 3.3.   Adding a fourth tier to McAdams's three tiers.

ferent levels of action, or different levels of personality; instead, the model focuses on temporal processes and changes occurring over the life span. Specifically, it tries to show how traits, goals, and selves causally impact each other over time. This presentation is very revealing.

Space here precludes thorough discussion of McCrae and Costa's model, which has some positive features. For present purposes, I would simply like to point out the basic assumptions behind the model, to show that the specter of reductionism arises among the different disciplines of personality, just as it arises concerning the different levels of analysis depicted in Fig. 2.1. Specifically, McCrae and Costa's model specifies that traits and "basic dispositions" (Level 2 in Fig. 3.3) are the primary elements of personality. These in turn give rise to "characteristic adaptations," a category that includes goals and strivings (Level 3 in Fig. 3.3). In turn, strivings are said to give rise to the self, including self-schemas and personal myths (Level 4 in Fig. 3.3). The implication of this arrangement is that strivings are "nothing more" than traits working themselves out, and selves are "nothing more" than strivings (in conjunction with biographical factors) working themselves out.

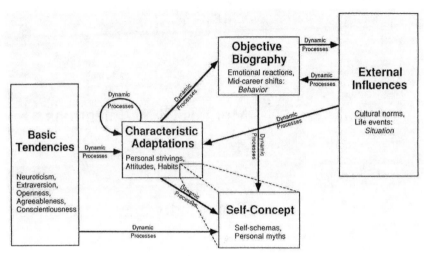

FIG. 3.4. McCrae and Costa's model of traits, goals, and selves. A five-factor theory of personality, with examples of specific content and arrows indicating the direction of major causal pathways mediated by dynamic processes. *From* Costa and McCrae (1994). "Set like plaster"? Evidence for the stability of adult personality. In T. Heatherton & J. Weinberger (Eds.), *Can personality change?* (pp. 21–40). Washington, DC: American Psychological Association. Reprinted with permission by The Guilford Press, New York, NY.

To further emphasize the point, consider that causality only flows from the bottom up in McCrae and Costa's model, as indicated by the arrows in the model. Traits, at the bottom of McAdams's hierarchy, can influence both strivings and selves. Strivings, at the next level up in McAdams's hierarchy, can influence selves (which are even further up), but not traits (which are below). Selves, at the top level of McAdams's hierarchy, can influence neither strivings nor traits (which are both below). In fact, it appears that the self influences *nothing* in this model—no arrows lead away from self-concept, and thus it apparently has no causal impact on the world.

Again, this is as we might expect, from a theoretical perspective focusing on a "lower" hierarchical level (in this case, the lowest level of McAdams's hierarchy). However, such reductionistic assumptions are exactly what McAdams (1996) was resisting, in his insistence that each of the three tiers of personality has unique effects on a person's life. Note that McCrae and Costa's assumptions also run directly counter to Carver and Scheier's more holistic model, in which high-level self-concepts (i.e., "me as a surgeon") are perhaps the most important causal influence upon long-term behavior. Finally, they also run counter to the hierarchical pluralist approach discussed in chapter 2, according to which each level of analysis can potentially be causal with respect to events at every other analysis.

THE MODEL OF PERSONALITY ADOPTED FOR CHAPTERS 4–7

Thus, I adopt Fig. 3.3 as a general framework for organizing personality, as I proceed to the rest of the book. In other words, I assume that to understand personality, we need to understand the basic human organism, individual differences in basic traits, individual differences in goals and intentions, and individual differences in selves and self-experience. I also assume that each of these characteristics of persons can influence the other types of characteristic, at different times or in different situations, in addition to differentially determining behavior, at different times or in different situations.

From the consilience perspective, a primary advantage of adopting Fig. 3.3 as the overarching model of personality is that the four levels it depicts can be inserted directly into Fig. 2.1 as sublevels at the level of personality, so that they might be considered in conjunction with the other human sciences and levels of analysis. This becomes reasonable once we make the assumption that each level has its own unique explanatory power for behavior (as does McAdams, if not McCrae and Costa), and also the assumption that the levels may be functionally related to each other, to a greater or lesser extent (as do I, if not McAdams).

In adopting Fig. 3.3 as the guiding configuration for chapters 4–7, will I be leaving Carver and Scheier's (Fig. 3.1) framework behind? No: The goals and intentions chapter (chap. 6) makes considerable use of it, for explicating "action-systemic" perspectives on optimal functioning. Also, the final chapter (chap. 10) makes use of Carver and Scheier's important concept of functional linkages between different levels of analysis as a general tool for understanding personal integration and optimal human being, and also for understanding optimal functioning among the human sciences.

4   The Universal Human Organism: Species-Typical Human Nature

In this chapter I attempt to elucidate the "organismic foundations" of personality, that is, the human nature that we all share. What needs, propensities, and characteristics do all humans have in common? In so doing, I focus on the bottom level of Fig. 3.3 (species-typical human nature), which I have suggested should be appended as a fourth (lowest) level of analysis within McAdams's (1996) hierarchical model of traits, goals, and self-narratives. Again, this four-level model can be viewed as a subhierarchy nested within the personality level of the total Fig. 2.1 hierarchy, and each level should in principle have unique explanatory status for understanding human behavior.

I first attempt to explain why personality psychologists should care about human universals. How might this focus help or complement personality psychology's traditional focus on individual differences? Then I consider what it means to say that a characteristic is universal—does this entail that everyone has it to the same amount, or that everyone has it but in perhaps differing amounts? That everyone has it all the time, or that people have differing amounts of it at different times? I then consider where universals come from, by discussing the evolutionary perspective on personality. I hope to show that the evolutionary perspective offers the best theoretical lens for viewing the question of human universals, as well as offering potentially powerful insights on the nature of optimal human being.

Then, in the second part of this chapter, I consider a variety of "candidate human universals," ranging from physiological needs to social-cognitive mechanisms to psychological needs to sociocultural practices. In addition to identifying promising candidate universals of each of these four types, I also consider the probable adaptive function of each universal. What was it about these characteristics that made them part of everyone's genome?

At the end of the chapter, I will attempt to identify human universals that are especially relevant to optimal human being. What needs and propensities do we all share, which, if satisfied or allowed expression, enable us to maximally fulfill ourselves? I also discuss the organismic philosophical perspective, which makes strong positive assumptions about basic human nature, and provides the meta-theory for much of the thinking in this book.

THREE FUNDAMENTAL AGENDAS
FOR PERSONALITY PSYCHOLOGY

One way of describing the theoretical agenda of personality psychology is to take note of the fact that every person is simultaneously (a) like all other persons, (b) like some other persons, and (c) like no other person (Kluckhohn & Murray, 1953). In other words, we are each all the same in some ways, somewhat different from each other in other ways, and entirely unique in other ways (McAdams, 2001). Kluckhohn and Murray suggested that all three issues are proper topics of study and theory for personality psychologists. However, contemporary personality researchers typically focus only on the second issue just mentioned, that is, on identifying, measuring, and understanding the ways in which people differ from each other (in particular, this is the focus of the trait approach, which is the topic of the next chapter). The first and third issues receive much less attention in contemporary personality psychology, for somewhat different reasons. Before proceeding further, it is instructive to consider these reasons, as it both helps to illustrate the "turf wars" that often dominate within academic discourse, and helps to illustrate what personality psychologists may gain by considering the level of organismic foundations, the topic of this chapter.

Why Personality Psychologists Resist Consideration
of How All Humans Are the Same

Personality psychologists typically do not study ways in which all people are the same, because this has traditionally been the domain of social and contextual psychologies, which attempt to identify fundamental social forces and group dynamics that condition all humans in the same way. For example, a social psychologist will try to identify the contextual conditions that cause "groupthink," or the interpersonal conditions that trigger a certain social response (such as "I'm sorry"), under the assumption that these conditions largely determine individual behavior. Or, a sociologist will attempt to identify the sociohistorical forces that prompt individuals to adopt certain roles, practices, or postures, again with the assumption that people are fundamentally conditioned by these forces.

Personality psychologists tend to resist such assumptions, as they seem to suggest that individuality is swallowed up by, or can be reduced to nothing more than, social-contextual forces. As mentioned earlier, strong turf wars have characterized the relations of social and personality psychologists (whose disciplines focus on adjacent levels of Fig. 2.1), as each perspective labors to legitimate its own claims regarding the causal determination of behavior (Funder & Ozer, 1983; Mischel, 1968). Personality psychologists fear that if they focus on how all persons respond in the same way, they may lose sight of their traditional subject matter—the differences between people. In addition, they may cede ground to the social psychological argument that personality differences may be dismissed as unimportant or inconsequential (Mischel, 1968).

I suggest that, in reality, personality researchers have nothing to fear—they will not be "reduced out of existence" by social or contextual psychologies. Part of this has to do with an empirical fact, that social and interpersonal factors have roughly equal causal influence on behavior, each accounting for about 10% of the variance (Funder & Ozer, 1983; the remaining variance is presumably accounted for by unmeasured causal factors or by random factors). That is, when personality and behavioral tendencies are measured with sufficient reliability, then personality is an equally strong predictor of behavior as social context (Epstein, 1979). In multilevel model terms, personality main effects are irreducible to social force main effects, because each refers to distinct and irreducible categories of phenomena.

Another reason social factors can never dominate the individual is another empirical fact, namely, that humans are not merely blank slates (or disks, to update the metaphor), ready to be written over by the environment. Instead they come with differential propensities, sensitivities, and preparednesses. Specifically, humans differ in their temperaments: that is, in their arousability, reactivity, emotionality, sensitivity to rewards and punishment, and sociability (Kagan, 1994). These inborn propensities send children in different developmental directions from the very beginning, helping to determine the kinds of environments and experiences to which the child will be exposed (Scarr & McCartney, 1983). In addition, they ensure that children will react differently, even if they are exposed to the very same social situation or stimulus (Rowe, 2001). These temperamental differences are part of personality, preceding exposure to social or contextual factors, and fundamentally condition the effects of such factors (see chap. 5 for further discussion of temperament).

Does the fact of inherited temperament mean that all behavior is reducible to genetics and the biochemical level of analysis? In other words, should personality psychologists fear a territorial attack from below, by the behavioral geneticists, if not from above, by the social psychologists? No—in fact, almost all behavioral geneticists take an interactionist position: that is, they assume that final outcomes and behaviors are a joint product of genetic preparedness taken in combination with particular encountered situations and contexts (Kagan, 1994). Individuals thus become "calibrated" to their environments, developing specific "basic adaptations" that correspond to their particular life context (McCrae & Costa, 1995). Furthermore, the developing action system within each individual begins to react not just to the environment, but also to its own productions, innovations, and interpretations (MacDonald, 1991). Thus, ultimately, people learn to calibrate and create themselves (Buss, 1997a), further removing their behavior from the possibility of simple prediction via genes. In short, genes influence, but certainly do not completely determine, behavior. The issue of interactionism is considered further later in the chapter, after the evolutionary perspective has been introduced.

Why Personality Psychologists Resist Consideration of How Each Human Is Unique

Let us return to the three ways of understanding personality mentioned by Kluckhohn and Murray (1953), briefly digressing from the main topic of the chapter (foundational human nature) to consider their third issue: how each person is entirely unique. Of course, this is an issue not easily understood from the biological perspective, which primarily concerns variations in the basic temperamental systems shared by all. In other words, biological perspectives assume that all humans have the same emotional and physiological systems, although they vary in their "settings" on these systems (Tooby & Cosmides, 1990). Obviously, one would not build "from the ground up" and seek to identify a completely unique emotional system, pattern of physiological arousal, or appetite within a particular person. Thus, the question of human uniqueness has received little attention from biologically oriented personality psychologists.

Indeed, few personality psychologists, of any theoretical persuasion, study the ways in which each person is unique, or unlike any other persons. In large part this is because the uniqueness approach sometimes seems to threaten foundational assumptions of psychological science—namely, the assumption that quantitative measurements can be made and that people can then be compared on the basis of those measurements. Fanning this fear, proponents of the "uniqueness" perspective sometimes argue that quantitative methodologies are fundamentally flawed—that by making and comparing measurements, psychologists lose sight of the individuals that they are studying, adopting a misguided focus on abstract psychological constructs, rather than on persons themselves (Jourard, 1974; Lamiell, 1997). "Uniqueness" proponents typically argue that case or small sample studies, focusing primarily on qualitative description and biography rather than quantitative prediction, are the most appropriate tools for the task of understanding personality (Runyan, 1997). However, most personality researchers are uncomfortable with such tools, assumptions, and their implications, and thus are reluctant to abandon their nomothetic quantitative approaches.

Just as I argued earlier that universalist perspectives do not threaten traditional personality psychology, I now suggest that uniqueness perspectives are also not a real threat. This is because it is possible to have both consideration of uniqueness and quantitative measurement, via mixed idiographic/nomothetic methodologies. As discussed in chapter 6 on goals and intentions, such methodologies offer excellent means of comparing people, while still taking account of their uniqueness (Emmons, 1989). For example, although each person can begin by listing his or her own distinct personal goals, the person can also be compared to other persons, after the goals have been coded into categories, or after participants have all rated their goals on the same conceptual dimensions. Thus, I do not agree that human unique-ness cannot be considered in a comparative sense. Instead I advocate a middle posi-tion, which addresses uniqueness but nevertheless extracts dimensions of commonality underlying the uniqueness (Sheldon, Joiner, Pettit, & Williams, 2003).

CONSIDERING THE NATURE OF HUMAN UNIVERSALS

It is time to turn to the primary topic of this chapter, namely, the underlying human nature that we all share (i.e., Kluckhohn and Murray's first agenda). Indeed, this question is alive and well within contemporary psychology (Buss, 2001; Deci & Ryan, 2000), and is perhaps more important than ever, given the increasing popu-larity of the evolutionary perspective within psychology (discussed later). Part of the purpose of this chapter is to identify some universals that are truly characteris-tic of every species member. However, I also attempt to identify some potential universals about which there is more controversy. Not surprisingly, these more controversial candidate universals tend to be located higher up on the Fig. 2.1 hier-archy, in the direction of social behavior and needs, rather than down at the level of physiological mechanisms and basic life-support. This is because, as discussed in chapter 2, higher level factors can be more difficult to define and measure pre-cisely, and are also seemingly more vulnerable to potential reduction to the many lower level factors on which they rest.

Before considering particular universals, it is important to consider what we mean by the word *universal*. I define a human universal as *a psychological process, need, or tendency that is evidenced by every human being*. For example, all humans have the same basic psychobiological needs, such as needs for food, water, and air; all humans desire attachments to nurturing others, at least as infants; and all humans are sensitive to the opinions and evaluations of others, and to their place within group hierarchies. Although there are many further distinctions or subtleties that could be made or relied on in considering or defining the topic of human universals (see Brown, 1991, chap. 2, for example), in this chapter I stick with this simple definition.

Of course, people may differ in the way that they engage in a tendency. These dif-ferences can be influenced by variations in immediate social contexts, variations in individual learning histories, variations in people's developmental stages, and varia-tions in cultural norms and practices, among other factors. For example, people cer-tainly prefer different foods, depending on their context, history, and culture. As another example, people certainly express their affection and attachments for others in very different ways, depending on their cultural group, their basic temperament, or their developmental stage. The crucial point here is that the basic tendencies or processes are common to everyone, regardless of how they are tangibly expressed.

In addition, people may also differ in how much of the tendency they have. That is, there is a continuum of variation, across the different human characteristics one might examine. For some characteristics, there is likely to be no variation at all: All members of the species possess it, all of the time, to an approximately equal extent, no matter what their culture or personality. Into this category fall autonomic mechanisms, basic hormonal systems, and primary physiological drives. Of course, it is very logical that there would be less variation at the level of physiological processes and needs, because these processes concern basic life support. Indeed, variation here might be deadly: Once a system (such as low blood glucose giving rise to a hunger drive) works, to have it be readily alterable by further mutation (Tooby & Cosmides, 1990) could be potentially disastrous, and genes allowing such mutation would tend to be selected out of the gene pool. Thus, certain human characteristics are likely to be almost completely invariant across individuals.

In contrast, for other characteristics there is likely to be substantial variation, such that individual members of the species differ considerably on how much they evidence the characteristic. Obviously, however, the more people differ in their level of a characteristic, the less we would say it is a universal feature of human nature. In other words, we would be more inclined to locate that feature at Level 2 of Fig. 3.3 (individual differences or traits), instead of at Level 1 (universal commonalities). For example, the fact that some people are very extraverted and gregarious, whereas others are more restrained and even averse to social contact, suggests that "gregariousness" is not an invariant feature of human nature, and should almost certainly be located at Level 2 (traits) rather than at Level 1 (universals). Notably, it may be quite difficult in practice to establish cutoff levels for particular characteristics or tendencies, such that below a certain level of variability the characteristic is considered universal, and above that level it is considered as an individual difference (Brown, 1991).

It is important to point out that the definition of universal proposed here is different from approaches that try to identify universal dimensions of individual differences. For example, McCrae (2001) considered universals in terms of a "trans-cultural level of analysis," in which the goal is to identify the basic traits on which all people vary, in every culture around the world. To illustrate, proponents of the "Big Five" model of personality attempt to establish, through lexical and factor analyses, that neuroticism, extraversion, agreeableness, conscientiousness, and openness to experience are the basic dimensions on which people differ, in every culture. Although this is an important research enterprise, it is a somewhat different matter to focus on basic dimensions of difference than it is to identify basic behavioral similarities across cultures and persons. Thus, although a Big Five theorist would like to show that any human personality can be described and located in the same factor space, depending on its level of each of the five traits, in the current approach, I would like to show that all human personalities are equivalent, in some basic ways. Again, chapter 5 addresses the trait perspective, that is, Level 2 of Fig. 3.3, in greater detail.

THE EVOLUTIONARY PERSPECTIVE UPON UNIVERSALS

The evolutionary perspective evidences the most concern with, and provides the best account of, human universals (Brown, 1991). Thus we now consider this perspective in some detail.

Species-Typical Human Nature

One important enterprise of evolutionary scientists is to identify the unique features and behaviors that characterize particular species. What characteristics or processes can be seen in every member of a given species? For example, all members of particular spider species weave particular types of web, all members of particular bird species emit particular songs or calls, and so on. Evolutionary psychology is the field that attempts to answer this question regarding human beings, and thus it is uniquely positioned to address the issue of universals. Evolutionary psychology can trace its lineage from Darwin himself, who in the last section of *The Origin of Species* said, "Psychology will be based on a new foundation." Evolutionary psychology can also trace its lineage through ethology, whose heyday was the 1950s and 1960s (although the field still exists today), and through sociobiology, whose heyday was in the 1970s and 1980s (a field now subsumed by evolutionary psychology).

Contemporary evolutionary psychologists typically assume that humans have large numbers of hard-wired cognitive modules and motivational propensities. Thus, in contrast to the "standard social science model" (Tooby & Cosmides, 1992; discussed in chap. 2), which views the human mind as a blank slate with very little preprogramming (Pinker, 2002), evolutionary perspectives assume that we have countless mental mechanisms, each of which evolved to help solve particular adaptive problems. Thus, we come prepared to do many things, including to pay attention to human faces, to form attachments and relationships, to join groups and form coalitions, to negotiate status hierarchies, to distinguish between in-group and out-group members, and to seek high-quality mating opportunities (Tooby & Cosmides, 1992). In this view, the mind is like a Swiss Army knife, equipped with a large number of blades, tools, and functions. The argument is that only with the help of such specialized adaptations can we account for the bewildering complexity of the computations that routinely occur within the human mind.

From this perspective, the primary research agenda of psychology should be to use evolutionary theory to derive predictions about the various mental mechanisms, and then conduct experiments that clearly demonstrate their existence and manner of operation (Buss, 1995). For example, Cosmides (1989) reasoned that humans needed to have an ability to recognize when others are taking advantage of them, a "cheater-detection" mechanism. To demonstrate the cheater-detection mechanism, Cosmides used a difficult logic problem, the Wason selection task, which only makes intuitive sense if it is framed in the context of detecting cheating within a social exchange. As predicted, people could easily solve the problem if it was framed in this manner, whereas they could not solve the problem phrased in the traditional manner. Apparently, people have a cognitive circuit that "kicks in" when they face this crucial social task, and the circuit is typically unavailable when this context is missing.

An important thing to point out is that Cosmides (1989) assumed and argued that this mechanism is a human universal—that is, it was selected for over the course of human history, until finally every member of the species had it (and continues to have it); it is part of the "psychic unity" of mankind (Tooby & Cosmides, 1992). Thus, a sensitivity to others' cheating is now a species-typical feature of human nature, in the same way that hoarding nuts is a species-typical feature of certain ground squirrels, weaving asymmetric webs is a species-typical feature of certain types of spiders, and so on. Again, although there may be variations in how the mechanism is expressed and regulated, the underlying sensitivity is assumed to be present, to an equal degree, in everyone. I believe Cosmides' (1989) research indeed told us something new and important about human nature and the basic human organism.

It is also important to note that evolutionary perspectives do not necessarily entail that everyone behaves in the same way, just because they all have the same mechanism; evolutionary psychologists typically take an *interactionist* perspective, just as do behavioral geneticists (Buss, 2001). Thus, the universal mechanisms are said to provide the basic cognitive and neural circuitry, which are calibrated by learning and culture. Accordingly, the circuits can lead to different very outputs, depending on their inputs. For example, in one culture or set of circumstances, the cheater-detection mechanism might become oriented toward one's place in the group, and whether one is giving up too much, personally, in the quest for group belongingness. In another culture or set of circumstances, the mechanism might become calibrated to focus on romantic relationships, and whether one is being exploited or cheated on by one's partner.

A crucial feature of evolutionary psychology is its focus on the adaptive function that the various features of human nature serve. Why was a particular characteristic, mechanism, or propensity selected for, in humans' evolutionary history? What advantage did it give those who possessed it, compared to those who did not—an advantage that was so important, that now everyone has it? Does it still confer benefit, in the present day? Typically, adaptive function or selective advantage is assessed with respect to either survival or reproduction. Thus, an evolved characteristic is one that either helped humans stay alive, or helped them to reproduce successfully, or both.

The adaptive function of the cheater-detection mechanism is obvious. As discussed in more detail in chapter 8, a primary adaptation for human beings is their ability to cooperate together, in very complex ways. As is well known in evolutionary game theory, cooperation is an effective strategy, but it brings vulnerability: Cooperative individuals can be exploited and deceived, and groups can become infested with parasites, that is, "free riders" (Axelrod, 1984). A cheater-detection mechanism is straightforwardly predicted by evolutionary theory, as a logical next step in the coevolutionary "arms race" between an adaptive social strategy (cooperation) and its potential undermining by noncooperators (Tooby & Cosmides, 1992).

Interestingly, adaptive function, the focus of evolutionary analyses, is an important potential criterion for optimal human being, and perhaps the most objective criterion of all. Although there may not be any "deeper meaning" to our lives and the universe, at the very least we can be sure that surviving and then reproducing are of primary importance, because that is what allowed us to exist to ask the question! Indeed, from the evolutionary perspective, any claimed form of optimal human being that involved humans working against their own survival or reproductive interests would inevitably be selected against, in the long term, and should disappear as a component of human nature. Thus, perhaps living long and having lots of children and grandchildren is the only true criterion for optimal human being! In the conclusion of this chapter, however, I argue that there is much more to optimal human being than this.

The Origin of Species-Typical Mechanisms

What conditions create species-typical or universal mechanisms? Geary and Huffman (2002) recently published a revealing analysis of this question. In a nutshell, they argued that inherited mental mechanisms are likely to be invariant when the adaptive problem that they evolved to solve was invariant across generations or the lifespan. For example, given basic game-theoretic considerations, it is likely that the problem of cheater-detection has been salient throughout *Homo sapiens* history—there is no getting around the possibility of being exploited in one's interdependent cooperative relationships. In addition, this possibility likely persists throughout the life span (from children being exploited by siblings, to women being exploited by their spouses, to elderly persons being exploited by con artists). Thus, from a cost-benefit perspective, it is perhaps most efficient to have such tendencies "hard-wired" into the genome. However, where there are large variations in environments or circumstances, it is perhaps more efficient to allow for more plasticity in the mechanism or propensity.

Note the subtle distinction between saying that a mechanism is hard-wired but can produce different outputs depending on the inputs to it or the way it is calibrated, and saying that there is no encapsulated mechanism at all due to that mechanism's historically inconsistent functionality, with the mechanism instead needing to be learned or acquired "from scratch" as needed. This distinction can easily become blurred, especially as one moves from the realm of physiology (where distinct mechanisms and regulatory processes have been empirically documented) to the realm of social cognition (where there are many more degrees of freedom for both inherited mechanisms and online learning to operate). This is perhaps an inevitable ambiguity, given that psychology is not yet able to demonstrate the specific neural mechanisms underlying mental acts (Kagan, 1994). Only when both specific behaviors and the corresponding neural processes can be measured with precision will it be possible to determine if there is a "core" or invariant mechanism underlying a particular category of behavior, which is merely differently calibrated according to the inputs to the mechanism, or whether rather, no such core mechanism exists. Again, Geary and Huffman's (2002) cost-benefit analysis suggests that which of the two is the case likely depends on how little the basic contours of the adaptive problem vary across generations and the life span. For some adaptive problems it might be most efficient to have a single general mechanism (in terms of the cheater-detection mechanism, the tendency to ask, "Is this person breaking the rule?"), which is easily modifiable by different inputs (i.e., it can be applied to very different types of rules). For other adaptive problems, a single cognitive mechanism might turn out to distort or over-simplify the situation, in which case multiple mechanisms might evolve, or no par-ticular mechanism evolves, with individuals instead relying on learning from scratch as necessary.

CONSIDERING FOUR TYPES OF HUMAN UNIVERSAL

In considering potential human universals I divide the discussion into four parts: physiological needs, social-cognitive mechanisms/biases, psychological needs, and socially evoked rituals and group processes. These correspond to potential universals that are relevant to low, middle, and higher levels of the Fig. 2.1 hierar-chy. Of course, there are likely to be considerable overlaps among these; that is, I do not assume that the four types of processes I describe are independent of, or completely distinct from, each other.

Universal Physical Needs

What are the universal physical or bodily needs? The candidates are obvious and limited: All humans need nutrition, water, oxygen, sleep, to be able to eliminate waste, and a proper environmental temperature range. Given these things, a human could remain alive indefinitely. Huge research literatures exist in each of these ar-eas, concerning the mechanisms and processes by which people satisfy these phys-iological needs. Indeed, drive theories of motivation, dominant in the 1940s and 1950s, were based almost entirely on such forces and processes (Weiner, 1992). Again, the typical assumption of such biologically oriented researchers is that there is little if any meaningful variation across humans in the way these processes occur, as such variability might prove disastrous for life support (Tooby & Cosmides, 1990).

Again, however, these biological motives can vary in their expression in differ-ent cultural or personal contexts; that is, there are also top-down chains of causal-ity that influence them. For example, a perfectionist with low self-efficacy (Bardone, Vohs, Abramson, Heatherton, & Joiner, 2000) may develop a very dif-ferent food-regulation style compared to most people, or a culture may develop a very different set of attitudes and motives toward food, compared to another cul-ture. Again, the interactionist perspective would expect this; inborn mechanisms and propensities combine with encountered circumstances and traditions, to help determine behavior. Nonetheless, my point here is that although they may be ex-pressed very differently at the behavioral level, there are still underlying biological constants. Hunger pangs are generated by deficiencies in blood glucose and moti-vate eating behavior, no matter which food, person, or culture.

As already noted, the list of definite universal physiological needs is indeed a short one. However, one can also perhaps expand the list to include bodily needs that are not as immediately essential to life. These include needs for exercise, for hygiene, to blink, to scratch, for optimal arousal, and perhaps for sex. These are states of satisfaction that people desire and strive for, but that are not necessarily life threatening if we do not get them. Still, it can be psychologically debilitating, or physically debilitating in the long term, not to get them. Also, even if these needs or processes are not necessary for life, this does not mean that they are inconsequential. All people suffer when they experience no stimulation at all, or when their eyelids are fixed open to prevent blinking, or when they are covered in filth—although, of course, their threshold levels of suffering may differ. Again, social and culture-level variables certainly moderate the levels, triggers, and behavioral routes chosen to obtain these needs, but the needs are present within everyone.

Social-Cognitive Mechanisms

Humans have a large number of innate cognitive abilities, including the ability to learn languages, to think abstractly, to model the future, and to generalize from experience (Pinker, 2002). In this section I focus specifically on social-cognitive mechanisms, as cognitive psychology per se is not as relevant to personality theory and the question of optimal personality functioning. A social-cognitive mechanism is a computational ability or decision-making bias that is relevant to social interaction. We already considered one important social-cognitive mechanism that is likely to occur in all human beings: a sensitivity to cheaters, that is, those who would violate implicit and explicit social contracts. According to Tooby and Cosmides (1992), this sensitivity is based on evolved neural hardware that (a) makes a person sensitive to the adaptive problem when it arises, and (b) gives the person the information-processing capacity necessary to solve the problem. However, contemporary evolutionary psychology also proposes many other social-cognitive mechanisms besides this one. I next consider just a few of the most discussed and best documented processes.

One undoubtedly important mechanism is the tendency to classify others as in-group members or out-group members. In other words, we seem to have an inborn propensity to try to figure out who is with us, like us, and coextensive with us, as compared to who is against us, not like us, and separate from us (Geary, 1998). This propensity constitutes the "sensitivity" mentioned earlier; it seems we automatically tend to perceive others in in-group/out-group terms. Furthermore, we appear to be innately inclined to make the calculation based on a small set of particular factors, such as race, gender, nationality, and family. These factors correspond to important features of the early human environment (the "environment of evolutionary adaptability" or EEA; Buss, 2001) that had relevance to survival and reproduction. In other words, if we assume, as most evolutionary theorists do, that humans evolved in small family or tribal groups, and that cooperation with these groups is an important adaptation in its own right, then it is logical that we develop strong tendencies to classify and prefer others on the basis of such features (Geary & Huffman, 2002). Conversely, it would be inefficient or even dangerous to indiscriminately cooperate with out-group members, and this tendency should have been selected against. Such social and group-level processes are considered in further detail in chapters 8 and 9.

Other seemingly evolved social-cognitive mechanisms include a tendency to select mates on the basis of their ability to provide important resources for child-rearing (with different factors, such as looks vs. financial resources, being differentially weighted by men and women, according to the somewhat different selective pressures faced by men and women; Buss, 1998); a tendency to be jealous at any perceived threat to one's mating relationship (again, triggered by different types of threats, for men and women—i.e., women are jealous at the thought of emotional infidelity, and men at the thought of sexual infidelity; Buss, Larsen, Westen, & Semelroth, 1992); and the ability of every human to both generate and recognize a few basic emotions as expressed on human faces (Ekman, 1972). In addition, all humans appear to be predisposed to make inferences about others' beliefs and desires, that is, to model the mental states of others (Geary, 1998), an ability that begins to develop in the first 3 years of life.

Another type of potential candidate social-cognitive universal is manifest in various decision-making biases, in which we prefer or give precedence to certain others, or features of others. For example, because of the selective pressures of inclusive fitness, we are predisposed to be more invested in and supportive of relatives. We are also predisposed to prefer male rather than female children, older rather than younger prepubescent children, and younger rather than older adult children, as these children are likely to bring a greater return on our investment, in terms of maximizing the spread of our genes into the next generation (Weiner, 1992). Of course, not all of these characteristics are unique to humans.

Importantly, many social and personality psychologists do not accept the evolutionary perspective upon social behavior. This resistance is based on at least two grounds: first, that it is not possible to experimentally test evolutionary hypotheses, because evolution happened in the past. Thus how do we know evolutionary explanations of human nature are not just post hoc "just so" stories? Second, mainstream social-personality psychologists criticize the evolutionists as likely overstating the degree of predetermination of the human mind. As discussed in chapter 2 and earlier in this chapter, psychologists, and personality psychologists in particular, bristle at the notion that human behavior is reducible to lower level or nonconscious forces.

The first criticism is generally not justified—with careful enough framing, experimental studies, based on hypotheses derivable only from evolutionary theory, can provide impressive support for such theories of basic human nature (Buss, 1995). The second criticism is a more open question, as debate rages within the evolutionary psychology camp itself regarding the extent to which cognition involves predetermined, hard-wired, highly specific modules, or whether the innate circuitry is instead more loosely configured, allowing, perhaps, for more plasticity and flexibility (MacDonald, 1991). Of course, proceeding even further along this continuum, one arrives at the "standard social science model," according to which cognitive skills and capacities are acquired and assembled from scratch during ontogeny, rather than being activated or unfolded from a preexisting or predetermined neural foundation (Tooby & Cosmides, 1992). According to the SSSM, the only true universal is a general ability to learn.

The debate concerning the nature and extent of modularity, and also the debate concerning the proper place of evolutionary theory within social/personality psychology, certainly cannot be resolved herein. Instead, I only restate my assumption that evolution must have had strong effects on human nature, and thus that this perspective cannot be ignored in a quest to understand optimal human being—the SSSM is not enough. Living things are intricately and exquisitely attuned to their environments, as reflected in their genetic heritages. It seems exceedingly unlikely that the human mind, perhaps the most intricate adaptation of all, was not profoundly shaped and prestructured by evolution.

Psychological Needs

By way of introducing this third category of human universals, it is useful to consider Malinowski's (1944) early proposed list of universal human needs and processes. His list contained the physiological needs named earlier, namely, for food, liquid, oxygen, proper temperature, and sleep. It also contained the "quasi" needs and presses listed, for sex, cleanliness, and exercise. Again, the latter needs veer further in the direction of psychology, in that they are more modifiable by personality and culture, and are not as necessary for physical existence. However, Malinoski's list also contained some even more psychological needs, such as a "need for physical health" and a "need for growth." These two seem potentially problematic, however: We can all think of individuals who display little or no concern for personal growth, or even for their own health.

Again, this highlights the difficulty of postulating universals at higher levels of analysis. Universal physiological needs and processes are relatively uncontroversial; however, universal cognitive processes are more controversial, as alluded to in the section on evolved social-cognitive mechanisms; and universal psychological needs, located even higher (at the level of personality), are perhaps the most controversial of all. This issue can be illustrated by considering the most prominent theory of psychological needs, that of Abraham Maslow (1971).

As is well known, Maslow proposed a hierarchy of five needs, ranging from physical needs to safety/security needs to relatedness/belongingness needs to self-esteem/competence needs to self-actualization needs. Maslow also proposed a contingent relationship between lower and higher levels of the hierarchy, such that as people solve or satisfy needs at one level of the hierarchy, they move "up" to work on the next higher, and typically more subtle, need. Also, needs at each successive level of the hierarchy are assumed to be more difficult to satisfy than the lower needs. Thus in Maslow's model there is a kind of filtering effect, such that only a minority of persons reach the "top" of the hierarchy (see chap. 1).

Although Maslow's model remains appealing, there has been little empirical support for his proposals concerning the contingencies between the different levels (Goebel & Brown, 1981). For example, many people sacrifice security needs for self-actualization needs, or, conversely, fail to move toward self-actualization, despite reasonable satisfaction of the lower level needs. However, Maslow's model may still remain useful as a potential list of universal organismic needs. We can ask, "Is Maslow's fivefold list the basic set of psychological needs for every human, or are there some needs that have been left off, or some that have been improperly included?" This question is considered momentarily.

Self-determination theory (SDT) provides a more contemporary account of organismic human needs, based on the concept of intrinsic motivation (Deci & Ryan, 1985, 2000). Specifically, SDT posits three organismic needs: for autonomy, competence, and relatedness. That is, all humans need and better thrive when they feel that they choose or at least endorse their behavior, when they feel that their behavior is effective and efficient, and when they feel connected to important others. SDT uses subjective well-being (SWB) as one criterion for identifying psychological needs, arguing that needs, if they truly are needs, should uniquely predict variation in measures of happiness and positive thriving, just as sun, soil, and water uniquely predict positive thriving for plants (Ryan, 1995).

What empirical support exists for the claim that autonomy, competence, and relatedness are the three basic organismic needs? The support is fairly good. For example, Sheldon, Ryan, and Reis (1996) and Reis, Sheldon, Ryan, Gable, and Roscoe (2000) showed that feelings of autonomy, competence, and relatedness all uniquely predicted variations in daily well-being. La Guardia, Ryan, Couchman, and Deci (2000) showed that each of the three needs uniquely predicted variations in the quality of attachment relationships, Baard, Deci, and Ryan (in press) showed that each of the three needs on the job predicted employee job satisfaction and performance on the job, and Deci et al. (2001) showed that need satisfaction predicted positive outcomes in a sample of Bulgarian workers.

Notably, none of the just cited research measured any alternative candidate needs, in addition to SDT's three. Thus, it is possible that SDT is "leaving some needs out." For example, how does SDT's set of three needs compare to Maslow's set of five needs?

One recent set of studies addressed this question, by comparing both the needs specified by SDT and the needs specified by Maslow's theory, using a single methodology. Specifically, Sheldon, Elliot, Kim, and Kasser (2001) asked participants to write a paragraph about "the most satisfying event" they had experienced in the last week, month, or year. Participants then rated the experience, in terms of 30 items representing 10 candidate psychological needs. Included within this set of needs were all five of Maslow's proposed needs (for physical health, security, relatedness, self-esteem, and self-actualization), as well as SDT's proposed three needs (relatedness, competence, and autonomy), as well as three other potential needs: for money/luxury, for popularity/influence, and for pleasure/stimulation.

Sheldon et al. (2001) found evidence for four basic needs, by two very different empirical standards. Specifically, autonomy, competence, relatedness, and self-esteem were most strongly manifest (in terms of having the highest means) within people's ratings of their satisfying event, and each of the four uniquely predicted positive mood associated with event (a component of SWB, which again, SDT argues, supplies a reasonable criterion for identifying needs). None of the other candidate needs emerged in the top group, by either of these two criteria. A fifth need emerged within the top group when participants were instead asked to describe and rate "what was unsatisfying about your most unsatisfying recent event": namely, the absence of security achieved comparable prominence with the absence of autonomy, competence, relatedness, and self-esteem in the case of unsatisfying events. These effects were also shown to emerge within a sample from a collectivist culture, South Korea, offering some support for the universality of these four (or five) needs.

Notably, three of Maslow's five proposed needs appeared within these final sets: the needs for self-esteem, security, and relatedness. However, Maslow's "physical health" need and his "self-actualization" need did not make the final sets. Although physical health may have been missing because most undergraduates have reasonably good health (i.e., in a geriatric sample health might have emerged as a more important component of "satisfying events"), the absence of self-actualization from the list suggests that not all individuals are concerned with growth and the ideal self. Instead, the master "self"-based need in this data was autonomy, the sense that one freely chose to engage in the satisfying event and was expressing one's values and interests during it. Of course, Maslow's model posits that self-actualization only becomes a need for a very small percentage of the population, namely, those who have fully satisfied the "lower" needs. Again, however, the empirical support for this contingent proposition is not good. Also noteworthy is the fact that Maslow's proposed self-actualization need does not fit the earlier definition of a universal characteristic, namely, that it is a characteristic that is manifested by everyone, not just by a very few people.

Another contemporary theory of psychological needs focuses on ontological security, or the lack of it: terror management theory (Greenberg, Pyszczynski, & Solomon, 1995). This theory, based in Ernest Becker's (1973) analysis of the "denial of death," maintains that the fundamental human need or motivation is to cope with the knowledge of one's own inevitable annihilation. The profound insecurity induced by this fact would derail us, if we did not develop means to cope with it. In the theorists' own words, in order to cope, people need "faith in a relatively benign cultural wordview … and the belief that one is living up to the standards of value prescribed by that worldview" (Greenberg et al., 1995, p. 75). In terms of the need concepts outlined earlier, it appears that this coping can achieved by a variety of different means, such as via self-esteem striving (coping by thinking of oneself as a person with value and permanence; Arndt & Greenberg, 1999), via relatedness/belongingness striving (coping by affirming one's attachments to secure others; Mikulincer, Florian, & Hirschberger, 2003), and even via self-actualization striving (coping by seeking to consolidate or even transcend one's ego in the face of death; Yalom, 1995). Thus, in a sense, terror management theory turns Maslovian need theory upside-down, putting security as the master need, which the other needs may serve, to a greater or lesser extent.

It is important to point out that not all social-personality psychologists accept the terror management account of organismic psychological human needs. For that matter, not all theorists accept SDT's account of universal needs, either, for a variety of reasons. Indeed, some contemporary evolutionary perspectives do not accept the idea of basic or domain-general human needs at all; instead, they argue that natural selection would have brought about many hundreds of domain-specific motives and propensities, rather than just a few global motives (Buss, 1991). However, MacDonald (1991), a prominent evolutionary theorist, suggested that a hierarchical control theory-type arrangement, in which the many social-cognitive mechanisms potentially serve a smaller set of basic needs or motives higher up in the action hierarchy, would solve many conceptual problems. Similarly, Deci and Ryan (2000) argued that evolutionary accounts do not as yet deal with the problem of how the many hard-wired mechanisms are integrated and coordinated into a coherent life and sense of self. Deci and Ryan's view was that a few basic self-related motives or needs help to supply this "glue," guiding humans in a generic way towards experiential satisfactions in important domains of adaptation, such as relationship formation and skill development. Put simply, those who sought out and were rewarded by experiences of competence, relatedness, and autonomy may have been most likely to survive, thrive, and pass their genes forward.

Obviously, the debate of whether a set of domain-general psychological needs could have evolved, and if so the debate over what the exact needs are, cannot be resolved here, either. To state my own assumptions for the remainder of the book: There are indeed fundamental organismic needs, common to all human beings, that must be acknowledged within any final account of optimal human being. The Sheldon et al. (2001) research described earlier may be the most definitive statement to date on what these basic needs are, as it is one of the few studies that comparatively examined a large set of candidate needs using rigorous empirical criteria. But of course, much more research is needed, both to better establish the basic set, and to examine its consistency within different national samples, different age group samples, and different socioeconomic samples. Notably, other research in the SDT tradition has begun to supply such data (see Deci & Ryan, 2000, for a summary).

Sociocultural Practices

In considering this fourth category of universals we arrive at the domain traditionally studied by cultural anthropologists. Within this field there has been considerable controversy regarding the topic of cultural universals, that is, features that are to be found in common in humans from every human culture. Indeed, during the majority of the 20th century, cultural anthropologists rejected the idea of universal mechanisms, instead adopting a doctrine of radical cultural relativism best stated in Ruth Benedict's *Patterns of Culture* (1934). In part this was due to anthropologists' steadfast rejection of the idea that cultural variations could be accounted for by lower levels of analysis, such as by physics, biology, or psychology. In terms of

Fig. 2.1, anthropologists were attempting to secure the cultural level of analysis as a legitimate one, distinct from processes occurring at other levels of the hierarchy. Not only did mid-century anthropologists argue that culture is not reducible to biology or psychology (i.e., no bottom-up determination), but some suggested that culture was instead the primary determinant of psychology, and to some extent biological functioning (top-down determination; see Kincaid, 1997). Again, I believe that rarely will a given level of analysis completely determine events at another level of analysis, and that each level's rhetorical quest for causal supremacy has slowed the overall progress of science.

Returning to sociocultural universals: What characteristic human behaviors are found in every culture? E. O. Wilson, in his 1978 book *On Human Nature,* pointed out that if we were comparing humans to ants (made hyperintelligent), the description of each species would be easily recognizable, and wholly distinct from the other species. Humans evidence "athletic sports, dancing, feasting, joking, modesty regarding natural functions, puberty customs, hair styles, religious ritual, mourning, and music," among many other characteristics. In contrast, ants evidence "body licking, cannibalism, caste determination, metamorphosis rites, mutual regurgitation, and queen obeisance," among many other characteristics (pp. 22–23).

In this level of comparison, at least, we can see that humans indeed have a distinctive "sociocultural nature," different from other species (Pinker, 2002). Indeed, the description of this nature could be made much longer; for example, Wilson's proposed characteristics of humans were taken from an authoritative list supplied by Murdock (1945) that included 67 different sociocultural universals, including the 10 just listed.

The idea that humans around the world all share these 67 (or however many) characteristics is of course difficult to prove. I do not venture into the question of how to prove universals here, but instead note that compelling evidence does exist. For example, Kidder (1940) pointed out the startling similarity in the evolution of Old World and New World cultures, including but not limited to their parallel development of cloth making, animal domestication, metalworking, and writing. Although this parallelism could perhaps be explained in terms of the very similar environments and tasks that Old and New World inhabitants faced, it is difficult to avoid the idea that these striking and complex behaviors were in some sense selected for within universal human nature, as a part of a species-typical suite of adaptations.

One might ask, "Aren't sociocultural universals, if they are universal, somehow represented within each person's genes? If so, does it make sense to talk about them at the sociocultural level? Might it be more parsimonious to simply speak of molecular biology and genetic inheritance, or of social-cognitive mechanisms, which constitute the sociocultural behavior?" Indeed, here lurks the very reductionism that the anthropologists feared. Although these sociocultural tendencies are doubtless encoded in some sense within the genome, consistent with the interactionist perspective, I believe that it requires the presence of an extended group of individuals, interacting together over time and creating a common history, to bring about the unique versions of sociocultural practice that we see around the world. Thus, for example, the Yiddish, Chinese, and Bantu cultures and their millennia-old religious traditions, tribal identities, and musical forms cannot simply be reduced to "genetic mechanisms." In terms of Fig. 2.1, emergent processes occur at the cultural level, processes whose effects on behavior cannot be subsumed by any other level of analysis (see chap. 9 for more detailed discussion of the relations between genetic and cultural evolution). Thus, although the human tendency to make music and to worship together may be universal, the particular ways in which humans do this is culturally and historically constrained. Both levels of analysis are required for a complete picture.

IMPLICATIONS OF THE ORGANISMIC FOUNDATION LEVEL FOR OPTIMAL HUMAN BEING

In this section I consider each of the four categories of organismic universal (i.e., physiological needs, sociocognitive mechanisms, psychological needs, and sociocultural practices) in conjunction with optimal human being. What is optimal human being, from each perspective developed above?

General Implications of the Organismic Perspective

Before exploring this, it is instructive to consider the organismic philosophical perspective more generally, as it makes strong universalistic assumptions concerning positive human nature. The organismic perspective views humans as self-organizing, dynamical systems that contain a natural and built-in impetus for positive development and change (Overton, 1976). In Piaget's (1971) theory of cognitive development, this built-in impetus was manifest in the child's curiosity and his or her desire to both assimilate and accommodate new information. In Goldstein's (1939) theory, this involved the attempt to maintain consistency and identity at the same time that one "comes to terms with" one's environment. In contemporary SDT (Deci & Ryan, 2000), the impetus is exemplified in the important concept of intrinsic motivation, wherein a person acts primarily for experiential, rather than instrumental, rewards; when intrinsic motivation predominates, maximal growth and cognitive integration tend to occur.

I believe that the organismic perspective offers the human sciences the most optimistic and theoretically inclusive vision of, and set of assumptions about, human beings. The perspective can accommodate to dynamic systems theories just as readily as it can to person-centered and humanistic theories, and is also essentially consistent with evolutionary perspectives, functional perspectives, and psychosocial perspectives. Although I do not often speak explicitly about organismic theory in this book, let me state now I share its basic assumptions: that humans are inherently growth oriented and prosocially oriented, until adaptation to problematic circumstances forestalls or forestays these impulses (Rogers, 1961; Sheldon, Arndt, & Houser-Marko, 2003). This assumption rests on a basic observation of life, especially human life: that there is a tendency toward synthesis, integration, unification, combination, and cooperation (i.e., toward increasing negentropy, as discussed in chap. 2). Sheldon and Schmuck (2001) referred to this inherent desire for higher order integration as the "holistic impulse." In terms of the Fig. 2.1 model, one might say that humans naturally yearn to extend their lives to higher levels and realms, namely, toward the social and cultural.

Physical Needs and Optimal Human Being

Let us consider the four types of universal just discussed and their possible prescriptions for optimal human being, in sequence. First, and most obviously, optimal human being would seem to require basic physical need satisfaction. As Maslow's model acknowledges and many others have pointed out (i.e., Oishi, Diener, Suh, & Lucas, 1999), it is hard to be a fully functioning person when one does not have enough food, water, air, warmth, and rest! Of course, although these commodities may be necessary components of optimal human being, they are far from sufficient. What else promotes optimal human being?

Evolved Social-Cognitive Mechanisms and Optimal Human Being

One type of candidate concerns the evolved social-cognitive mechanisms already discussed. Notably, these are not as easily tied to optimal human being as they are viewed as species-typical means to the ends of successful survival and reproduction, rather than being direct sources of individual human thriving. Bearing this perspective in mind, optimal human being might be viewed as a state in which the social-cognitive mechanisms are efficiently and effectively serving the enactment of survival and reproductive tasks. The prescription would be to "Hone your evolved mechanisms so they serve your characteristic adaptations, and better calibrate them to your actual circumstances." For example, optimal human being might involve using one's "theory of mind" mechanism to effectively predict a rival's behavior, using one's in-group/out-group mechanism to cement one's social standing within personally important groups, and using one's cheater-detection mechanism to become aware of a partner's lack of fealty.

What about when one's sociocognitive mechanisms get one in trouble—for example, when one is too rigidly supportive of one's group and condemning of outgroup members, or too suspicious of the intentions of others? This leads us to another potential prescription for optimal human being, also based on the evolutionary perspective, offered by Buss (2000): Learn to keep distress-causing evolved mechanisms (such as jealousy and competitiveness) in check, while more frequently activating happiness-causing mechanisms (such as cooperation and reciprocity). This prescription suggests that we may need to "wrestle" with our evolved nature, learning to apply it appropriately and to control its problematic elements so as to maximize our happiness.

Buss's analysis suggests that using one's sociocognitive mechanisms in service of survival and reproductive purposes is not the ultimate prescription for optimal human being, as such tendencies may sometimes misfire and work counter to happiness and thriving. Thus, it appears that we need something in addition to survival and reproduction in order to thrive, just as we need more than our physical needs met. What is this something more?

Psychological Needs and Optimal Human Being

To answer this question we may perhaps turn to the psychological needs. Indeed, the concept of psychological need is directly tailored to address the question of optimal human being: Needs are qualities of experience that humans presumably require in order to maximize their motivation, growth, and well-being (Deci & Ryan, 2000). From this perspective, optimal human being involves living life in a way such that one obtains as many of certain kinds of high-quality experience as possible. Again, the leading contemporary candidates for positive psychological needs are security, autonomy, competence, relatedness, and self-esteem (Sheldon et al., 2001). A person who simultaneously maximizes the experience of all five of these experiences might be said to be experiencing optimal human being.

Of course, this prescription may be easier said than done. Many factors influence the extent to which people experience psychological need satisfaction, including the quality of their social context and interpersonal relations, their basic personality traits and dispositions, and the ways in which they interpret and construe their experiences (Deci & Ryan, 2000). As an example of the latter factor, individuals trying to learn a new skill (such as rock-climbing) may primarily focus on their ability relative to accomplished others, thereby feeling incompetent and inadequate; or, they may focus on their ability relative to their own past levels of performance, thereby feeling a sense of progress and growing competence (Elliot, McGregor, & Thrash, 2002). As this example illustrates, psychological need satisfaction may to some extent depend on one's attitude toward one's experience, in addition to the experience itself. It also illustrates that need satisfaction may be to some extent controllable by the individual, as he or she works to contextualize his or her life and experiences in more positive and self-nurturing ways.

At this point, some readers may be wondering: Are psychological needs really invariant, or do they differ across cultures, such that there are perhaps no truly "universal" needs after all? For example, might it be the case that needs for belongingness and relatedness are stronger in some cultures, and needs for autonomy strongest in other cultures? If so, must we abandon the idea of a universal human nature?

In considering this question, we should first notice that the needs might still be universal, even though they are expressed and satisfied in different ways in different cultures. In this view, all humans have the needs, but their cultures constrain them to obtain satisfaction in differing ways. We should also notice that the needs might still be universal even if people in some cultures are receiving less current satisfaction of the needs than people in other cultures. In other words, just because people are not having a particular type of experience does not mean that they do not need it. In this vein, Diener and Suh (2000) suggested that the average level of

well-being experienced within a country or cultural group might form a valid index for judging the culture's health and potential longevity. I suggest that the same
holds true for psychological need satisfaction.

To further address this issue of the universality of the needs, let us consider
SDT's proposed need for autonomy, as this need has been most controversial in the
recent literature (in contrast, the proposals that all humans need to feel competent
and related are more widely accepted). For example, Markus et al. (1996) and
Triandis (2001) suggested that individuals in collectivist cultures are socialized to
develop a more interpersonal orientation, and simply never develop the strong desire for autonomy that characterizes those raised in individualist cultures (the distinction between individualism and collectivism receives more detailed treatment
in chap. 9). In this view, psychological autonomy is an acquired preference, rather
than a universal need; one might easily do without it, in a culture that de-
emphasizes it. Indeed, some cross-cultural theorists have suggested that those who
desire autonomy might actually be worse off in cultural settings that deemphasize
autonomy (Markus et al., 1996).

However, as discussed earlier in this chapter, SDT insists that autonomy (the
need to endorse one's behavioral choices) is not the same thing as independence
(the desire to be free of influence by others). Neither is autonomy the same thing as
individualism, self-efficacy, internal locus of control, or self-esteem. Also, autonomy and social connectedness are not antithetical, as many assume; in fact, they
are typically quite highly correlated (Deci & Ryan, 2000; Bettencourt & Sheldon,
2001). Furthermore, there is considerable emerging evidence that autonomy, defined and measured in SDT terms, is important in every culture (see Deci & Ryan,
2000, for a review). As one example, Sheldon, Elliot, Ryan, Chirkov, Kim, Wu,
Demir, and Sun (2004) assessed goal autonomy in four different cultures, including China, Taiwan, South Korea, and the United States. This research found similar associations between autonomy and measures of psychological well-being in
every one of these cultures. Also, there were no negative associations, as one might
expect if autonomy is actually maladaptive in some cultural contexts. Thus, once
again, it appears that satisfying innate psychological needs (including that for autonomy) may provide an important foundational prescription for optimal human
being. This idea is considered further in chapter 10.

Sociocultural Practices and Optimal Human Being

How does the fourth category of organismic universals, sociocultural practices, relate to optimal human being? It seems apparent that dancing, joking, music making, and other communal activities are part of "the good life" (Seligman, 2002),
that is, a life full of both enjoyment and meaning. In other words, humans may have
needs to express these sociocultural universals, just as they may have psychological needs for certain types of experiences. From this perspective, the prescription
for optimal human being would be to create a cultural matrix that supported and
promoted the enactment of most if not all of the practices listed above. A "healthy"
culture would be one that afforded many such opportunities.

Why would a rich assortment of sociocultural practices contribute to optir ... human being, at the individual level? Presumably because they afford many opportunities for psychological need-satisfaction, especially experiences of relatedness, security, and group belongingness (Baumeister & Leary, 1995). In addition, such practices would help to cement social bonds and enhance group cooperation, contributing, ultimately, to the survival and reproductive needs of individuals as well as their psychological needs (see chap. 8).

BEYOND THE FOUNDATIONAL ORGANISM

Whatever the exact universal needs, propensities, and requirements, it seems apparent that optimal human being requires more than expressing or satisfying this foundational level. People also have personality traits, personal goals, and enduring self-identities (Levels 2–4 in Fig. 3.3) by which they differ from each other, and these can also presumably be "optimized" to a greater or lesser extent. Also, individuals exist within widely varying social and cultural networks, which provide very different sets of optimization problems. Although these problems (and the drive to solve them, and the reinforcement for solving them) may be echoed in the psychological needs, they also raise issues that go far beyond psychological needs and the other constants within human nature. In the next chapter, we turn specifically to the question of personality traits and enduring individual differences (Level 2 in Fig. 3.3). What are the crucial distinctions at this level of analysis, how does the level fit with the other levels, and how does the level relate to optimal human being?

5 Personality Traits and Individual Differences: The Meaning of Variability

The previous chapter addressed the universal or species-typical features of human nature, concluding with discussion of how optimal human being might be achieved, according to this level of analysis. How are all people the same, and what do all people need to thrive? This chapter instead focuses on how people differ from each other, and concludes with discussion of how these differences impact the recommendations for optimal human being. For example, how might optimal human being differ for someone with a neurotic as compared to a sunny disposition, or for someone with an introverted as compared to a gregarious disposition? Before addressing the optimal human being question, however, the chapter first provides a thorough analysis of the personality trait construct.

In an edited book on the topic of consilience (2001), David Rowe, a behavioral geneticist, wrote a chapter arguing for the importance of individual differences in any overarching or comprehensive theory of human nature. In particular, Rowe pointed out the substantial extent to which individual experience and behavior are influenced by genetic variations. More specifically, as discussed in detail later, considerable heritability has now been shown for many different traits and response dispositions. If we want to understand and predict human behavior, says Rowe, our theory must take these large effects into account. And indeed, Fig. 2.1 encompasses such effects, at the "personality" level of analysis (located at Level 2 in Fig. 3.3).

The predominant goal of this chapter is to consider this particular level of personality in detail. What is a personality trait, and what role do traits play in the overall causal account of human behavior? Might trait effects perhaps be reducible to other factors or forces, such that the trait level of analysis becomes unnecessary in the "final" model? These questions refer to the ontological status of the trait concept within the causal account of human behavior. After concluding that personality traits indeed have legitimate ontological status, I venture a redefinition of the trait construct, which formalizes this fact and may solve some problems for trait theorists. I then use this definition to consider the question of what other existing individual difference constructs (i.e., motive dispositions, unconscious attitudes, social value orientations?) ought to be included in the trait category. Finally, at the end of the chapter, I consider the implications of personality trait concepts for the question of optimal human being.

DEFINING PERSONALITY TRAITS

An Example Trait Profile

Our first task is to define the concept of a "personality trait." In some ways this is very easy, but in other ways it is quite difficult. To illustrate, let's start with an example: the case of "Allison."

> Since she was a girl, Allison has been emotional and intense—stimulating and engaging, but also needy and stormy. No matter what the event, Allison seems to react with strong emotions. In addition, she always seems to be wrestling with "issues"—fears of being abandoned by close others, worries about her own abilities and capacities, and the like. Nevertheless, those who know her tend to agree that she is a very talented and capable person. She is also quite receptive to new experiences, having tried everything there was to try in college, and having spent two years in Africa, in the Peace Corps. Furthermore, Allison has always been a "people" person, with a remarkable ability to draw people out and elicit self-disclosures from them. This does not mean that she is always warm and pleasant, however! Indeed, she has a history of short and intense friendships that fade over time, in part because others grow weary of coping with her challenges to them, and with her emotions. Finally, Allison is a perfectionist, taking her duties and responsibilities very seriously. She does not rest until "the job is done right."

In just these few short sentences, you, the reader, have gained a rather vivid sense of Allison's personality (perhaps you even know somebody like her). In McAdams's (2001) words, "traits talk"—they catch our attention, because they are interesting and because they can quickly provide us with useful information about new people we encounter. Humans like to gossip (Wilson, Wilczynski, Wells, & Weiser, 2000), and trait talk provides one of the readiest means to do so. "Oh, you can't rely on him—he's a procrastinator." "Have you noticed how bitchy Mary can be?" "That's Joe for you—slow but steady." "No, she wasn't snubbing you—she's a naturally quiet and introverted person."

As these examples illustrate, in everyday life we have natural tendency to describe people in terms of traits. In addition, we have a natural interest in personality profiles based on traits (John, 1990). To condense the profile of Allison given above, we might say that Allison is high in the traits of *neuroticism* (i.e., reactivity and negative emotionality), *extraversion* (i.e., sociability and positive emotionality), *openness to experience* (i.e., sensation seeking and creativity), and *conscientiousness* (i.e., diligence and achievement orientation), and that she is low in the trait of *agreeableness* (i.e., cooperativeness and acquiescence; these terms come from the "Big Five" model of personality, the dominant contemporary trait perspective, which is discussed later in the chapter). Such labels and descriptors provide a valuable shorthand for conveying information about people. Indeed, the value of trait terms is attested to by how many of them there are: Allport and Oddbert (1936) identified almost 18,000 different trait or trait-related adjectives in the English language! Surely there would not be so many trait words, unless they played some important role in human affairs and interactions.

Another thing to point out is that in everyday usage, we typically assume that traits are *causal*—that is, that a person's trait can provide the explanation for their behavior. Why did Allison join the Peace Corps? Because she is open to experience. Why does she seek out new relationships with people? Because she is extraverted. Why does she always worry about herself and her capabilities? Because she is neurotic. People's (especially Westerners') tendency to assume that traits are causal is also evidenced by the well-known "fundamental attribution error," in which people are too prone to attribute the cause of others' behaviors to internal dispositions, rather than considering the situational forces that were impacting them (Jones & Nisbett, 1972).

As the term *error* implies, the assumption that personality traits have a causal role in behavior is nowhere near as clear and unambiguous as people commonly assume (Mischel, 1968). Indeed, as shown later, some theoretical perspectives view traits as mere summary descriptive labels or social fictions, with no corresponding psychic or biological reality. This would considerably limit their scientific utility! To illustrate the issue, let us consider some theoretical perspectives upon personality traits.

A Formal Definition, and Four Theoretical Positions on Personality Traits

Let us begin with this formal definition: that a *trait* is a consistent disposition to think, feel, or act in certain ways (Pervin & John, 2001). Traits are thought to describe or characterize a person's personality over a wide variety of situations, and are also assumed to be relatively stable over time. In addition, traits are typically viewed as continuous dimensions on which people can be located (i.e., low, medium, high), and their scores can be used to compare them to other people. Furthermore, traits are relatively independent of each other. Thus, one can be high or low on one trait, and have an equal chance of being either high or low on another trait. In terms of the example, Allison shows high intensity in almost all situations, and has been intense since childhood. Moreover, she has shown more consistent and long-lasting emotionality than most other people in her age group. Although she is intense, still, she could just as easily have been low in conscientiousness and openness to experience, rather than high in them, as in the description above.

What is a personality trait, exactly? McAdams (2001) identified four different theoretical positions on the nature of personality traits. One position is that traits are "biological patternings in the central nervous system that cause behavior to occur and account for the consistencies in socio-emotional functioning from situation to the next and over time" (Allport, 1937; Zuckerman, 1991). From this perspective, personality traits are the outward manifestations of physiological and biological regularities built into the person's brain and nervous system.

A second position is that traits are "tendencies to act, think, or feel in consistent ways.... Trait attributions can be used both to describe behavior summaries and to suggest causal or generative mechanisms for behavior" (McCrae & Costa, 1990). From this perspective, traits have a definite reality, but no strong claims are made regarding the grounding of those realities in biology. Still, they are at least based on consistent ways of feeling and thinking, which presumably involve particular and consistent patterns of brain function.

A third position is that "traits are descriptive summary categories for behavior acts. Acts that have the same functional properties may be grouped together into families, with some acts being more prototypical of the general family features than others" (Buss & Craik, 1983). From this perspective, traits are simply the abstract categories into which we group conceptually similar behaviors. Notice that this definition begins to take leave of the idea that traits are something internal to the person, and moves toward a different idea, that traits are merely descriptive concepts constructed by external observers. However, this definition still assumes that the behavioral regularities really do exist.

The fourth position is that "traits are convenient fictions devised by people to categorize the diversity of human behavior. Traits do not exist outside the mind of the observer, and therefore they can have no causal influence. Through social interaction and discourse, people construct meanings for trait terms" (Mischel, 1968; Shweder, 1975). According to this view traits have no inherent reality at all; instead, they are merely arbitrary fictions that observers create, perhaps because of needs to categorize events or to label others.

SCIENTIFIC PROBLEMS WITH THE SECOND, THIRD, AND FOURTH POSITIONS ON TRAITS

Failure to Identify Processes Inside the Person

From a scientific perspective, there are potential problems with the second, third, and fourth views of traits, becoming worse with each succeeding definition. First, if personality traits are to be valid explanatory constructs at the person level of analysis, then presumably they must at least have some real basis inside the person. Otherwise, they could likely be reduced to some other effect, which has nothing to do with personality as it is typically defined. The third and fourth definitions are both vulnerable to such a reduction, as they define traits in terms of the observer, rather than the actor. Indeed, the fourth definition explicitly proposes that traits have nothing to do with personality!

Failure to Explain Behavior Noncircularly

Another conceptual problem with the second and third definitions is that if there is no possibility of defining or measuring traits apart from the behaviors they are supposed to explain, then the concept of a trait quickly becomes circular. "How do we know Allison is an extravert? Because she manifests extraverted behaviors. Why does she manifest extraverted behaviors? Because she is an extravert." The danger is that theorists will reify the phenomenon they wish to explain, using the reified label as the explanation for that which prompted the assignment of the label in the first place. In contrast, the first definition avoids this problem.

To illustrate the latter problem more concretely, consider Costa and McCrae's path model described in chapter 3 (See Fig. 3.4). As can be seen, Costa and Mc-Crae's path model asserts that traits have a foundational causal role, helping to determine people's strivings, attitudes, self-concepts, and ultimately their objective biographies and life courses. Obviously, however, if traits are simply descriptive tallies of behavior, or socially constructed labels with no inherent meaning or true object of reference, then it would be difficult to understand how they could play the foundational causal role that Costa and McCrae propose they do. Of course, there are many reasons that traits might remain interesting or useful even if they were reconstrued purely as effects rather than as causes. Personality profiles can be a lot of fun, and they can convey considerable information quickly. In addition, traits might still be quite useful for predicting people's behavior, even if they are not useful for explaining it. Still, if traits cannot be construed as causes, then perhaps they do not belong in Fig. 2.1, which refers to "potential influences on behavior."

Undermining the Foundations of Science

Another conceptual problem with the fourth definition is its more general alignment with social constructivist perspectives. Consistent with the doctrine of cultural relativism discussed in chapter 2, social constructionist perspectives tend to assume that social and cultural meanings are arbitrary and are also largely unconstrained by factors below them. Also, the social constructivist position tends to cut off its phenomenon from the rest of the universe and from biology, in exactly the way that Wilson (1998) lamented, as he pondered the nonconsilient state of the social sciences. Finally, the social constructivist position, if taken to its logical conclusion, indicates that there is no objective psychological reality to detect—only negotiated subjectivities, which should not be accepted as facts, but instead should be carefully scanned for political agendas. This kind of position is of limited scientific usefulness.

HOW CAN TRAITS BE SHOWN TO HAVE CAUSAL FORCE?

To return to the orienting question for the chapter: How can we show that personality traits are real entities that have a causal impact on human behavior, rather than being mere descriptive summaries of behavior? One answer is that one must find something about them that is different from the actual regularities in thinking, feeling, and acting that are observed. What, if any, realities undergird the observed regularities, and might be said to give rise to them? I consider two broad possibilities: genetic/temperamental dispositions, and learning/developmental histories.

Perhaps the best way to causally ground personality trait concepts would be to show that they are based in inherited temperamental differences (as in the first definition of traits already given). This would provide a tie to molecular biology and underlying brain systems, entities that are of course quite different from the observed behaviors, thoughts, and feelings themselves. For example, if we can show that people with a certain gene or set of genes tend to become extraverted and gregarious, whereas people with another gene or sets of genes become introverted and retiring, then we would have a way of affirming the reality of the extraversion versus introversion trait construct in terms other than the manifest extraverted or introverted behaviors.

This suggestion may seem to raise the question of reductionism. Couldn't the behavioral geneticist, armed with data such as that just described, argue that personality traits are nothing more than amalgamations of biochemical and molecular factors, with no effects that cannot be reduced to these factors? No. As discussed later, genetic factors can supply some of the story, but by no means all of it—environmental and social-contextual main effects upon traits are also large. In addition, environmental and contextual also interact with genetic factors, so that their combined effect is more than the sum of both taken alone. Finally, people's experiences of their traits (and their experience of the behaviors to which traits give rise) play their own part in the story, feeding back into the mix to help determine subsequent behavior in a way not reducible to simple biology.

Temperament as a Cause of Traits

With these ideas in mind, let us tour consensual knowledge regarding temperamental traits, which are most directly tied to genetics, and which may also provide the firmest grounding for the trait level of analysis. Temperament can be defined as "any moderately stable, differentiating emotional or behavioral quality whose appearance in childhood is influenced by inherited biology, including differences in brain neurochemistry" (Kagan, 1994, p. xvii). Theories of temperament go back to the ancient Greek times and the "four humours" or temperamental styles: sanguine (stable and cheerful), melancholic (moody and anxious), choleric (irritable and restless), and phlegmatic (steady and stoic). In the first half of the 20th century, Sheldon (1940; no relation) defined three temperamental styles: visceratonia (hedonistic and comfort-loving), somatotonia (adventurous, aggressive), and cerebrotonia (inhibited, fearful). These correspond to the body types of endomorphic (soft and round), mesomorphic (hard and muscular), and ectomorphic (thin and fragile). Although these concepts are interesting relics, the field is now dominated by newer and better supported conceptions of temperament. We turn to these concepts below.

Modern research on temperament began with the New York Longitudinal Study of children (Thomas & Chess, 1977), which distinguished between "easy" babies (active, happy), "difficult" babies (irritable, unhappy), and "slow-to-warm-up" babies (reticent, shy). Allison, in the earlier example, would likely have been judged to be in the difficult category, given her intensity and sometimes disagreeableness. Supporting the idea that they are biologically based, Thomas and Chess showed that children's styles persisted over time, evidencing very good stability across early childhood. Buss and Plomin (1984) postulated that these three styles were in part constituted by differences in the temperamental dimensions of emotionality, activity, impulsivity, and sociability.

Jerome Kagan is probably the best known contemporary temperament researcher, and he has also best crossed the gap between behavior and biology. Kagan began with the distinction between inhibited and uninhibited babies, who react differently to novel stimuli. Specifically, inhibited or reactive babies showed more fearful behavior when exposed to something new. In addition, inhibited babies showed higher blood pressure, more heart acceleration, and greater right hemisphere reactivity in the face of the unfamiliar. Furthermore, these biological differences have been shown to persist years later, and to be predictive of later psychological and behavioral characteristics, such as shyness, smiling, and talkativeness (see Kagan, 1994, for a review). Such findings suggest that at least some personality traits have firm biological bases, and thus that traits may indeed be more than mere "descriptive categories" and "sociological fictions."

Further support for the potency of biological temperament comes from twin studies, which have determined that the heritability coefficients for emotionality and impulsivity are in the .40 to .45 range whereas the coefficients for sociability and activity are around .25 (Dunn & Plomin, 1990). These coefficients, taken together, indicate that approximately 40% of the population variance in temperamental traits represents a main effect of genes, which presumably have their effects via biological processes (Loehlin, 1992). Thus, a particularly nervous or irritable person has considerable likelihood of remaining that way all through life, because his or her psychobiological systems are innately calibrated in this direction. As discussed at the beginning of the chapter, Rowe (2001) argued that such facts suggest that personality theory must have a place in any consilient theory of human nature.

It is important to point out, however, we should not read genetic destiny into these findings. Kagan (1994) emphasized that temperament is not a "life sentence." Thus, although there is considerable consistency over childhood, he also finds that some children switch categories. Indeed, it only makes sense that there would be considerable plasticity in trait expression. First, genes do not directly determine behavior, instead indirectly influencing it by helping to set the biological context. This leaves large degrees of freedom for phenotypic expression. Second, there are large variations in the experiences that people have in life, which undoubtedly have large effects on who they become. To illustrate the latter fact, we turn to the topic of environmental effects.

Environment as a Cause of Traits

Environment and variations in developmental environments provide a second possible grounding for personality traits. In behavioral genetic studies, two kinds of environmental effects can be estimated: that due to shared environments (i.e., being raised in the same household as another person), and that due to unshared environments (i.e., being exposed to different conditions within that household, compared to others within that household). Surprisingly, shared environment effects are quite small. Identical twins raised together are hardly more similar than identical twins raised apart (Dunn & Plomin, 1990)! A larger determinant of final outcomes is unshared environments, which again are conditions and circumstances that vary across persons, even though they live in the same physical environment (notably, these factors are typically not measured, but instead are assumed to reside in the residual of the regression equation—they are all that is left).

Rowe (1999) listed six categories of unshared environmental effects: perinatal trauma (i.e., injuries before birth), accidental or low-probability events (ranging from physical injuries to unusual awards, occurring during childhood), family constellation (i.e., birth order, birth spacing), sibling mutual interaction (i.e., distinctive alliances and conflicts among the siblings), unequal parental treatment (i.e., parents have favorites, or treat daughters very differently from sons), and influences outside the family (i.e., peers and teachers). Differences between siblings based on these six factors tend to differentially shape personality, driving siblings in different developmental directions.

Most importantly for the current argument, all environmental effects, taken together, account for about the same percentage of population variance (40%) as genetic effects (Dunn & Plomin, 1990). This is significant both because it further suggests that genes are not destiny, and because it provides another foundation for the concept of personality traits in addition to genetic inheritance. Indeed, given that gene and environment effects are about of the same size, when we say a person's trait caused him or her to do something, we might just as easily be saying that the person's developmental history caused him or her to do it as saying that their genetic constitution caused the person to do it.

Two other facts are worth pointing out here. First, construed in terms of Fig. 2.1, the data concerning unshared environment effects well demonstrate the powerful influence that the "social interaction" level of analysis can have upon personality. More generally, they show how important holistic explanations can be (in which one explains a phenomenon by going "up" in the Fig. 2.1 hierarchy). Children with similar genes turn out differently, depending on the local family context in which they are reared; the gene's-eye view cannot account for such emergent effects. Social interaction effects also emerge outside the family system, as children's inter-actions with peers (the sixth category of unshared environment alluded to above) may have an even larger influence on children's personalities than the influence of experiences inside of their family (Harris, 1995). Again, these social-level effects are not reducible to any other level of analysis.

A second thing to point out, consistent with the discussion of multilevel models and cross-level interactions in chapter 2, is that there are not merely simple main effects of genes and environments upon personality; in addition, these two levels of analysis to some extent interact to determine behavior. That is, genes and envi-ronment influence each other's influence. Three categories of gene–environment influence have been identified (Dunn & Plomin, 1990). First, a child may interpret the same environmental event in a different way, depending on his or her genetic predispositions. Thus, a child prone to negative affectivity might interpret her par-ents' divorce as being her own fault, influencing her self-concept and development relative to her siblings. Second, a child may elicit different responses from the en-vironment, depending on his or her genes and the nature of that environment. Thus, an irritable child might elicit angrier responses from parents, compared to the re-sponses his siblings elicit. Third, a child may select different kinds of situations or environments to enter based on genetic predispositions, thereby affecting the envi-ronment's effect on himself. Thus, a sociable child might form and lead a "neigh-borhood gang" of children, providing a different social environment for himself than the one his siblings experience.

The example of Allison can be used to illustrate these ideas more concretely. In terms of the first point just mentioned, suppose that as a girl, Allison was much more likely to react strongly to a particular experience or situation than her brother, who was a much more easygoing child. In other words, her genetic dispositions led her to perceive more threat or challenge in a given event, compared to her brother. This led her in a somewhat different developmental direction. Second, Allison, the difficult baby, typically elicited very different responses from her parents com-pared to the responses elicited by her brother. This was especially the case follow-ing a family tragedy, when parents and other relatives had reduced emotional resources for Allison. Allison's neediness and disagreeableness surged at this time, a trend that continued into her stormy teenage years; in contrast, her brother became the "quiet and rational" child. Third, another part of the problem was Allison's tendency to explicitly seek out or create situations providing strong emo-tional experiences, specifically by challenging and provoking family members. It seemed that she craved strong emotional responses from others.

To summarize: We began this section trying to find a basis for imputing causal force to personality traits. Do they *do* anything, or are they instead simply out-comes—the very behavioral regularities that we might try to explain, using other constructs? I concluded that temperament, based on inherited variations in bio-logical systems, may help to ground trait concepts as causal entities. I also con-cluded that people's developmental histories may provide another foundation for personality traits, helping to constitute and explain people's enduring propensi-ties to act and react in particular ways. Because temperament and developmental history have causal force of their own, they can lend causal force to the concept of the "personality trait."

REDEFINING THE TRAIT CONCEPT

As we have seen, personality traits appear to be a legitimate level of analysis, with their own unique influence on human behavior. Moreover, this influence is to a large extent based on genetic and historical factors. But at this point, let us ask once again: Why should we say that genes and history are *foundations* for traits, helping to give them legitimacy and causal force, instead of saying that genes and history are the *determinants* of traits, such that traits can perhaps be reduced to, or redescribed in terms of, genes and history? In other words, might personality traits yet be depicted as "only effects, never causes," with no influence that could not, in principle, be attributed to the effects of lower level factors? If so, then perhaps the personality trait level of analysis does not belong in Fig. 2.1, which refers to possible influences on human behavior.

Three Suggestions

I have three suggestions regarding this issue, which lead toward a redefinition of the personality trait. First, I believe the personality trait concept provides a useful shortcut for conceptualizing the impact of stable genetic and historical influences on human behavior. However, we should not lose sight of the fact that personality traits are based on these factors; that is, we should not reify traits as something more or different than these. To this end, we might expand the general definition of a trait given at the beginning of the chapter ("a disposition to think, feel, and act in certain ways"; Pervin & John, 2001), lengthening it to "a disposition to think, feel, and act in certain ways based on one's biological constitution and developmental history." With this definition, the latter two factors are acknowledged as providing the causal force behind traits.

As a second suggestion, I also believe that the personality trait enterprise may work better if we exclude *action* from the definition of traits, so that the definition becomes "a disposition to think and feel in certain ways based on one's biological constitution and developmental history." Why? Because, as noted earlier, "behavioral regularities" are in large part precisely the thing we are trying to explain! If behavioral regularities are included in the definition of traits, then it becomes impossible to use traits as explanations for behavior (as in Fig. 2.1) without circularity. However, if we instead define traits as cognitive or emotional regularities, then we have at least located processes inside the person, separate from behavior itself, presumably supported or constituted by brain functioning and/or developmental history, which can potentially cause behaviors.

The primary problem with this second suggestion, for trait theorists, is that in moving toward a more subjectivist definition of traits based on internal processes, one begins to blur the distinction between traits and the next level up in McAdams's hierarchy, motives and goals (i.e., between Levels 2 and 3 in Fig. 3.2).

What is the difference between saying a person has recurrent thoughts and feelings about meeting task obligations (i.e., high trait conscientiousness, in McCrae and Costa's [1995] terms), and saying that he or she has an enduring internal motive to do well at socially valued tasks (i.e., high achievement motivation, in McClelland and Atkinson's terms; McClelland, Atkinson, Clark, & Lowell, 1953)? Perhaps there is relatively little. Indeed, the potential overlap between trait and motive constructs has long vexed personality theorists, beginning with Allport (1937), and continuing through Murray (1938) to the present day (Pervin, 1994). Excluding behavior from the definition of traits accentuates this overlap.

This leads to my third suggestion: I propose that there is no important distinction between personality traits and chronic motives, and thus that chronic motives should be included within the category of personality traits. In terms of Fig. 3.3, chronic motives should "moved down" to Level 2, rather than being located within the category of goals and intentions (Level 3).

To illustrate the convergence of trait and motive constructs more concretely, let us consider the motive disposition constructs. These are stable tendencies to seek particular classes of behavioral incentives, such as achievement, intimacy, power, or affiliation (McAdams, 2001). These tendencies develop very early, as a result of formative experiences and reinforcements (McClelland, Koestner, & Weinberger, 1989). Notice that motive dispositions are in many ways very similar to traits, as they concern stable patterns of thinking and feeling, patterns that vary across people and that have roots in people's developmental histories. Conversely, as discussed earlier, traits share similarities with motive dispositions in that they imply chronic tendencies to seek out certain incentives and experiences (Read & Miller, 1989). That is, the trait of conscientiousness implies a stable motive to try to do well and responsibly in one's tasks, not just tendencies to think about doing well and to feel emotions concerning doing well. Thus, I am suggesting that both types of construct should be included in the same overarching category—the traits/individual differences level of analysis.

A Summary Definition and Its Applicability to Other Personality Constructs

The foregoing reasoning suggests, then, that the best definition of a personality trait may be as follows: " *a disposition to think, feel, and be motivated in certain ways based on one's biological constitution and developmental history.*"

At this point some readers may ask: "What about the fact that motive dispositions are typically viewed as nonconscious, such that they must be measured via projective tests such as the Thematic Apperception Test? This distinguishes them from conventional personality traits, which are typically assumed to be measurable by self-report." I believe this is not a problem, as a "stable disposition to think, feel, and be motivated in certain ways based on one's biological constitution and developmental history" might be either conscious or unconscious. The latter is undoubtedly an important dichotomy (Wilson, Lindsey, & Schooler, 2000), but one that does not change the core definition of traits.

In this context, it is worth briefly mentioning the "implicit attitudes" measured by the Implicit Associates Test, by lexical decision tasks, by Stroop tasks, and the like (Fazio & Olson, 2003). Similarly to motive dispositions, these are defined as emotion-relevant response dispositions that are activated automatically, often without the person's conscious knowledge. For example, the IAT (Implicit Associates Test; Greenwald, Nosek, & Banaji, 2003) might indicate that a particular person very readily associates minorities with negative words, and research suggests that such nonconscious attitudes, presumably acquired early in development, can have important behavioral consequences (McConnell & Leibold, 2001). Based on this reasoning, I suggest that implicit attitudes fall into the personality trait category just as do motive dispositions, as implicit attitudes also involve dispositions to think, feel, and be motivated in certain ways based on one's developmental history. Again, the fact that they may be nonconscious does not affect their placement in this category.

Indeed, a wide variety of individual difference constructs employed by personality psychologists, both conscious and nonconscious, could fit the above definition and thus be located at Level 2 of Fig. 3.3. These might include attachment styles, social value orientations, Meyers–Briggs types, and Minnesota Multiphasic Personality Inventory (MMPI) profiles. They might also include many more specific traits, such as self-monitoring, Machiavellianism, self-consciousness, and narcissism. The underlying commonality: All involve "a disposition to think, feel, and be motivated in certain ways based on one's biological constitution and developmental history."

Finally, it is worth reconsidering the universal organismic needs, discussed in the preceding chapter, in light of the above definition and discussion. Organismic needs might be viewed as motive dispositions in the same sense as the needs for achievement, intimacy, and power; after all, both are personality dispositions that affect what people think, feel, and are motivated toward. Does this mean the needs should also go at Level 2 in Fig. 3.3? No—there are two important differences between motive dispositions and organismic needs. First, the organismic needs are assumed not to vary significantly across individuals (Deci & Ryan, 2000), whereas the motive dispositions listed earlier (i.e., for achievement, intimacy, power) do vary. Also, the organismic needs are not based on developmental history or temperament, but rather are assumed to be based on selection pressures that shaped all humans in the same way. As a result, the organismic needs would not be viewed as trait/individual difference constructs (located at Level 2 of Fig. 3.3), but would instead remain at Level 1 of Fig. 3.3, which concerns species-typical features of human nature.

THE BIG FIVE MODEL OF PERSONALITY TRAITS

With these ideas in mind, it is now time to turn to the predominant contemporary theory of personality traits: the Big Five model. This model of adult personality traits has received impressive empirical support in the past 15 years, and thus it will be instructive to try to apply the above analysis to the model. Can the Big Five traits be grounded in temperamental and environmental factors, thereby confirming my suggestion that personality traits have legitimate causal force?

The Basic Traits

The Big Five model asserts that a personality can be comprehensively described in terms of five major traits or dimensions. These traits were already alluded to, in the trait profile given for Allison, earlier in the chapter—again, Allison might be characterized as high on neuroticism (i.e., reactivity and negative emotionality), high in extraversion (i.e., sociability and positive emotionality), high in openness to experience (i.e., sensation-seeking and creativity), high in conscientiousness (i.e., diligence and achievement orientation), and low in agreeableness (i.e., cooperativeness and acquiescence).

Much research on the Big Five is based on the "lexical" hypothesis regarding traits, which states that the major dimensions on which humans vary should be represented in all human tongues (Goldberg, 1990), as language evolved, in large part, in order to describe variations in the world. From this perspective, how does one discover the fundamental human traits, if there are any? By finding that the same basic traits and clusters of traits emerge in every language and culture. In contrast, if one finds very different traits and factors in different cultures and languages, then one would legitimately question whether there really are any fundamental human traits.

In this light, one of the more significant accomplishments of Big Five researchers has been to show that the same five superfactors (those listed earlier) consistently emerge when one analyzes a broad spectrum of trait adjectives within many different languages and countries, including Germany, Italy, Hungary, Poland, Czechoslovakia, Russia, China, Japan, and the Philippines (DeRaad, Perugini, Hrebickova, & Szarota, 1998). In other words, these five factors appear to be "transcultural universals," species-typical dimensions on which all human beings vary (McCrae, 2001). It should be said that there are some exceptions in the published data, however. For example, the openness to experience factor emerges least consistently across cultures, and some studies suggest that in some cultures, other factors besides those named in the Big Five might be included in the "basic" set (Pervin, 2003). Still, it is safe to say that most personality psychologists are impressed with the degree of cross-cultural generalizability that has been shown for the Big Five traits.

Biological Basis of the Big Five

What is the biological basis of the Big Five traits? It appears that all five have significant genetic underpinnings, as heritabilities in the .41 to .61 range have been reported for the five traits (summarized in Pervin, 2003). These are of approximately the same magnitude as the heritabilities for temperamental traits, reported above. Coefficients of this size suggest that a person (like Allison) might be expected to maintain the same basic trait profile across the life span. And indeed, impressive

30-year stability has been demonstrated for each of the Big Five traits, with test–retest coefficients reaching the .60s. On the basis of such findings, McCrae and Costa (1990) suggested that personality is "set in plaster" by the age of 30, and that little rank-order change in trait scores occurs afterward.

Can the five factors be linked to underlying biological or temperamental variables, such as emotionality, activity, impulsivity, and sociability? Yes. One line of evidence comes from studies of autonomic arousal and temperamental traits, begun by Eysenck in the 1940s. Eysenck theorized that all humans have a similar point of "optimal arousal," a species-typical level of psychophysiological arousal at which both their mood and their performance are maximized. In this view, being either underaroused or overaroused is aversive and detrimental. Moreover, Eysenck theorized that people vary in their typical or baseline level of arousal. Some people tend by nature to be chronically underaroused, and other people tend to be chronically overaroused. In fact, Eysenck's definition of an extrovert is a person who is underaroused at baseline and who has evolved a stimulating style of life designed to procure the missing stimulation. Conversely, an introvert is a person who is overaroused at baseline and who has evolved a calming style of life designed to reduce the predominant overstimulation (Eysenck, 1990).

Eysenck (1973, 1990) cited considerable psychophysiological evidence consistent with the proposal that the trait of extraversion is based on people's psychobiology. For example, introverts (who are presumably overstimulated at baseline) require more antidepressants to reach a given level of sedation compared to extraverts (who are understimulated). Also, compared to introverts, extraverts show less salivary reaction to taste stimulation, show less pupillary contraction to a bright light, choose more noise stimulation in a learning task, and perform better in the presence of intense noise. Evidence also exists for the biological basis of neuroticism, as those high in neuroticism have been shown to be highly reactive to emotional stimuli in specific brain areas, and to have strong right-hemisphere dominance, in general.

Applying these ideas to the "Allison" example, we might say that she has been understimulated all of her life, and that she has developed various ways of coping. This effort began in her childhood, in her tendency to try to provoke strong emotional responses from family members, and in her tendency to react more extremely to particular events than her siblings. It continued through her teenage and early adult years, as she learned to seek out intense social relationships and encounters, and to seek out novel experiences in general (i.e., by joining the Peace Corps).

In what other ways can biology and the Big Five be connected, in addition to demonstrating co-activation of biological systems and traits? Another fruitful avenue would be to show historical connections between infant temperament and later trait profiles. If the Big Five traits are biologically based and develop out of temperament, then it should be possible to chart a developmental sequence by which babies with certain combinations of temperamental variables turn into children with certain combinations of Big Five traits.

Caspi (1998) made a number of interesting suggestions concerning this important question, focusing on the temperamental traits of activity, positive affect, inhibition, negative affect, and persistence. Specifically, Caspi proposed that high activity may help give rise to high extraversion and low conscientiousness; that high positive affect may help give rise to high extraversion and high agreeableness; that high inhibition may help give rise to high neuroticism and low extraversion; that high negative affect may help give rise to high neuroticism and low agreeableness; and that high persistence may help give rise to high agreeableness, conscientiousness, and openness to experience. Caspi (1998) also proposed six "mechanisms of developmental elaboration," by which temperament gradually develops into the adult personality traits: learning processes, environmental elicitation, environmental construal, social and temporal comparisons, environmental selection, and environmental manipulation. Unfortunately, there are as yet little data to test Caspi's interesting developmental hypotheses.

The Evolutionary Basis of the Big Five

Yet another way to perhaps demonstrate a biological basis for the Big Five is to take an evolutionary perspective on the traits. Might these five dimensions of behavior have been somehow selected for in humanity's evolutionary past, due to the adaptive advantages they conveyed? Buss (1991) suggested several ways in which this may be the case. First, selective advantage may have accrued to those who were able to accurately evaluate others on the traits. For example, those able to detect that a new acquaintance is low in conscientiousness may derive a selective advantage, in terms of knowing whom to rely on for important work. Similarly, being able to detect and select individuals high in agreeableness may convey considerable advantages in terms of enabling cohesive and cooperative functioning in one's social groups (as discussed further in chap. 8).

Note that such an adaptive mechanism does not explain the evolution of the traits themselves, but rather the evolution of the ability to perceive them in others. Obviously, the more important question is: Why are the traits there in the first place? That is, why would natural selection have left wide variability in particular personality styles within the gene pool, given that variability on a particular trait within the gene pool is typically reduced over time (Tooby & Cosmides, 1990)?

Buss (1991) put forth an intriguing proposal, suggesting that the bipolar extremes of Big Five traits represent heritable alternative behavioral strategies, which are maintained in the population because they give selective advantage at least in some times, or in at least some types of social environments. For example, high extraversion might be an adaptive life strategy at a time when energy and camaraderie are needed, or when the ability to quickly make contacts with others is important. In contrast, extraversion may not be such a good strategy at a time when caution, self-reliance, and self-restraint are needed. Similarly, there are a variety of niches available within the overall social ecology, and enthusiastic extraversion may be adaptive in some of these niches (i.e., if one is a talk-show host), and less adaptive in other niches (i.e., if one is a mortician).

The former example, concerning variations in the adaptiveness of a trait over time, demonstrates that *frequency-dependent selection* may sometimes influence the prevalence of traits. Frequency-dependent selection occurs when the adaptiveness of a trait depends on how many others also have that trait within the population, or when adaptiveness depends on the frequency of some other linked trait within the population. When there is frequency dependence, the percentage of people evidencing the trait tends to cycle up and down over time. For example, the trait of low agreeableness/high competitiveness might be quite adaptive if most people are fairly agreeable (or gullible), as this situation offers easy niches for exploitation (Tooby & Cosmides, 1992). However, once the population shifts so far toward intragroup competition that successful group functioning became very difficult, then agreeableness might again become an adaptive trait, enabling those who possessed it to derive the substantial benefits of coherent group functioning (this process is discussed further in chap. 8). Notably, frequency dependence between linked traits is another excellent example of a higher level or "holistic" theoretical concept, describing a social-level factor that affects outcomes in ways not reducible to lower levels of analysis.

Buss (1991) also suggested another way in which the Big Five traits may have an evolutionary basis. Specifically, adult differences in the Big Five may represent "developmental calibration of psychological mechanisms." In this view, humans arrive in the world with the potential for variation in their levels of various traits, such that they might end up in the low or the high ends of their potential "reaction range" (Plomin, 1995). Which way they go depends on the developmental environment they encounter. For example, a child raised in an insecure or depriving environment may develop a personality higher in agreeableness or higher in neuroticism, which might prove adaptive in that environment, as it helps the child to get along with the caretakers, or to anticipate and avoid trouble with them. As another example, a child reared in a very traditional or even repressive family may develop a personality lower in openness to experience, in order to better fit in within that family. In keeping with the general evolutionary psychological approach (discussed in the preceding chapter), Buss's assumption is that the neural circuitry for either outcome is already in place, merely waiting activation and calibration. This hypothesis again illustrates the strong impact that environments can have on people's trait scores. As pointed out earlier in the chapter, such higher level factors account for about as much variation in trait scores as do genetic factors.

In sum, the Big Five model does well in terms of many of the criteria for asserting a causal role for traits, outlined earlier. First, the Big Five traits seem to have a considerable biological basis, with substantial heritabilities and longitudinal stabilities, and also with considerable data linking psychobiological and temperamental functioning to the traits. In addition, the five traits can be construed as evolved dimensions of human difference, which emerged because of their adaptive relevance. Furthermore, the Big Five traits can also be construed as based in part on people's developmental histories—again, history may provide as good a basis for grounding traits as does genetics. Finally, consistent with my earlier suggestions concerning the redefinition of traits, the Big Five can be construed as internal cognitive, emotional, and motivational dispositions, and not just as explicit behavioral dispositions, enhancing their explanatory potential. Thus, I believe that the Big Five personality traits are indeed "real entities" (rather than being mere linguistic or sociological fictions), which can doubtless contribute to a consilient causal account of human behavior (Rowe, 2001).

LIMITATIONS OF TRAIT APPROACHES

Still, it would not do to finish this section before also taking note of some limitations of the trait construct. One important limitation is that although personality traits are reasonably good predictors of people's average behavior over time, they are not very good predictors of behavior at a single instant in time (Epstein, 1979). Thus, for example, knowing that the "killer" described at the beginning of chapter 2 was low in the trait of agreeableness and high in the trait of neuroticism would not have given us a basis for predicting this particular aggressive behavior at this particular time, although it might lead us to say that the behavior was more likely for this person than for another person. In this vein, some critics (Briggs, 1989) have argued that the Big Five's focus on very global, abstract traits may limit predictive ability, as more specific traits might be better predictors of specific behaviors (i.e., the trait of "jealousy" might better predict the murder of a lover than the trait of "neuroticism").

A related limitation of the trait approach is that trait scores are assumed to remain largely invariant across situations and across the life span (McCrae & Costa, 1990). What this means is that they give the same prediction in every situation, and at every phase of life. Thus, on the basis of her trait profile, we would expect Allison to seek out emotional intensity in all parts of her life, at all times. But surely she fluctuates in this characteristic, manifesting more or less of it at different times or in different situations, or while playing different roles (Fleeson, 2001)? For example, people who know Allison have observed that she becomes most emotional when the subject turns to her childhood and the family tragedy, and least emotional when she is playing the social roles of "employee" or "student" (see Sheldon, Ryan, Rawsthorne, & Ilardi, 1997).

Unfortunately, the trait perspective gives no basis for predicting such between-situation variations in trait behaviors. Indeed, trait researchers have tended to resist acknowledgment of such within-subject variation, instead treating it as inconvenient "noise" in their models (Smith & Williams, 1992). But it is likely that there is much signal in such noise, information that is simply inaccessible to the trait perspective. In order to access these signals and enhance predictability, one would probably need to go beyond trait scores, to consider people's specific and situationally grounded thoughts, feelings, and perceptions.

Which leads us to a third critique: that the trait approach is, in large part, a "psychology of the stranger" (McAdams, 1996). That is, traits provide the kind of information you would want about a totally new person in order to begin to get an initial sense of him or her, but this information does not take us beyond the level of relatively superficial description, and gives no deeper sense of what makes a person tick. In other words, this approach says little about the dynamics of personality, nor about the organization of the various features of personality into a more-or-less unified whole (Sheldon et al., 1997). To illustrate, again consider McCrae and Costa's (1995) temporal model, presented in Fig. 3.4. Although it makes reference to several "dynamic processes," the trait perspective says nothing about what these are or how they work.

To illustrate this third criticism more concretely: By this time you, the reader, would probably like to know more about Allison than her standing on the Big Five traits. What is she trying to do in her life, what are her dreams and ambitions, and how does she think of herself as a person? How has she construed her emotional struggles over her lifetime, and how has she integrated this facet of herself into a workable whole? What does she make of the fact that her friendships are typically intense, but relatively short-lived? In McAdams's terms (see Fig. 3.2), we also need to know about her goals and intentions, as well as her self-concepts and life stories, to round out the picture. Again, such information would likely give considerably more basis for predicting what she will do in a particular situation, beyond the information given by her Big Five trait scores.

A final limitation of trait approaches is that they typically do not focus on the factors that mediate between traits and behaviors. For example, we know that Allison is high in extraversion. How does she get from this generic trait to the specific behaviors that express it? Why does she express the trait one way in one context, and another way in another context? Why do her traits seem to dominate her behavior at some times, and not at other times? Some theorists have suggested that answering these kinds of questions requires knowledge of "if–then contingencies" within personality, by which people are configured to behave differently depending on different contextual circumstances (i.e., Mischel & Shoda's 1998 "cognitive-affective personality system"). Trait models are largely silent on such issues.

PERSONALITY TRAITS AND OPTIMAL HUMAN BEING

Working Toward More or Less of Certain Traits

What definitions of optimal human being, or prescriptions for optimal human being, emerge from the personality trait level of analysis? There are several interesting possibilities. One very promising possibility is based on the fact that the Big Five traits are differentially correlated with psychological well-being and happiness (although, of course, these are not the only indicators of optimal human being). Specifically, extraversion and agreeableness are positively correlated with well-being, and neuroticism is negatively correlated with well-being (DeNeve & Cooper, 1998). Based on this information, perhaps the prescription for optimal human being is as simple as this: Strive to become more extraverted and agreeable, and strive to become less neurotic.

But is this possible? Again, one of the hallmarks of the personality trait construct is longitudinal stability—thus personality may, to a considerable extent, be "set in plaster" by the age of 30 (McCrae & Costa, 1990). However, closer scrutiny of the data indicates that this idea is not necessarily true. Thirty-year stability coefficients of .55 to .60 are indeed impressive, but they also leave substantial room for rank-order change. For example, a person who is high in neuroticism at the age of 30 relative to his cohort can potentially move a considerable distance toward the lower end of the spectrum, by age 60. Notably, Big Five theory gives no information on how a person might do this, as it has focused more on demonstrating stability rather than explaining change.

It is also important to realize that rank-order change is not the only way to manifest positive improvement in traits. Even if people do not switch places with each other over time, still, everyone could change their levels of traits over time, while maintaining the same rank-order relative to others. In other words, the population mean level of various traits may shift up or down, as the population ages. And in fact, there is considerable evidence that this occurs. For example, researchers have reported longitudinal sample-wide declines in neuroticism and longitudinal increases in agreeableness and conscientiousness (McGue, Bacon, & Lykken, 1993; Robins, Fraley, Roberts, & Trzesniewski, 2001; Watson & Walker, 1996). Furthermore, these trends appear to be consistent across cultures (Costa et al., 2000).

Recently, Costa and McCrae have extended their thinking, attempting to account for such positive change. Specifically, McCrae et al. (2000) posited an "intrinsic maturational" process, in which "personality traits, like temperaments, are endogenous dispositions that follow intrinsic paths of development essentially independent of environmental influences" (p. 173). The idea is that personality tends to develop in certain ways over the life span, regardless of the environments and experiences that people encounter. This development takes the form of the observed decreases in neuroticism and openness, and the increases in agreeableness and conscientiousness. The "intrinsic maturation" idea is consistent with other developmental models of personality, such as Erik Erikson's (1963) epigenetic assumptions regarding inherent trends toward psychosocial maturation. However, one cannot help but think that Costa and McCrae were trying to stretch their concepts in ways they will not really go, given their overall commitment to demonstrating longitudinal stability for the Big Five. Also, they have not yet provided a good account of why the "intrinsic maturational push" would go in the positive directions it does. Why decreasing neuroticism and increasing conscientiousness, instead of vice versa? As discussed at the end of chapter 4, I believe that the organismic theoretical perspective, which assumes that all humans have inherent tendencies toward growth, health, and development, is needed to explain such normative positive changes.

Working Toward Optimal Arousal

Other prescriptions for optimal human being are also derivable from trait theory. One approach takes note of the biological basis of the traits. For example, recall Eysenck's (1990) idea that extraverts have developed their social personalities and stimulating mode of life in order to cope with chronic underarousal, and vice versa for introverts. From this perspective, everyone is seeking to achieve an optimal level of arousal. Accordingly, a successful person is one who succeeds in regulating his or her life so that he or she stays as close as possible to the optimal level, as often as possible.

However, this is a rather simplistic notion of optimal human being. First, levels of arousal above or below one's median level can doubtless be useful and adaptive at times. For example, it is probably better to be somewhat arousal oriented when one is seeking leisure and entertainment, and somewhat less arousal oriented when one is trying to be careful in an important work task (as in Apter's 2001 reversal theory). A second way in which this definition of optimal human being seems somewhat simplistic is that it ignores meaning and psychological fulfillment, that is, eudaemonia. Instead, it promotes a rather hedonistic and reductionistic account of optimal human being, in which fulfillment is found simply by properly calibrating one's autonomic nervous system. Surely there is more to the human spirit than this.

Being True to One's Traits

More complex prescriptions for optimal human being are also derivable from trait theory. For example, if we assume that people's traits reflect their underlying biological nature, then perhaps optimal human being involves developing a style of life that provides one with experiences that are consistent with one's traits and biological nature. However, the prescription of being "true to one's traits" (McGregor, McAdams, & Little, 2003) can be applied even more broadly. Perhaps extraverts should try to structure their lives to receive lots of social stimulation, those high in agreeableness should try to surround themselves with amiable people, those high in openness to experience should try to continually experience new things, and so on. Conversely, those low in extraversion should seek solitude, those low in agreeableness should seek situations of social conflict, and those low in openness to experience should seek sameness and predictability.

Notice that this model of optimal human being is different from saying that optimal human being involves moving toward the traits most associated with well-being. Instead, it says that optimal human being involves intensifying, satisfying, or expressing one's traits, whether or not those traits are associated with happiness and well-being. Each person has a unique genetic and socioemotional nature, which they should structure their lives in accordance with.

There are at least two problems with the "be true to your traits" perspective, which likely limit its usefulness. One concerns "negative" traits, such as neuroticism. If a person tends to overreact to threat, to worry unduly, and to experience anxiety for no objectively valid reason, should he or she try to make it so that these experiences occur more often? Given that neuroticism is associated with a variety of negative effects and outcomes, this seems like a bizarre prescription for optimal human being! Similarly, consider the trait of agreeableness. The "be true to your traits" model would counsel a person low in this trait (i.e., one who is exploitative and argumentative) to give fuller expression to his antisocial nature. As another example, the "be true to your traits" model would counsel a slovenly or irresponsible person (who is low in conscientiousness) to indulge these preferences as much as possible. This hardly seems like wise counsel!

A second problem with the "be true to your traits" model involves the general notion that one should try to strengthen and reinforce one's dominant tendencies. Arguably, it is just as important to modulate and even alter those tendencies, for the sake of balance, or even to try to develop in the opposite direction. Indeed, this was a predominant prescription for optimal human being within Carl Jung's theory of personality, according to which we must seek to know the "shadow" sides of ourselves, in addition to the sides most in the spotlight. To illustrate, suppose that Allison, by the age of 40, has brought her negative emotionality under much more control, and has also reduced her dependency on social stimulation as a route to autonomic arousal. Thus one way of depicting the positive changes that have occurred in Allison's life is to say that she has learned to compensate for the more extreme aspects of her personality, so that her traits no longer dominate as before. Again, such intentional processes implicate a different level of analysis within personality, involving the person's goals and intentions (as discussed in the next chapter).

In sum, the most defensible prescription for optimal human being, from the personality trait level of analysis, appears to be this: Work toward higher levels of conscientiousness, extraversion, openness, and agreeableness, and toward lower levels of neuroticism. Less defensible are prescriptions to seek a certain optimal arousal level, no matter what the circumstances, and to try to be true to one's traits, whatever they are.

THE HERITABILITY OF HAPPINESS AND THE QUEST FOR OPTIMAL HUMAN BEING

A final, somewhat different question is worthy of discussion, as we consider the implications of the personality trait approach for optimal human being. Although the question does not concern personality traits per se, I discuss it here because it fits well with this chapter's focus on people's unalterable temperaments, which help to ground personality traits. Here is the question: Is it even possible to sustainably increase one's psychological health and well-being? Might it instead be the case that one's general mental state and level of functioning are stable and unchangeable, such that efforts to improve them are futile or even counterproductive? The latter conjecture, if true, would certainly have discouraging implications for two fundamental premises of this book: that optimal human being to some extent arises from the person's intentional attitude, and, that people thus have considerable potential control over the optimality of their mode of being. Accordingly, I try to show, in this section, that the conjecture is false.

This general issue arises because, as discussed earlier in the chapter, many personality characteristics have demonstrated considerable heritability. Psychological well-being (i.e., happiness) appears to be one of these, with heritability estimates of .50 or even greater (Diener & Lucas, 1999). Based on such data, Lykken and Tellegen (1996) argued that individuals have a "setpoint" for happiness—a genetically determined chronic happiness (or unhappiness) level, to which they will keep tending to return, no matter how things might improve (or worsen) in their lives. Again, if so, this would have discouraging implications for people's search for greater happiness and more optimal circumstances.

Lykken and Tellegen (1996) argued that such longitudinal stability occurs for at least two reasons. First, one's basic temperament typically does not change over the life span. A person who is by nature irritable, moody, and/or reactive will tend to keep evidencing those characteristics, no matter what their circumstances (Costa et al., 2000), and conversely, a person who is by nature cheerful, optimistic, and sociable will tend to stay that way, also. Second, hedonic adaptation automatically limits the happiness-producing effects of any life change. Hedonic adaptation is the idea that even if one experiences radical positive changes in one's life, one will quickly become accustomed to them, so that they no longer have the positive effect they did initially. Consistent with this claim, studies of lottery winners have shown that after the initial euphoria wears off winners are no better off than when they started, and are sometimes worse off (Brickman, Coates, & Janoff-Bulman, 1978; Nissle & Bschor, 2002). Although this may seem depressing, remember that the same reasoning also applies to radical negative changes; for example, becoming a paraplegic or losing a spouse may not have permanent negative effects on one's happiness.

One implication of the happiness set-point concept is that trying to become happier is no more meaningful or possible than is trying to become taller (Lykken & Tellegen, 1996)! Thus, although the Declaration of Independence guarantees Americans the right to "pursue happiness," perhaps this is a futile ambition—people might be better off accepting their current level of happiness, rather than striving for greater happiness (Gaskins, 1999). Of course, it is not such a long distance from "happiness" to "optimal human being," the topic of this book. By implication, might it also be useless to strive for a more optimal state of being? Perhaps one's general state of being is largely determined at birth, and there is no altering it.

This is probably put too strongly (Lykken, 2000). As discussed earlier, even highly heritable traits are subject to considerable environmental influence, and, people can switch places in the distribution of such traits. Also, even heritable traits evidence some mean-level change across the life span, such that individuals tend to move, on average, in happiness-congruent directions (McCrae et al., 2000). However, the latter effects are rather small, indicating that people do not necessarily succeed in moving in positive directions over the life span. This raises the question: How *does* positive change in happiness-relevant traits occur, and what can go wrong so that it does not occur?

Lyubomirsky, Sheldon, and Schkade (in press) recently proposed a model of "the architecture of sustainable happiness," which offers some suggestions. Specifically, Lyubomirsky et al. distinguished between three categories of influence on well-being: the happiness setpoint, which is genetically determined and which specifies the most likely or expected value for the person at time t; circumstantial change (i.e., winning the lottery, moving to California, buying a new car), which may give one a momentary happiness boost, raising one above the setpoint; and activity change (i.e., setting and pursuing meaningful new goals, adopting positive new attitudes or habits of mind, adopting happiness-relevant behavioral practices), which may also provide happiness boosts above the setpoint. A key assumption of the model is that the happiness-boosting effects of circumstantial changes more quickly fade because of hedonic adaptation—as noted earlier, even lottery winners tend to "come back down," eventually. In contrast, the happiness-boosting effects of activity change have a greater potential to persist, because there are a variety of ways that activities can "stay fresh" and thus counter adaptation. In other words, one can vary where, how, when, with whom, and how well one does an activity, maintaining its ability to create positive states. From this perspective, one of the things that can go wrong in people's quest for happiness is that they rely too much on changing the static external circumstances of their lives, and not enough on changing their habits, activities, and practices (Sheldon & Lyubomirsky, in press).

Some recent data supports the idea that activity change provides a potentially effective route to sustainable new happiness. Sheldon and Lyubomirsky (2004) conducted several longitudinal studies of self-reported well-being (positive affect, life satisfaction, and happiness), and found good support for a model in which positive circumstantial changes predict only temporary boosts in well-being, whereas positive activity changes predict longer lasting boosts. As shown in the path model of Fig. 5.1 (taken from one of their studies), although positive activity and circumstantial changes between Time 1 and Time 2 had equivalent positive effects on changes in well-being at Time 2, only the activity effect remained significant at Time 3.

Notably, Sheldon and Lyubomirsky's (2004) studies only considered the relatively short period of three months, and remains to be tested over longer periods of

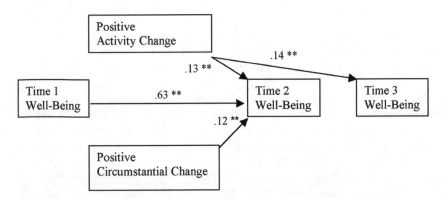

FIG. 5.1. Longitudinal path model predicting maintained changes in well-being. From Sheldon and Lyubomirsky (2004), with permission.

time. Also, the effects need to be generalized to other measures of optimal functioning besides well-being, such as physical health or interpersonal relationships. Still, the implication of this theory and research is that it is worthwhile taking action to improve one's life. By being successful in those actions, one can achieve and maintain new levels of psychological well-being, and perhaps more optimal human being.

This conclusion provides a good transition to the subject of the next chapter: Goals and intentional activity. I argue that this level of analysis is perhaps the most important of all for understanding optimal human being, because it is the means by which individuals can "take the reins" of their lives, shaping it in more positive ways.

6

Goals and Intentions: The Method of Self-Organization

This chapter focuses on Level 3 of Fig. 3.3, the realm of goals, tasks, intentions, concerns, projects, and purposes. This is a large area of personality theory, including of all of the many attempts to deal theoretically with the fact that people are intentional actors, proactively shaping their environments and lives. This domain potentially includes the achievement motivation and test anxiety literature; the intrinsic and extrinsic motivation literature; the goal-setting and personal goal literatures; the European action theory literature; the social-cognitive literature; and many other literatures besides.

Rather than canvassing the entire field, this chapter will focus in depth on the domain I believe may be most relevant to the question of understanding optimal human being—the personal goal literature. This domain well captures people's attempts to be causal agents within their own lives—in terms of Fig. 2.1, their attempt to use the personality level of influence on human behavior, on their own behalf. Thus, consideration of this literature may cast considerable light on what it means to optimize one's being and how to best strive toward greater optimality in one's being. Specifically, in this chapter I provide a detailed summary of the emerging longitudinal goal-studies literature. What can this literature teach us about the *process of attaining* more optimal human being?

DEFINING PERSONAL GOALS

What is a personal goal? Herein, I define it as "a relatively chronic attempt to bring about some outcome or set of outcomes within one's life." The word *chronic* implies that a personal goal is not just something that arises within a particular time or situation, but rather is something that lasts (or at least is intended to last) for at least a few weeks or months. This definition includes the abstract personal strivings that are characteristic of a person's personality throughout his or her life span, such as the strivings to achieve a particular ideal self-image or to find a higher spiritual meaning in life (Emmons, 1989). However it also includes shorter term and more concrete projects, such as the goal of completing a landscaping project or making an "A" in a course (Little, 1993). Stated in terms of Carver and Scheier's control theory model (1998; see Fig. 3.1), personal goals can be located at the system, the principle, or the program levels of control. Below the program level of control are more concrete skills, or mere motor and behavioral sequences, which typically would not fall into the personal goal category.

The reader may be wondering: Does everyone have goals? What about people who don't verbalize goals, or who don't make lists, or who don't seem to be achievement oriented? Personal goal theorists assume that even the latter types have goals—intentions emerge and then to some extent control behavior, whether or not the person is preoccupied with them or gives words to them (Emmons, 1989). Indeed, without goals and intentions, behavior would be random and chaotic (Carver & Scheier, 1998). Of course, goals may perhaps be more effectively enacted if they are verbalized and made explicit, but this is an empirical, not a definitional, question.

Readers may also wonder: Do goals have to be conscious, that is, must the person know about them as he or she works on them? Not necessarily—again, goals need not be activated within conscious awareness to have influence. In terms of Carver and Scheier's model, higher levels of control are typically implicit, remaining in the back of awareness until attention is required at that level, as when one questions or changes one's broader objectives (see chap. 3). Further indicating that goals need not occupy awareness to influence behavior, Bargh and colleagues have shown that people can be induced to pursue short-term goals purely via subliminal priming (Bargh, Gollwitzer, Lee-Chai, Barndollar, & Troetschel, 2001). In short, I assume that we all pursue goals, although there can of course be large differences in what goals we pursue, how we pursue them, why we pursue them, how aware we are of them, and how well we pursue them.

In more functional terms, a personal goal is a recurring cognitive image or symbol that serves as a behavioral standard or instigator with respect to behavior. In Carver and Scheier's holistic teleological model, such images provide the top-down standards that create the discrepancies that we try to reduce. As such, goals are a special type of mental representation, invested with motivational energy—goals and intentions literally move us (Ford & Lerner, 1992). To return to the concept of negentropy discussed in chapter 3, goals are a vital means, and perhaps the most important means, by which human beings create new life organizations, thus establishing themselves within the future. In other words, goals allow people to arrive in possible futures that would have been extremely unlikely to occur otherwise (Sheldon & Vansteenkiste, in press), in the process "dissipating entropy" (i.e., counteracting random and destabilizing influences that might stand in the way of getting where one wants to go). Again, from the evolutionary perspective, the action system may be viewed as an essential human adaptation that allows us to engage in extended serial courses of behavior—courses that can enhance organization and make life better not only for ourselves, but also for our associates (MacDonald, 1991). Thus, effective goal striving must certainly be part of any comprehensive account of optimal human being.

What are the limitations on the effectiveness of goal striving? In other words, why might some individuals be unable to create better life circumstances and personal well-being for themselves, via intentional activity? Or said yet another way, why does the action system sometimes fail in its mission of enhancing the person's life? This question occupies most of the remainder of this chapter, because of its important implications for understanding optimal human being. In addressing it, I consider two basic types of theoretical explanation (Sheldon & Kasser, 1995). The first focuses on the *systemic functioning of the action system.* How is the process coordinated, or perhaps miscoordinated, such that the person either achieves, or fails to achieve, his or her goals? Systemic perspectives tend to focus on the cognitive level of analysis (see Fig. 2.1), and lend themselves to reductionistic and mechanistic models of behavior. The second theoretical perspective, based on the organismic philosophical perspective discussed in chapter 4, focuses on the *organismic needs of the person who has the action system.* What are the goals the person pursues, and why did he or she choose them? Are they the right goals for that person, or for human personalities more generally? Do the goals help to further the person's health, well-being, and personal growth, or do they perhaps work against these outcomes, in some fashion? Organismic perspectives tend to focus on the personality level of analysis in Fig. 2.1 (especially the self level), and lend themselves to holistic and humanistic models of behavior.

SYSTEMIC PERSPECTIVES ON OPTIMAL GOAL FUNCTIONING

Carver and Scheier's (1998) control theory model provides a good framework from which to consider systemic perspectives on optimal goal functioning (but see Shah & Kruglanski, 2000, for a review of other recent goal-systems perspectives). Recall that in Carver and Scheier's model, there are multiple levels of control within the action system (i.e., a goal may be a short-term project, a more abstract longer term principle, or a most abstract global system image). In addition, there are likely to be multiple agendas within each level of control (i.e., people have a variety of personal projects at a particular time, a variety of enduring personal strivings, and a variety of possible self images). Action occurs via establishment of functional linkages between lower and higher levels of the system, initiating behavior such that discrepancies between actual and desired states are reduced. Starting from this foundation, one can identify a number of potential problems that might occur within an action system. These are considered next.

Insufficient Skills

First, the person may have insufficient skills or abilities relevant to goal pursuit. In terms of Fig. 3.1, a person may not have the "sequences" in place to enact programs. For example, a man's project may be to lead a successful fund-raising drive for his group. However he may not have the accounting skills or the organizational skills necessary to achieve this goal, and thus the discrepancy between the present state (no funds) and the desired state (achieved funds) may not be reduced.

What are the crucial skills and abilities for goal strivers to have? This is a difficult question, as it depends in part on what the particular goals are, how one defines skills, and what kinds of constructs are included in the skills category. For example, does intelligence count as a skill? What about the ability to take a positive attitude, or the ability to put one's goals aside and relax? As one approach to this question, Sheldon and Kasser (1998) studied 10 candidate life skills that they believed would be relevant to effective goal attainment. Participants rated their possession of each of the 10 life skills. The ten skills formed two higher order factors: six social skills (specifically, the ability to play different roles as situations require; to perceive social norms; to create rapport with others; to express oneself and communicate effectively; to use one's emotions as information; and to be assertive when necessary), and four self-regulatory skills (specifically, the ability to budget one's time effectively; to concentrate when necessary; to forgo immediate gratification for longer-term rewards; and to conceive of an appropriate plan to obtain goals). Both groups of skills were correlated with longitudinal attainment of personal projects over a 6-week study (Sheldon & Kasser, 1998), suggesting that social and self-regulatory skill possession indeed forwards goal pursuit. Of course, there are doubtless many other skills and abilities relevant to effective goal pursuit.

Lack of Vertical Coherence

The preceding paragraph concerned the problems that may arise when one does not possess relevant lower level discrepancy-reducing units, that is, certain skills. However, one may also have relevant skills or abilities but fail to apply them. Here, the problem is not the absence of a lower level action unit, but rather, the absence of a functional linkage between lower and higher level action units. In Sheldon and Kasser's (1995) terminology, a person may not have "vertical coherence" in his action system, such that lower and higher level action units fail to contact each other.

For example, at the more concrete levels of the action system, vertical incoherence might be said to exist when a person does not apply relevant skills (i.e., the ability to be a persuasive public speaker) to the higher level goal (i.e., of obtaining donations for the fund drive). For example, rather than seeking public-speaking opportunities, the person might instead only think to send out bulk mail and e-mail. Vertical incoherence might also occur if a person does not remember to apply his or her skills, or enact his or her concrete plans and intentions, at the specific time that they are relevant. In this vein, Gollwitzer (1999) showed that behavior in service of goals is better enacted if one creates an "implementation intention," of the form "I will perform behavior x in situation y." For example, a person might say, "I will ask the boss about my raise the next time I see her in the hallway." This memory technique helps to make a concrete linkage between the goal, the specific behavior designed to serve it, and the specific situation in which the behavior will be cued to occur.

At more abstract levels of the action system, vertical coherence might be lacking when one's daily projects and behaviors are irrelevant to one's broader ambitions (i.e., a graduate student may spend much time on projects that have nothing to do with his or her primary goal of completing the doctoral thesis). It might also occur when one's higher level goals are too vague or nebulous, such that it is not clear how to go about attaining them. For example, the goals of "Find that inner solace and higher mind" and "Seek new definitions for my life, what is good, desirable, realistic" may be too high-level and abstract, such that the person does not know what to do (i.e., what programs to implement) in order to approach them (Emmons, 1992). Another form of vertical incoherence occurs when concrete behaviors and goals directly conflict with higher level goals (i.e., a person's typical behavioral goal of "ignoring panhandlers" might conflict with the person's desired future self goal of "me as a compassionate, altruistic person"). In this case, the person has not succeeded in making his or her behavioral goals consistent with his or her avowed longer term purposes.

Lack of Horizontal Coherence

In addition, there can be conflict between goals at the same level of the action system (Emmons & King, 1988). Sheldon and Kasser (1995) referred to same-level conflict as a lack of *horizontal* coherence. For example, on the day when I began this chapter my goals were to make a good start, to prepare for a conference talk, to prepare for and attend a faculty meeting, and to finish designing a research paradigm. These goals conflicted because of time limitations, such that I only accomplished the first and third goals. Fortunately, however, my goals did not also conflict in terms of content; that is, they were not logically as well as temporally inconsistent with each other (Wilensky, 1983). At least I was not also pursuing the goals of trying to get out of going to the conference, or to the faculty meeting! Although this may sound absurd, people frequently suffer from ambivalence of this kind. Such approach-avoidance conflicts can bring about heightened stress and reduced well-being (Emmons & King, 1988).

A related way of considering the horizontal coherence or consistency of the person's goals at a particular level of the action system has been provided by Kuhl (1986), in his analysis of how people handle ambivalence. Kuhl noted that some goals are more intrinsically appealing than others, and that important but less appealing goals may need to be "shielded" from the more appealing goals, so that they are not usurped by them. In other words, people need *motivational maintenance* skills, by which they keep their focus on particular goals, resisting their undermining by other goals at the same level of the action system. Kuhl discussed a variety of motivational maintenance mechanisms, such as attention control, motivational control, encoding control, and environmental control, which can be applied to protect unappealing intentions. For example, someone might try to quit smoking by intentionally avoiding other smokers, turning the magazine page when a smoking ad is encountered, and thinking about the health benefits he or she will receive from quitting (Emmons, King, & Sheldon, 1993). When we consider later the organismic congruence of goals, we explore some important reasons why some goals may be less appealing, and more vulnerable to being usurped.

What is the optimal same-level arrangement between goals? From the horizontal coherence perspective, it is good when one's various projects are consistent with each other, so that working on one does not take away from another. Better yet is when one's projects mutually reinforce each other—as when one can simultaneously pursue the goals of disseminating one's research findings, developing new theory on a topic of interest, and finally taking the time to analyze new data, all by preparing a conference talk. Emmons and King (1989) showed that striving systems can be more or less differentiated, that is, more or less distinct and independent of each other. In the case of extreme differentiation, people may have the most difficulty integrating their various goals into a coherent whole, and the most difficulty pursuing them efficiently (Sheldon & Emmons, 1995). Conversely, it is likely easier to effectively run one's goal system when one's goals are all very similar to one another. Intuition suggests, however, that a person who is too "monothematic" in life may sometimes encounter other difficulties, in terms of burnout, relationship problems, or missed growth opportunities. Thus, there is more to systemic coherence than a mere lack of differentiation (Sheldon & Emmons, 1995).

Approach Versus Avoidance Framing

A final systemic perspective on goal failures comes via the distinction between approach framing and avoidance framing. Most goals could be framed in either approach terms (i.e., "Eat better and exercise more") or avoidance terms (i.e., "Eat less and stay off the couch"). Does it matter which framing is chosen? Yes, framing indeed has significant implications for how well goals are attained. Specifically, Elliot and colleagues (Elliot & Sheldon, 1996, 1998; Elliot, Sheldon, & Church, 1997) showed that people do worse at attaining avoidance goals. Elliot, McGregor, and Thrash (2002) suggested that this is for reasons similar to the reasons people do worse at overly vague and abstract goals (Emmons, 1992)—namely, that it is less clear how to achieve an avoidance goal than an approach goal. For example, if one wishes to eat better or exercise more, one can set subtargets of where to shop, what food to buy, or when to include a workout in one's schedule. However, it is less clear what concrete steps to take in order to avoid eating, or to keep from being a couch potato. Stated differently, it is easier (and perhaps more self-reinforcing) to try to find a single path toward a desired outcome, than to try to block all possible paths toward an undesired outcome. In short, the negative effects of avoidance goals may be construed in terms of a lack of vertical coherence between lower and higher level action units, in that the person does not know how to take action to close the gap between actual states and desired outcomes. Vertically integrated goal systems should capitalize on this fact, by containing predominantly approach goals that can specify clear routes to follow.

Back to the Medical Student

To concretely apply these systemic conceptions of optimal functioning, let us return to the example used in chapter 3 of a medical student driving to the Health Sciences Library to acquire a book. In this case, vertical coherence likely exists from the bottom to the top of the action system. The person has the requisite lower skills for the goal (i.e., the ability to drive, and the ability to find the way to a particular place). Also, the goal is vertically coherent with higher level goals (getting an A in the class, getting a good residency, and becoming a surgeon), and in fact directly serves to reduce the discrepancy between the present state and these higher level personal goals. In addition, the goal is framed in approach rather than avoidance terms, which allows for clear specification of a path to the goal. More information would be required to evaluate the horizontal coherence within the student's action system; horizontal coherence would be higher if, for example, the behavior of driving across town also served other daily goals such as picking up the dry-cleaning or returning a video.

ORGANISMIC PERSPECTIVES
ON OPTIMAL GOAL FUNCTIONING

In sum, systemic perspectives address the question of the "fully functioning person" (Rogers, 1961) by asking whether there is efficient and effective functioning by the action system. However, readers may have observed that the control-theory perspectives do not consider some other potentially important questions relevant to optimal human being (as also discussed in chap. 3). For example, what are the goals that the person is striving for? Are some types or contents of goals (such as goals for personal growth, emotional intimacy, or community contribution) more healthy or beneficial than other goal types or contents (such as goals for material success, social popularity, or an attractive image)? Also, why is the person striving for the goals? Does the person feel a sense of pressure or a sense of being controlled by external forces, or does he or she instead feel that the goals are intrinsically interesting, valuable, and important?

The latter considerations bring us to the concept of *organismic congruence* (Sheldon & Kasser, 1995). The question is, do the person's goals allow the person to meet organismic psychological needs, or are they instead irrelevant to such needs, or perhaps directly incompatible with those needs? Sheldon and Kasser (1995) identified two types of organismic congruence. One type focuses on the *content* of goals (the "what" of goals), and the other type focuses on the *reasons* for goals (the "why" of goals; see also Ryan, Sheldon, Kasser, & Deci, 1996, or Deci & Ryan, 2000). I first consider the "what" of goals, and then the "why" of goals. Later in the chapter, I also consider the conceptual relations between goal contents and goal reasons. Notably, most of the work discussed in the next few pages uses subjective well-being as the positive outcome of interest (Ryan, 1995); again, this is just one possible indicator of optimality, although as discussed in chapter 1, subjective well-being is likely to covary with many other types of positive outcomes.

The "What" of Goals and the Intrinsic/Extrinsic Values Model

Considerable research now demonstrates that the content of the goals a person pursues has ramifications for her happiness or well-being. For example, Kasser and Ryan (1993) showed that there may be a "dark side" to the American dream, or at least to one version of the dream—the ideal of attaining wealth and luxury. Specifically, participants who valued financial success (which Kasser and Ryan called an *extrinsic* goal) more strongly than they valued emotional intimacy, community feeling, and personal growth (which Kasser and Ryan called *intrinsic* goals) reported lower well-being, and also showed more evidence of psychopathology during interviews with clinicians. Kasser and Ryan (1996, 2001) extended these ideas, showing that those who strongly value social popularity and physical attractiveness (two more purported extrinsic goals) also evidenced lower well-being. Importantly, factor analyses supported the idea that money, beauty, and popularity tend to go together, while intimacy, growth, and community tend to go together (Kasser & Ryan, 1996). Thus, intrinsic and extrinsic goal contents are empirically distinguishable categories or syndromes, which have reliable relations with concurrent well-being (see Kasser, 2002, for a review of this literature).

Sheldon and Kasser (1998) extended these cross-sectional results by conducting a longitudinal study of goal attainment and its effect on changes in well-being. They showed that attaining goals helpfully linked to extrinsic "possible futures" involving money, popularity, or attractiveness had no effect on increasing well-being, whereas attaining goals that were helpfully linked to intrinsic futures involving intimacy, community, and growth did have a positive effect on longitudinal well-being. These findings suggest that some types of vertical coherence may be more beneficial than others; it depends on what higher level goals the person's lower level goals are functionally linked to. Again, this issue is typically not represented within purely systemic perspectives on optimal functioning.

It is important to point out that these results do *not* indicate that desiring money, popularity, or beauty is "bad" per se; instead, they indicate that desiring these outcomes more than one desires growth, intimacy, and community may be problematic. In the latter case there may be an imbalance in the goal system, such that person is overfocused on goals that may be less satisfying in the long run, even if they are attained (Kasser, 2002).

What is the source of the content-to-well-being effects? Kasser (2002) theorized that the overpursuit of extrinsic goals may fail to meet universal organismic needs, such as those discussed in chapter 4— for security, autonomy, competence, and relatedness. For example, a person who is fixated on acquiring wealth or fame may ignore deeper interests and passions, and may often feel pressure and tension to perform behaviors he or she does not really want to do (reduced autonomy); also, he or she may often focus on the possibility of negative evaluations by others, or may objectify others, perceiving them as means to self-centered ends (reduced relatedness); and finally, he or she may feel that wealth or fame outcomes are difficult to attain (reduced competence; see Kasser, 2002, for a more detailed discussion of these dynamics). Notably, however, no published research directly tests the idea that reduced need satisfaction mediates the negative effects of extrinsic goal content on well-being (although such data do exist regarding the "why" of goals, as shown in a later section).

Still, there are considerable data that are indirectly consistent with the idea that intrinsic goals are more need-satisfying, besides the fact that strong intrinsic valuing is associated with well-being. First, people generally report valuing the intrinsic goals more strongly than the extrinsic goals. This is as would be expected, if we assume that people try, for the most part, to align themselves with sources of satisfaction (Kasser, 2002). Second, when people change in their valuation of goals, they typically move toward intrinsic goals and away from extrinsic goals. Specifically, Sheldon, Arndt, and Houser-Marko (2003) showed, via repeated assessments of goals over periods ranging from 20 minutes to 6 weeks, that there is a "biased shift" toward intrinsic and away from extrinsic goals, and Sheldon (in press) showed such a similar shift in students' values over the 4 years of college.

The second point is worthy of further discussion, because it helps to illustrate the general assumptions of the organismic theoretical approach to understanding human thriving, first discussed in chapter 4. Sheldon, Arndt, and Houser-Marko (2003) and Sheldon (in press) interpreted these biased shifts toward intrinsic values and away from extrinsic values as revealing the influence of an *organismic valuing process* (OVP). The OVP is a concept that was first proposed by Carl Rogers (1961) but that had not been empirically evaluated before. As discussed in chapter 1, Rogers argued that the OVP automatically tends to orient people in healthy and well-being-relevant directions, assuming that their environments are reasonably supportive of this process. The OVP is said to come into play when people are given opportunities to reconsider or revise their choices, and its cumulative effects presumably help to account for the small but significant tendency for people to approach greater well-being as they age (Argyle, 1999; Sheldon & Kasser, 2001; discussed later). The emerging data indicate that an OVP may indeed be a component of positive human nature.

The "Why" of Goals and the Self-Concordance Concept

A second major issue relevant to organismic congruence concerns the "why" of goals—that is, the quality of the underlying reasons that people pursue goals (Sheldon & Kasser, 1995). Again, the systemic perspective on effective functioning typically does not consider people's dynamic reasons for striving. The discussion that follows is based on self-determination theory's *perceived locus of causality* concept (PLOC; deCharms, 1968; Deci & Ryan, 1991, 2000). From the self-determination theory perspective the question is, does the person perceive him- or herself to be the cause or origin of his or her own behavior (internal perceived locus of causality, or I-PLOC), or does he or she instead believe that external factors cause his or her behavior (E-PLOC)? In terms of the free will issue discussed in chapter 2, the question is, does the person believe that goals were chosen of his or her own free will, or instead, that the goals were determined by forces over which he or she has little control or choice?

The free will issue is worthy of further consideration in this context. My position is that free will is neither fact nor fiction, but rather is a *variable*—some people have more of it than others, depending in part on their attitudes and beliefs regarding their own personal goals and initiatives. In terms of Fig. 2.1, those who believe that *they* are the cause of their intentional behavior are more likely to behave in ways that are consistent with their internal personalities, thereby giving the personality level of analysis potentially greater influence on their behavior. In contrast, those who believe that external forces dictate their goals and behavior are more likely to allow themselves to be controlled directly by such forces, reducing the potential causal influence of their own personalities and needs on behavior.

Sheldon and colleagues (Sheldon & Elliot, 1999; Sheldon & Houser-Marko, 2001; Sheldon, 2002) referred to the feeling that one's goals are internally caused as *self-concordance*. In this case, the person has more likely chosen the goal based on his or her deeper values, interests, needs, and personality preferences. In contrast, if a person feels that he or she has chosen the goal because of external forces or internal compulsions, then the goal is less likely to correctly his or her represent deeper personality and needs. From this perspective, being able to correctly intuit one's own needs and values, and also being able to select and act on goals that are consistent with these, are important skills that are highly relevant to optimal human being (Sheldon, 2002).

Let us return to the "going to get a book at the Health Sciences Library" example, to consider the self-concordance issue more concretely. We saw that the medical student was getting the book, ultimately, in order to approach "being a surgeon." The question is, why does he or she want to become a surgeon? There are a variety of possibilities: for example, because the person sees this goal as a route to wealth, or as something that his or her parents expect or demand, or as something that will prove his or her worth and value to others. Alternatively, the person may see this goal as a route to helping others, as an expression of prosocial values and ideals, or as a pursuit that is inherently fascinating and exciting. According to Sheldon (2002), the latter reasons are more self-concordant, and are thus more likely to be relevant to attaining well-being via the goal. In contrast, a person trying to become a doctor primarily for the money, or because that is what his or her parents expect, or because the person hopes that this will finally prove his or her intelligence, may not derive as much satisfaction from pursuing and attaining the goal. Perhaps the person would be better off pursuing some other career goal, such as interpreting history, mastering the cello, or becoming a firefighter.

Self-concordance is operationally defined as the extent to which you pursue the goal "because you endorse it freely and value it wholeheartedly" (identified motivation) and "because of the enjoyment or stimulation which that goal provides you" (intrinsic motivation), rather than "because somebody else wants you to or because the situation seems to compel it" (external motivation) and "because you compel yourself because you would feel ashamed, guilty, or anxious if you didn't" (introjected motivation; Ryan & Connell, 1989). According to self-determination theory (Deci & Ryan, 1991, 2000), the former two motive types are internalized and self-concordant, and the latter two motive types are noninternalized and potentially nonconcordant. Participants in self-concordance studies first list a set of (5 to 15) goals, then make each of the four ratings just described concerning each goal. An aggregate self-concordance score is then computed for each participant by summing identified and intrinsic ratings across goals, and subtracting external and introjected ratings. Because of the self-concordance construct's relevance to optimal human being and because it is the focus of my own work, I next spend some time summarizing the published research concerning the construct.

The Association of Self-Concordance and Subjective Well-Being

Given the assumption that self-concordant goals better represent the individual's deeper needs and personality, it is logical to hypothesize that those who are pursuing self-concordant goals should be thriving in many different ways. Sheldon and Kasser (1995) tested this assumption in a goal-based study of personality integration. Specifically, they measured the self-concordance of participants' self-generated personal strivings (Emmons, 1989), which represent what people are "typically trying to do in daily life" (strivings may be located at the "principle" level of control, in Carver and Scheier's Fig. 3.1 hierarchy). Sheldon and Kasser (1995) found that striving self-concordance was concurrently associated with a wide variety of healthy personality characteristics, such as vitality, empathy, autonomy orientation, role-system integration, and openness to experience, as well as with several conventional measures of subjective well-being.

As a next step, Sheldon and Elliot (1998) conducted a month-long longitudinal study to examine the prospective influence of self-concordance on goal attainment. For this study they chose the personal project construct, which represents individuals' shorter-term and more concrete initiatives (Little, 1993; locatable at the "program" level of control in Carver and Scheier's Fig. 3.1 hierarchy). Sheldon and Elliot also used an objective methodology for assessing goal-attainment, namely, goal-attainment scaling, in which categories of possible negative and positive outcomes are clearly specified in advance and are later used to evaluate the person's success at achieving the goal (Kiresuk, Smith, & Cardillo, 1994).

In this study, Sheldon and Elliot (1998) found that although people intended to devote strong effort to highly nonconcordant goals, this intention had faded 2 and 4 weeks later, resulting in a failure to attain such goals. In contrast, highly self-concordant goals were associated both with strong initial intentions and with sustained effort over time, which led to greater goal attainment at the end of the study. Sheldon and Elliot (1998) argued that self-concordant goals receive longer term effort because they better represent stable facets and trends within the personality. Thus, they are more enduringly energized (Gollwitzer, 1990) and are better protected from other, potentially usurping goals (Kuhl, 1986). In contrast, nonconcordant goals may represent failures to discriminate transient impulses from deeper and more enduring interests, explaining why initial effort intentions regarding such goals tend to fade over time.

To extend the model further, Sheldon and Kasser (1998) conducted a longitudinal study to explore the effects of goal-attainment on changes in well-being, especially as moderated by self-concordance. Consistent with Brunstein's (1993) earlier longitudinal results, they found that people who attained their goals experienced increases in general positive mood and life satisfaction, and decreases in negative mood, from the beginning to the end of the study. More importantly, they found the predicted interaction: The more the participant's projects were self-concordant, the more the participant benefited when he or she attained those projects (in terms of measured increases in positive mood and life satisfaction, and reductions in negative mood and depression). In contrast, attaining nonconcordant goals had little positive effect on well-being. Sheldon and Kasser suggested that self-concordant goals are more satisfying of psychological needs when obtained, and thus they have a larger impact on the person's well-being. However, Sheldon and Kasser (1998) did not actually measure psychological need satisfaction in their study.

More recently, Sheldon and Elliot (1999) introduced an integrative longitudinal model that subsumed all of the relationships just cited, and that also included need satisfaction. Their summary path model is presented in Fig. 6.1, which contains the coefficients generated in a successful semester-long test of the model (see Sheldon & Elliot, 1999, Study 2). As can be seen, self-concordance predicted sustained effort over time, and hence greater longitudinal goal attainment. Attainment in turn predicted strong psychological need satisfaction during the semester (i.e., many daily experiences of autonomy, competence, and relatedness, measured at eight different points during the semester). In addition, extending the finding of

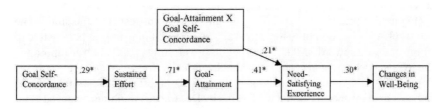

FIG. 6.1. Longitudinal path model predicting enhanced well-being from self-concordant goal pursuit and organismic need satisfaction. *From* Sheldon, K. M., and Elliot, A. J. Goal striving, need–satisfaction, and longitudinal well-being: The self-concordance model. *Journal of Personality and Social Psychology, 76,* p. 492. Copyright © 1999 by the American Psychological Association. Reprinted with permission.

Sheldon and Kasser (1998) already described, self-concordance moderated the impact of goal-attainment on need satisfaction—that is, attaining self-concordant goals led to the most satisfaction for participants. Finally, cumulative need satisfaction predicted positive changes in global well-being from the beginning to the end of the semester. Notably, the latter step in the model is consistent with "bottom-up" theories of well-being (Diener, 1994), according to which people estimate their global well-being with reference to how many recent positive experiences they can recall. Having many daily experiences of autonomy, competence, and relatedness (i.e., much organismic need satisfaction) can presumably supply the grist for such a process.

In addition to validating their basic model, Sheldon and Elliot (1999) also showed that the positive effects of self-concordance were not reducible to the also significant effects of strong life skills (Sheldon & Kasser, 1998), efficacy expectations (Bandura, 1997), implementation intentions (Gollwitzer, 1999), or approach versus avoidance framing of goals (Elliot & Sheldon, 1996). Thus, self-concordance provided motivational resources that are "more than" the combination of these important systemic factors.

Sheldon and Houser-Marko (2001) recently took this research program even further, attempting to understand the longer term effects of self-concordant motivation. Specifically, they examined the self-concordance of freshman students' goals for their first semester in college, as a predictor of adjustment and academic performance that semester. More importantly, they examined how these first-semester outcomes might "feed back into" the system, leading to even more positive outcomes in the second semester. Although no other longitudinal goal research has examined linkages between successive cycles of striving in this manner, we believe that such studies are long overdue. At stake were a number of important issues, including (a) the longer term effects of self-concordant motivation; (b) whether goal-related gains in well-being and adjustment last, or whether successful strivers instead tend to fall back to their original baselines (as suggested by happiness setpoint theories, discussed in chap. 5); and (c) whether one can increase one's level of self-concordance as a result of successful striving, perhaps enabling one to do even better in subsequent cycles. In other words, is it possible to enter a self-sustaining growth trajectory, assuming only that one begins with the "correct" set of goals for oneself?

Figure 6.2 presents the specific path model that was tested in the study. The model provided a good fit to the data, suggesting that it may indeed be possible to climb onto an "upward spiral," if one begins by selecting goals which are appropriate to one's deeper values and interests. Specifically, freshmen with self-concordant initial motivation better attained their first-semester goals, which lead to enhanced social and emotional well-being by December. Attainment also led to increased self-concordance for the second semester's goals, controlling for the first semester's self-concordance score. Second-semester self-concordance then led to increased second-semester attainment, controlling for first-semester attainment. Finally, increased attainment led to even further increases in well-being by the end of the freshman year. Of particular relevance for the question of whether increases

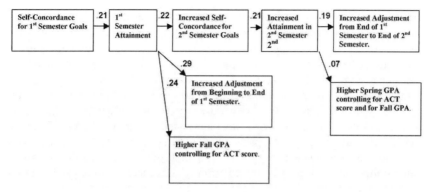

FIG. 6.2. Longitudinal path model depicting the relations between self-concordance, goal attainment, and enhanced well-being and performance over two striving cycles. *From* Sheldon, K. M., and Houser-Marko, L. Self-concordance, goal-attainment, and the pursuit of happiness: Can there be an upward spiral? *Journal of Personality and Social Psychology, 80,* p. 160. Copyright © 2001 by the American Psychological Association. Reprinted with permission.

in well-being are theoretically sustainable, some students were able to both increase their levels of well-being in the first semester and then maintain that change over the second semester—specifically, those who did very well in their goals during each of the two semesters. Those who did well in the first semester but who did not do well in the second semester tended to slip back to their initial level of well-being. Thus, maintained change in well-being is possible, but it takes continued successful intentional effort.

Interventions for Enhancing Self-Concordance

The potential importance of self-concordance leads to the question of whether self-concordance may be changed by psychotherapeutic interventions. Are there techniques or counseling approaches that can help people to select more self-appropriate goals and purposes, or to feel more sense of ownership regarding whatever set of goals they pursue? I believe so, and indeed, this would seem to be one of the primary purposes of psychodynamic and insight-based therapies. However, only one published study has directly addressed this issue in the context of the self-concordance construct. Specifically, Sheldon, Kasser, Smith, and Share (2002) attempted to create an experimental intervention to enhance participants' self-concordance. The findings of this study were complex but suggestive.

Participants in this study first generated and rated goals, and also rated their initial well-being. They were then randomly assigned either to an irrelevant control condition or to an intervention condition. The intervention included both a group session run by a counselor, in which relevant material was presented and discussed with other participants, and a one-on-one session, in which intervention participants spoke in detail with a counselor. The intervention presented four strategies for enhancing goal functioning, including two strategies relevant to self-concordance: "make it fun" (designed to perhaps enhance intrinsic motivation), and "own the goal" (designed to perhaps enhance identified motivation). Afterward, participants rerated the self-concordance of their goals. Two months later they rated their semester-long goal attainment, and also rerated their well-being.

Interestingly, there was no main effect of participating in the intervention on increases in self-concordance. In other words, participants could not simply be "persuaded" to better identify with or enjoy their goals. This may reflect the fact that, because of study design issues, participants were not encouraged to change their goals—perhaps those who began with the "wrong" goals (i.e., goals that did not fit their implicit personalities) could not simply turn them into the "right" goals merely by intending to do so. However, a significant interaction did emerge: Supporting a "prepared to benefit" model, participants who were already self-concordant and who also received the intervention later reported the greatest attainment of their goals. As in previous studies, longitudinal attainment, in turn, led to increased well-being from the beginning to the end of the study.

These results suggest that presented strategies for pursuing goals may only be effective if the person has already succeeded in identifying appropriate personal goals; otherwise, they may be of limited use, perhaps because the person does not have the energy or resolve to apply them (as discussed earlier). Future research will need to examine the issue of how to help those who are most in "need of improvement," as well as those who are most "prepared to benefit." I suggest that encouraging people to change to new goals, rather than simply encouraging them to change their attitude toward their old goals, offers a promising approach. The work cited concerning the OVP (Sheldon, Arndt, & Houser-Marko, 2003), which biases people to shift toward more positive goal-contents over time, further suggests that this is a potentially fruitful approach.

Self-Concordance and Chronological Age

Several of the results discussed above suggest that people can become more self-concordant over time. Does this hold for the life span as a whole? In other words, as time goes by, do people better learn which goals best fit their personalities, needs, and interests, while learning to better resist the pressures that might cause them to ignore these deeper personality factors? Some theoretical perspectives indeed predict such positive long-term movement, including Erik Erikson's (1963) theory of normative personality development across the life span, George Vaillant's (1977) theory of normative movement toward more mature defenses across the life span, and Midlarsky and Kahana's (1994) theory of normative movement toward altruism and social integration across the life span. All of these theories are consistent with the organismic theoretical perspective (discussed in chap. 4), which assumes that humans are fundamentally proactive and growth oriented, with a propensity to move toward greater internal consistency and self-regulation over time, as they gradually master the challenges they encounter.

Recently, new empirical data has been collected regarding the issue of positive personality change over the life span. Specifically, Sheldon and Kasser (2001) and Sheldon, Kasser, Houser-Marko, and Jones (2004) tested the hypothesis that people's sense of self-concordance increases as they age, by seeking a positive correlation between chronological age and measured self-concordance. Finding such a correlation would support the idea that progression wins out on average, presumably because of the innate drive toward greater organization and integration built into humans. And indeed, positive correlations were shown in a cross-sectional study of the goals of adults ranging from 18 to 82 (Sheldon & Kasser, 2001), in a comparison of the goals of college students to the goals of their own parents, and in a comparison of parents' current goals to their recollected goals at their child's age (Sheldon, Kasser, Houser-Marko, & Jones, 2004).

Notably, the associations of age with self-concordance were rather modest (effect sizes in the .20 to .25 range), indicating that not everyone moves toward greater self-concordance as they age—there are plenty of exceptions. Organismic theory (discussed in chap. 4) would expect such exceptions, to the extent that people's environments do not support, or perhaps even overpower, the basic growth impulse. Still, the reliability of the effect supports the optimistic assumption that there is indeed normative improvement with age—that is, on average, life experience teaches people what their true values and interests are, what pursuits are most likely to satisfy, and how to resist social pressures that might derail them from these pursuits.

It is important to note that the finding that people become more self-concordant as they age does not necessarily mean that people become more selfish and self-centered as they age. As was noted earlier in the chapter, people also tend to move toward intrinsic goals over time, that is, toward greater community contribution, generativity, and emotional intimacy (McAdams & de St. Aubin, 1992; Sheldon, 2003; Sheldon, Arndt, & Houser-Marko, 2003; Sheldon & Kasser, 2001). Thus, it appears that positive change over the life span may be normative for both aspects of organismic congruence—both in what people pursue, and in why they pursue it.

The Relationship Between Self-Concordant Reasons and Intrinsic Content

In this section I discuss the relationship between the "what" and "why" of goals, the two major organismic factors discussed earlier. How do the reasons for striving (in self-determination theory terms, whether the goals are self-concordant or not) relate to the contents of striving (in self-determination theory terms, whether the goals aim toward intrinsic or extrinsic values)? Are they distinct and independent factors?

Indeed, there is a positive association between self-concordant reasons for striving and intrinsic goal content, although the association is not large (typically about .30). This suggests that it is quite possible to pursue intrinsic goals for nonconcordant reasons, or extrinsic goals for self-concordant reasons. For example, a person may devote time to a humanitarian cause (an intrinsic goal) primarily in order to impress his or her liberal friends (external motivation; nonconcordant), and/or to assuage guilt over his or her inherited wealth (introjected motivation; nonconcordant). Conversely, a person with inherited wealth may spend time trying to increase his or her wealth by playing the stock market (an extrinsic goal) because he or she finds the "money game" to be inherently interesting and enjoyable (intrinsic motivation; concordant) and/or because the person affirms and believes in the values of capitalism (identified motivation; concordant).

Is being strongly oriented toward extrinsic goals "okay," as long as one pursues the extrinsic goals for internalized reasons (i.e., the stockbroker who enjoys and believes in the work)? In other words, might the negative effects of extrinsic content be entirely reducible to the fact that people are more likely to pursue such goals "for the wrong reasons," such that if reasons are taken into account, content no longer has an effect? Some authors have made this argument. For example, Srivastava, Locke, and Bartol (2001) suggested that "it's not the money, it's the motives"—that the insecure motives that often underlie materialistic goals account for their association with negative well-being, rather than anything about materialistic content per se. Carver and Baird (1998) made a similar argument.

However, the data of both of these research groups had significant limitations and methodological weaknesses, and thus Sheldon, Ryan, Deci, and Kasser (2004) have recently examined this issue in greater detail. Sheldon, Ryan, Deci, and Kasser (2004) discovered, in both cross-sectional and longitudinal studies, that the reasons for and contents of goals had independent effects on well-being. Specifically, people's reported happiness and life satisfaction were an additive function of both the contents of their goals and the reasons behind their goals (no interactions were found). In terms of the preceding example, these data suggest that the self-concordant stockbroker, despite enjoying and identifying with his or her goals, would experience lower well-being than the self-concordant philanthropist. The self-concordant philanthropist would be happiest of all, and the nonconcordant stockbroker would be least happy.

The Sheldon, Ryan, Deci, and Kasser (2004) findings thus support the organismic theoretical perspective that both what goals people pursue and the reasons why they pursue the goals are important for psychological need satisfaction and well-being (Ryan et al., 1996). Again, however, it is important to point out that external motivation and materialistic goals are not necessarily problematic—the problem mainly comes when such goals and reasons dominate within a person's goal system. This is a point that many critics seem to miss.

GOAL FUNCTIONING AND OPTIMAL HUMAN BEING

Basic Recommendations

What is the best route to optimal human being, according to the concepts developed in this chapter? Generalizing from the data on goal functioning and psychological well-being, a variety of "suggestions for striving" can be made (Sheldon & Schmuck, 2001) First, people would be advised to attend carefully to their intentional life, as it provides perhaps the most direct way of effecting positive life change. Like it or not, we are responsible for making things work, and those who fully grasp this fact may be in the best position to optimize their lives.

From the systemic perspective, optimal human being also involves selecting goals that are consistent with each other, that are supported by relevant skills, and that are nonconflicting with or even enhancing of other goals, at either the same or at different levels of the action hierarchy. In addition, it involves remembering to enact one's behavioral intentions at the right time, and remembering to check whether one's current state matches one's goals and ambitions. Finally, it involves selecting approach rather than avoidance goals, feeling a sense of self-efficacy regarding one's goals, and maintaining one's important but nonenjoyable goals, so that they are not usurped by other goals. Most generally, the systemic perspective suggests that one should try to be as efficient as possible in pursuing whatever goals and ambitions one selects. That is, in keeping with the mechanistic orientation of systemic perspectives, one should try to be a "highly effective robot" that makes steady progress toward its higher level targets (Carver & Scheier, 1990), no matter what those targets are.

From the organismic perspective, however, there are a number of other important considerations influencing the "optimality" of a person's intentional life. First, optimal human being would involve selecting goal targets that are most consistent with one's enduring interests, core values, and deepest beliefs. Although robots are passively programmed by their environments, human beings have internal dispositions and psychological needs, which may necessitate considerable self-programming to meet. Indeed, taking account of one's internal states and needs may sometimes require one to resist programming coming from the social environment. A second important consideration for optimal human being, according to the organismic perspective, involves what goals the person pursues. Although money, beauty, fame, and popularity have their place, they should not occupy more important positions in the person's system than intimacy, community, and growth values. Stated in terms of the top three levels of Fig. 2.1, people appear to thrive best when they actively strive to enhance their personalities, relationships, and societies—that is, when they enhance their sense of being "holistically linked" to the higher levels of the systems in which they are embedded (Sheldon & Schmuck, 2001).

More Complex Considerations and Recommendations

Of course, it is not really this simple! In the remainder of this chapter I discuss three more difficult issues and questions relevant to goals, intentionality, and optimal human being, to illustrate the complexity of this topic. The first question is, why do people strongly pursue nonconcordant and extrinsic goals if they are so unsatisfying? In other words, how do people get off track and end up stuck there? Second, what does self-concordance really mean—that a person has managed to select goals that fit his or her deeper personality, or instead that a person is taking appropriate existential responsibility for his or her goals, whatever they may be? This gets at the suggestion that optimal human being involves a particular type of intentional attitude, as discussed in chapter 1, and also raises the question of whether one might have the "right" intentional attitude but have it with respect to the "wrong" goals. Third, what is the optimal relationship of the goal-striving level of personality to the other three levels of personality, depicted in Fig. 3.3? Which is most important—that goals be consistent with the person's organismic needs, with his or her enduring temperamental and personality traits, or with his or her narrative self-images and life stories?

Why Do People Pursue Unsatisfying Goals?

Starting with the first question, if highly extrinsic or nonconcordant goals are less rewarding, then why do people pursue them? This is a difficult issue, with ties to the more general question of why people sometimes engage in maladaptive or self-defeating behavior. There are many possible answers, but in the discussion here, I focus on the issue of *insecurity*. Maslow (1971) provided one of the best ways of thinking about this question, with his proposal that people have a need for security (i.e., basic psychological safety, consistency, and social approval). Only after this need is satisfied, said Maslow, can people proceed to work on the higher level, more sophisticated, and more deeply satisfying needs. According to his model, when they lack security, people may be unable to focus on or concern themselves with higher level needs, and may also have difficulty concentrating and functioning effectively.

This analysis suggests that there are at least two problems with being caught in the throes of insecurity. First, it can orient the person toward "taking whatever he can get." It is as if the person says, "True relatedness is impossible in this situation or environment. Let me at least try to get people to think I am okay." In such a quest for basic social acceptance, people can focus overmuch on external symbols of worth, such as money, fame, or beauty. And indeed, they can certainly derive *some* satisfaction from achieving these—in self-determination theory terms, they can thereby at least satisfy the need for competence, if not the needs for autonomy and relatedness. Stated somewhat differently, it is probably better to at least be motivated, even if one feels programmed by external forces, than it is to exist in a state of amotivation, in which one feels no sense of control at all over outcomes (Deci & Ryan, 1985). Still, preoccupation with external symbols of worth is likely to detract from happiness and personality development in the long term (Kasser, 2002; Rogers, 1961).

The second problem with rampant insecurity is that it makes people anxious, and unable to focus clearly either on their own needs or on the deeper structure of the situation (Kuhl & Kazen, 1994). Thus, a person in the grip of materialistic or appearance-based pursuits may be incapable of the more objective and self-reflective thought that is necessary to break out of this condition. In other words, people can get locked in a "vicious cycle" in which their strivings are not bringing them satisfaction but they are afraid of making changes that might make things even worse. Or, they may try to make changes but lack the internal resources to do so effectively (see Sheldon, 2001, for further discussion). Thus, they keep on doing the only thing they know how.

Of course, people can also be stuck in objectively horrific circumstances (such as living in a refugee camp), such that insecurity, the delay of deeper satisfaction, and the attempt to get money and status may be wholly appropriate (at least to some extent). I do not mean to minimize such problems; instead, the preceding discussion is aimed more at the case where an unhappy person with a reasonably adequate situation fails to move toward a more fulfilling way of being.

Two Meanings of Self-Concordance

Turning to the second more complex question, let us consider two possible meanings of the term *self-concordance,* which have very different implications for the question of how to achieve optimal human being. Again, Sheldon (2002) argued that a person with a high self-concordance score has succeeded in identifying goals that are consistent with that person's internal needs and personality. In this case, intuition and the OVP have spoken, such that "deep" personality is correctly expressed and represented by the goals. However it is also possible to imagine a person who has not succeeded in this important endeavor—that is, the person has not succeeded in selecting the best or most appropriate goals for him- or herself, perhaps because he or she does not yet have sufficient self-insight to do so. Still, this person could feel authentically self-concordant regarding the selected goals, because he or she willfully accepts and owns them—he or she knows that this is the most appropriate and effective way to be an intentional agent. In other words, the person might say to him- or herself, "If I'm going to pursue a goal, I should at least have the gumption to stand fully behind it!"

Although this is an admirable intentional attitude, seemingly quite relevant to optimal human being, it may be misguided in some cases. For example, the medical student who is studying only because his father expects him to might declare a state of total identification with the goal, mindful of the potential benefits of doing this. Such a person might appear very self-concordant according to self-report, while perhaps not being self-concordant in some deeper sense (i.e., because his goals conflict with his emotional dispositions, in that he becomes squeamish at the sight of blood). Would he be expected to benefit from this act of misguided existential responsibility taking?

In analyzing such cases, I believe it is useful to consider which of the other three levels of personality, besides goals and intentions, are involved (see Fig. 3.3). One form of concordance might be said to exist when the person's goals and intentions fit his or her personality traits, and another form of concordance might exist when the person's goals fit his or her sense of self, and yet another form of concordance might exist when the person's goals fit his or her organismic needs. In the "aspiring surgeon" case, in which the person mistakenly claims that he has "the right goals for me," there might be concordance between the person's goals and his self-concept, but not concordance between the person's goals and his personality traits and organismic needs. Of course, concordance between goals and selves likely has its own benefits, but perhaps not the same benefits that come when goals match one's deeper personality and needs.

Matches Between Goals and Other Levels of Personality

This leads us to the third more complex question, mentioned earlier: In terms of Fig. 3.3, with what level of personality (if any) is it most important for goals to be consistent? Chapter 10 more fully considers this issue of integration between different levels of personality. For now, I simply suggest that it is most important for goals to be consistent with organismic needs, located at the bottom tier of personality. Thus, even if a woman's goals are inconsistent with her personality traits or with her self-concepts, she might still receive considerable benefit if her goals provide her with the regular experiences of autonomy, competence, relatedness, self-esteem, and security that all humans seem to need. Given that such is the case, one can withstand doing things that are not directly congruent with one's traits (i.e., an introvert may behave in an extraverted way to achieve a valued goal, to no detriment, as long as need satisfaction results), or that are not directly congruent with one's sense of self (i.e., a person who thinks of him- or herself as uncoordinated may pursue an athletic goal, but to no detriment, as long as need satisfaction results; see Little, 1996, for further discussion of these dynamics).

As the latter example suggests, it is quite conceivable that a goal that does not match one's self-concept might be "beneficial" nonetheless, especially if such goals represent a person's attempt to break free of self-confining beliefs and personal histories (or "foreclosed identities," in the language of Eriksonian ego-developmental theory). In control-theory terms (Carver & Scheier, 1998), having a vertically coherent action system, in which goals are functionally linked to higher order selves, may do a person little good if the "wrong" higher level self-images are involved (Sheldon & Kasser, 1995, 1998).

This discussion illustrates the profound importance of "being in touch" with oneself, that is, of developing a self that is aware of both its organismic needs and its personality dispositions. Chapter 7 focuses in more detail on the self level of analysis within personality, and what it might really mean to "get in touch" with oneself.

7 The Self-Homunculus: Fictional but Functional

In this chapter we consider the self, located at the top level of personality (see Fig. 3.3). Rather than simply reviewing the self literature in conventional terms, I first propose a novel way of conceptualizing the self, based on the concept of a psychological homunculus. I then canvass the literature to show the consistency of this understanding with some existing social- and personality-psychological theories of self, and also with some recent neurobiological and philosophical approaches to the self. I also try to show that the conception helps with several perennial problems within self-theory, such as the nature of the psychological "I," the question of the causal efficacy of the self, the potential functions of the self, and what it means to be "in touch with oneself." Finally, I discuss the question of optimal human being in terms of the concepts developed during the chapter.

DEFINING THE SELF: CONCEPTUAL AND CAUSAL CONUNDRUMS

Defining the word "self" is surprisingly difficult to do. Definitions and views of the self vary on an astounding number of dimensions, ranging from magical to mundane, spiritual to neurobiological, computational to phenomenological, and evolutionary to social constructivist. To illustrate the differences more concretely, consider that within the field of social-personality psychology, the self has at different times or places been referred to as a concept or image (Brown, 1998); as a standard that guides action (Carver & Scheier, 1990); as a theory (Epstein, 1973); as a dynamic process (Markus & Ruvolo, 1989); as a set of motives, especially growth motives (Deci & Ryan, 1991); as a mental controller or agent (Blasi, 1988);

as a source of energy (Brehm & Self, 1989); as a story or narrative (McAdams, 1996); and even as a society (Nowak, Vallacher, Tesser, & Borkowski, 2000).

As can be seen from this partial list, there are a bewildering variety of definitions of self out there. Which definitions are correct, or most scientifically useful? Perhaps none of them—and thus, perhaps, the word *self* should be banished from scientific discourse altogether. Recognizing the problem, Tesser, Martin, and Cornell (1996) referred to this multiplicity of definitions of self (and self-esteem) as a "zoo," which badly needs taming. In the same vein, Greenwald (1986) argued that achieving consensus on the meaning and usage of the term *self* might forward the disciplines of social and personality psychology more than any other theoretical development. One ambition of this chapter is to suggest some ways in which this task might be accomplished.

Another important task for this chapter, relevant to the goal of evaluating the scientific status of each successive level of analysis, is to ask whether the self has any *causal force*. From a lived perspective, most of us feel that it does—that is, we believe that the phenomenon we experience ourselves to be has at least some ability to make choices and to guide its life in particular directions. But is this feeling of free will correct and appropriate, or is the self instead merely an epiphenomenon, an ineffectual "ghost in the machine," with no causal efficacy? This question mirrors the one asked of personality traits in chapter 5, but refers to the scientific basis for saying that the psychological self belongs in Fig. 2.1, rather than the scientific basis for saying that personality traits belong there. Can self-level effects on behavior be entirely reduced to effects at lower levels of analysis, levels that have nothing to do with phenomenology and self-experience? If so, then perhaps theories of self need not be included in a "final" model of human behavior.

Consistent with the epiphenomenon position, some prominent social psychologists have recently argued that psychologists should severely limit or abandon the idea that the conscious self has causal impact on the mind and world (Bargh & Ferguson, 2000; Wegner & Wheatley, 1999). Instead, they argue, behavior is determined by implicit cognitive processes, to which the self has no direct access (in terms of Fig. 2.1, nonconscious cognitive and neural processes are said to determine behavior, rather than personality or self-level processes). From this reductionistic perspective, feelings of self-agency are a mere comforting illusion, which theorists should seek to uproot from their causal explanations (Skinner, 1971). Similar disempowering conclusions are reached by social-constructionist theorists, who argue that the self is but a political narrative with biases toward self-enhancement and the accumulation of power (Gergen, 1991); by cross-cultural theorists, who question the individualist assumptions underlying much Western psychological theorizing (Markus, Kitayama, & Heiman, 1996); by terror management theorists, who view the self as a defensive structure struggling to deceive itself regarding its own true significance and permanence (Greenberg, Pyszczynski, & Solomon, 1995); and by evolutionary theorists, who argue that self-deception and inauthenticity may be the norm, because they help humans to deceive and out-compete each other (Krebs, Denton, & Higgins, 1988). But again, most of us operate with the belief that our sense of self-integrity and self-agency *is* real and important. That is, we feel that we are living our lives, as honorably as we know how, via the choices that we make. How can this affirming, everyday view of the self be reconciled with the skeptical theoretical perspectives on the self, described earlier? Hopefully, considering the ontological basis of the self level of analysis will help resolve this issue.

Yet another aim for this chapter is to resolve the puzzle suggested by common sayings such as "Just be yourself." Although this statement has immediate intuitive meaning, contemporary social-cognitive theory has no way to make sense of it. How can we help but be ourselves? What is one being when one is not being oneself? Or this: "Be true to yourself." Here is another statement we can all resonate to, which is similarly mysterious, on closer examination. What is one being "true to" when one is being true to one's "self"? Or finally, "Get in touch with yourself." What is the deeper "something" that we should try to contact? Can this something possibly be measured or quantified? Hopefully, considering the self level of analysis in conjunction with the other three levels of personality (in the final part of this chapter) clarifies what it means to "be yourself."

THE "I" VERSUS THE "ME"

The "Me"

One reason social psychologists have few conceptual tools for understanding sayings such as "be yourself" is that most empirical research on the self has focused on people's cognitive self-representations and self-concepts (their "Me's," to use William James' well-known [1890/1950] terminology), rather than on their subjective sense of *being* a self (the "I," in James's terminology). To illustrate the distinction, let's first consider the "Me."

"Me's" come in many different shapes and forms, corresponding to people's images and conceptions of themselves within the many different domains and spheres in which they move. For example, people have self-concepts corresponding to their gender, ethnicity, physical attributes, psychological attributes, job occupations, and marital/family status. They also have more elaborate self-concepts corresponding to their values and beliefs, their goals and ambitions, and their biographies and life histories. These "Me's" are typically viewed as a set of nodes or schemata within semantic memory, which can become linked via spreading activation (Kihlstrom, 1997). For example, a friend's teasing may remind one of a social gaffe one made earlier that day, which reminds one of a negative image of "self-as-social-bumbler," which reminds one of feelings of inferiority in childhood, and so on. Whatever their content, cognitive self-images are typically assumed to be relatively static and stable features of the person, and to characterize particular personalities over time.

Where do self-concepts and self-images come from? According to conventional social psychology, which focuses on the social interaction level of analysis, people mostly derive their "Me's" from externally mediated processes such as reflected appraisal, social comparison, and social modeling. That is, social environments have large influences on self-concepts, both because they dictate the kinds of self-related stimuli that people are exposed to, and, because they tend to dictate how people should respond to those stimuli. Cooley's (1902) concept of the "looking-glass self" was an early representative of the idea that people's self-concepts simply mirror the concepts that others have of them. For example, a little boy who is constantly told "you are stupid" or "you are special" might begin to see himself in such ways.

Conceiving of the self as a set of self-concepts or beliefs (i.e., "Me's") has some obvious empirical advantages. For one, "Me's" are relatively easy to measure, simply by asking people about their own perceived attributes. Once measured, scientists can ask a wide variety of questions about these self-beliefs. For example, they can study the temporal stability of the beliefs; the social and cultural genesis of the beliefs; the association of beliefs with various outcomes; the cognitive processes underlying the beliefs; and even the neuropsychological correlates of the beliefs. As the latter example illustrates, stable self-concepts and "Me's" should (in principle) eventually be locatable within the nervous system, as particular recurring patterns of neural activation or as particular nodes within the semantic memory network (Kihlstrom, 1997). This consilience potential considerably boosts their appeal.

Notice that cognitively oriented "Me" theories cross the boundary between body and mind, by crossing the boundary between the nervous system and cognition, as discussed in chapter 2. This reflects an important paradigm shift in psychology, the "cognitive revolution," which in the early 1960s won much wider acceptance for mentalistic explanations of behavior (Baars, 1986). "Me" theories also begin to bridge the boundary between the cognition and personality levels of analysis, by referring to the person's cognitions about his or her personality. Finally, they also bring in the social interaction level of analysis, by assuming that social stimuli help determine the content of the "Me's." Notably, however, "Me" theories still do not fully cross the barrier between the impersonal and the personal (or the objective and the subjective), because they typically do not refer to the experiencer, but rather to a particular type of mental content that is experienced.

The "I"

In contrast, "I" theories make specific reference to the subjective aspects of selfhood. How does it feel to be a self, and to make choices about how to express that self in the world? How do we manage to pull all of the various facets of our minds together, into a relatively unified whole? Can people have a weaker subjective feeling of self at some times compared to other times, or can some people have weaker selves, overall, compared to other people? Do such momentary or chronic self-differences perhaps correspond to momentary or chronic failures or breakdowns in functioning or self-regulation?

As the latter statements imply, "I" theories typically refer to the self as an integrator, organizer, or synthesizer of experience—as that which helps to give the mind coherence, and which coordinates the mind's various processes (Deci & Ryan, 2000). In Blasi's (1988) view, the I is "a grand function responsible for human intentionality and wholeness" (McAdams, 2001). Thus, "I" theories typically ascribe some degree of ontological and causal reality to the self, assuming that there is at least some veracity to the "I's" feelings of reality and agency, although, as discussed in chapter 6, people's sense of causing their own behavior can fluctuate at different times and in different circumstances (Deci & Ryan, 2000).

Problems With "I" Theories

Obviously, "I's" are much more difficult to pin down and quantify than "Me's." Rather than referring to distinct, static self-images, "I" theories refer instead to a fluid mental entity, waxing and waning over time. In addition, "I" perspectives in some ways seem to threaten the deterministic foundations of psychological science. Rather than explaining behavior via objective, externally viewable factors, they instead move explanation into a necessarily subjective and teleological realm, in which intentions are to be granted causal force (an issue discussed in chap. 2).

Perhaps most important for this chapter, "I" perspectives are problematic because they begin to move toward a homunculus concept, that is, the idea of an inner mental being residing within the head. This idea has long been rejected by philosophers (Dennett, 1991), on logical and other grounds. The primary logical problem is that of infinite regress—if we invoke a mental "I" to explain physical behavior, must we then evoke a second mental "I" inside the first mental "I" to explain the first "I's" behavior, and so on down the line? Another problem with positing a homunculus lies in the strong temptation to reify it, that is, to view the homunculus as a tangible and stable "entity" somehow perched in the brain, consuming space and resources. It is but a small step further from this idea to the idea of an immaterial and perhaps eternal soul existing separate from the brain (Popper & Eccles, 1977), an idea that is clearly untenable from a scientific perspective.

Nevertheless, by overlooking the "I," it seems that "Me"-based self-theories have limited ability to understand the lived self, that is, the conscious person that each of us feels ourselves to be. Also, as already noted, purely cognitively oriented self-theories may be limited in their ability to address vital issues that arise at the level of personality (see Fig. 2.1), issues such as the nature of psychological integrity, personal growth, and optimal human being, and also the meaning of sayings such as "be yourself." In addition, "Me" theories may be limited in their ability to address the dynamic processes by which personalities are internally coordinated and integrated. Finally, they may offer only limited perspectives on the vital question of free will and the question of whether we (selves) have free will or not, and if we do, to what extent, and in what circumstances. In short, an adequate understanding of positive human nature may elude us until we are finally able to address the difficult questions posed by the "I" (Kihlstrom, 1997).

THE SELF AS A HOMUNCULUS

In this section I develop a conception of the I-self that may help reconcile and integrate these many theoretical perspectives. The model explicitly focuses on the self as a *mental homunculus*—an emergent and more or less stable mental character that is projected into moment-to-moment experience. Although psychologists and philosophers have long avoided the "specter of the homunculus," I argue that we are now in a position to use the concept without misusing it.

Readers may ask, "Why stir up the philosophical problems associated with the homunculus concept? Why not simply call the mental entity the 'self,' or the 'I?'" Although I continue to use the latter two terms in this chapter, I believe that the term *homunculus* may be a useful summary term, for several reasons. First, the concept of "self" is too multifarious, multifaceted, and all-inclusive, as was discussed in the opening paragraphs of this chapter. It has too much baggage. Second, the term *I* is too cryptic, and risks becoming confused with the first person perspective of the speaker or writer. Also, the term *the I* sounds overly magical or all-seeing (i.e., "the eye"). Third, neither *self* nor *I* conveys the idea that the lived mental entity is computable (even if it may not be predictable in advance; see chap. 2), nor the idea that it is a projection of the underlying organism into an ongoing mental simulation of itself. Fourth, the scientific paradox of the homunculus concept readily conveys and reflects the existential paradox of the self, pointed out by Sartre (1965): that we are doomed to create ourselves from moment to moment, with no certain knowledge of our own reality or legitimacy. In other words, the somewhat questionable status of the homunculus within scientific theory highlights the somewhat questionable status of the mental self within the physical world. Of course, the term *homunculus* is awkward, and thus the terms *self* or *I* may be preferable for most purposes. However, I contend that the exercise of thinking of the self as a homunculus may enable a fresh approach to some intractable problems in the literature, and thus, that the exercise is worth attempting.

In the following discussion, I first provide further discussion of the homunculus concept. I then compare this view with the "I" theories that currently exist within psychology, showing that although the view is consistent with these theories, it may also clarify some issues for the theories. Next, I consider four important functions that the self homunculus serves, including terror management, social projection, action control, and organismic perception. Finally, in the last part of the chapter, I discuss the relevance of the homunculus conception of self to the question of optimal human being. What (or how) is the self being, when it is functioning to optimize the person's being?

Defining the Homunculus

The psychological homunculus can be defined as *the felt agent within experience*—that is, the perceiving and responding entity that we feel ourselves to be, at a particular moment in time. Thus, this definition is necessarily phenomenological (i.e., it refers to the experience and first-person perspective of the person). However, this definition does not assume that the homunculus is nonphysical, somehow occupying some separate realm of soul or spirit. As discussed in chapter 1, the self is definitely of the physical world—it is part of what the brain does, and thus it presumably passes away when the brain passes away. Thus the homunculus should, in principle, be locatable in neural dynamics, just as static self-concepts or "Me's" should (although these dynamics may be considerably more complex).

In cognitive terms, what is the self homunculus? I view it as a mental projection, the means by which the organism represents itself within each moment's experience. To use an analogy, the homunculus is like a character in a movie, a character who is lived from a first-person perspective, a character that is pregnant with meanings, intentions, emotions, and histories, a character whose experiences and inflections flicker from moment to moment, as different concepts, percepts, and images are activated and appropriated. The homunculus is rooted in bodily experience, but also has inputs from higher cortical processes that selectively attend to and interpret bodily experiences. Thus, the homunculus is an important means by which the human brain pays attention to itself, detecting, modeling, and interpreting its own internal state. In addition, the homunculus has inputs from memory, and the longer term concepts and goals contained within memory. Thus, the homunculus is an important means by which the human brain can direct and organize itself with respect to the future.

Another perspective is that the homunculus is a stance taken by the person in the world (Blasi, 1988), a subjective position from which experience is ongoingly consolidated and organized into a single point. Stated differently, the homunculus is an ongoing relationship, between an "I" and its circumstances, or between an "I" and other mental contents. Tremendous computing capacity is likely required to create and maintain the mental character, but it is now apparent that our brains have the necessary capacity (Marcel, 1993).

Is the homunculus "real"? Yes and no. On the no side, the emergent self-simulation is, in an important sense, a fiction. This is reflected in the fact that the serial contents and temporal structure of the self often follow the rules of narrative fiction (McAdams, 1993); in the fact that particular selves can be somewhat randomly or nonlinearly determined (Nowak et al., 2000); in the fact that selves can be self-deceived in their beliefs and intuitions about themselves (Greenwald, 1986); and in the fact that selves may fail to accurately represent or mirror the organism in which they are contained (Sheldon, 2002; discussed here further). Another reason why the self homunculus may be viewed as a delusion or an epiphenomenon is the fact that it is historically conditioned—as Baumeister (1987) pointed out, the idea of an internal mental entity, with the power to define itself and to make choices for itself, may be a relatively recent phenomenon within Western history (see also Jaynes, 1976, for arguments concerning the radically less integrated subjectivity of the ancient Greeks).

However, I suggest that the possibility that the human self is a relatively new phenomenon within human culture and history does not necessarily mean that it is unreal, a mere mental delusion; the internal combustion engine, the smallpox vaccine, and the personal computer are equally historically contingent, but nobody would say that they are unreal! Further speaking to the reality of the homunculus is the fact that it is far from powerless. Although fictional, it has many important functions (as discussed later), and exerts considerable top-down control over a host of cognitive and volitional processes. Finally, although the homunculus is built from brain and cognitive processes, it is important to point out that the homunculus is not just these processes. Returning to the concept of higher level organization discussed in chapter 2, momentary selves have emergent properties that cannot be derived merely by knowledge of their components (Sperry, 1993). In other words, there are rules, structures, and processes operative at the level of the experiencing self that cannot be reduced to the effects of rules at lower levels of analysis.

Still, the homunculus does not have total control, and sometimes may have very little control. Also, it may be wrong about the amount of influence that it does have over its own behavior, overestimating or perhaps underestimating its own control. Thus, scientists do not necessarily have to take the self's experiences and beliefs about itself and its own behavior at face value. Furthermore, they do not have to assume that the homunculus is always causal with respect to behavior. Indeed, it is likely that the causal effects of self-level processes on human behavior vary in different times, places, persons, and circumstances, just as the effects of explanatory constructs at other levels of analysis also vary. It is the job of empirical science to sort out the when, how, and how much of the self's effect on behavior.

In sum, I am proposing that we focus primarily on the "I" (rather than the "Me") as we consider the self level of analysis. Moreover, I am suggesting that we think of the "I" as a mental homunculus, a dynamic and changing mental character that the person constructs and then lives inside of, from moment to moment. The homunculus is a process, not an entity, although the process may involve thinking of oneself as an entity. The chief advantage of introducing the homunculus terminology is that it impels recognition of the existential paradox of the self; although selves are not as tangible and stable as they would like to believe they are, nevertheless, their belief in their own solidity helps give people considerable control over their lives.

Damasio's Theory and the Homunculus

Damasio's recent neurobiologically grounded theorizing concerning "the feeling of what happens" (1999) is quite consistent with the current view of the self, and thus it is worth considering these perspectives together. According to Damasio, there are three meanings for the word *self*. First, there is the *proto-self,* which provides the background for self-awareness. It is the implicit neural representation of the organism's underlying bodily and psychophysical state, which suffuses consciousness. For example, a moment ago, the drone of an airplane flying over was present at the back of my mind, although "I" was unaware of it. Nevertheless, the sensation was contained within my organism, awaiting attention. Second, there is the *core self,* which is the lived character that we are conscious of being. This emergent mental entity is to some extent constructed from moment to moment, and thus it may not contain all of the elements contained within the proto-self. For example, "I" just became aware of myself as perceiving the airplane's drone, as I sought for illustrations of the distinction between the proto-self and core self.

The core self has no lasting reality, but instead arises in the interaction between the proto-self, online cognitive processes, and particular objects of awareness (be they percepts, images, goals, or memories). According to Damasio, the core self is the means by which the organism cognitively relates itself to itself and to the world from moment to moment.

Damasio's third definition of self is the *extended self,* built from autobiographical memory. It consists of the enduring self-images, self-beliefs, and self-narratives, encompassing both remembered past and hoped-for future selves, that help to form our identities. Damasio (1999) argued that the core self can momentarily extend its own scope by relating itself to stable self-beliefs and narratives (i.e., "Me's") contained within long-term memory. In other words, the self can be more or less extended and stable, depending on how well it can integrate extended and stable mental constructs into the current "dynamic self-system" (Markus & Ruvolo, 1989). For example, a young teenager who successfully remembers her longer term goals and values in a situation that tempts her to premature sex might thereby shield her overall organism from the consequences of taking the potentially maladaptive actions being considered by her momentary core self. The extended self is one means by which the core self, transient though it is, can achieve a sense of stability and can contribute to the enactment of the person's longer-term goals and projects.

An important aspect of Damasio's neurobiological model is that it has a clear place for the "underlying organism," via its reference to a primary or proto-self, wherein primary assessments and emotional reactions occur, often beneath or at the fringe of awareness. As discussed in chapter 4, such organismic perspectives have been slow to win acceptance in "hard-core" research circles, and thus it is encouraging to see such a perspective within a prominent neurobiological theory of selfhood. Damasio's distinction between core self and proto-self also allows us to ask an important question, which is considered later in much detail: To what extent is the phenomenal self consistent with, or inclusive with respect to, the underlying organism? This question plays an important role in the consideration of optimal human being from the self level of analysis, in the final part of the chapter.

How is the current conception of the homunculus different from Damasio's conception of the core self? Actually, the two ideas are not much different. I am using the term *homunculus* here primarily in order to emphasize the core self's somewhat illusory sense of mental solidity, and also to emphasize the curious position of the core self—that it is to some extent self-constructed and independent of lower level factors, giving it both the power to act and the potential to inadequately model the underlying totality from which it springs. The momentary self, like Adam, has been cast out of its home, with the freedom to ignore its creator.

The Formation and Causal Efficacy of the Homunculus

How, exactly, is the homunculus formed and maintained? Largely through its appropriation of cognitive elements (Allport, 1937). As percepts and concepts arise through the mind, the current or regnant self either identifies with them ("I'm that") or rejects them ("I'm not that"). When elements are accepted, subsequent selves then view events from "inside" the frames they provide. In this way, "I" am continuously regenerated, at the same time that "I" am updated of my own situation. Indeed, Allport (1961) was so impressed with the importance of this appropriation function that he used the term *proprium* as a general term to refer to the self.

How do ongoing self-appropriations influence the stream of behavior? In part by reminding the person of his or her goals, and his or her distance from them. In terms of the control-theory concepts developed in chapters 3 and 6, "I's" can help in the detection of discrepancies between current and future states, by clearly indicating what the current state is. "I's" can also make salient one's ideal or desired relationship to that type of situation; recall that the homunculus can be viewed as a relationship, between the "I" and mental contents (Blasi, 1988). When the "I" corresponds to the current state and the mental contents correspond to future goals or ideals, action to reduce the discrepancy is readily energized and initiated.

This observation illustrates an important characteristic of the psychological homunculus: that it represents or "stands in for" the organism. That is, the mental self-simulation has access to, and control over, bodily resources. As this suggests, self-regulatory brain events often take the form of an inner phenomenal executive, which has mentally distinguished itself from the world and from the past, and which has the authority to implement new or changed courses of action. In return for being given the "reins of the biocognitive machinery," the momentary homunculus is charged with the duty of satisfying the needs of the organism in which it is housed. In this sense, the homunculus is like Freud's concept of the ego, which, according to Freud, is charged with balancing the demands of the other parts of the mind.

Another part of the potential causal efficacy of the phenomenal self, I suggest, comes from the fact that the momentary homunculus can to some extent consciously choose what to identify with, given sufficient effort and appropriate habits of mind. The self, living in an only partially constrained mental world, has significant degrees of freedom with which to influence its own self-construction. In dynamical systems terms, new conscious self-investments may have nonlinear effects on subsequent system configurations, pushing them into new functional regimes that were unpredictable in advance (Nowak et al., 2000). For example, consider a woman who says to herself, "I am no longer going to allow him to take advantage of me like that. I deserve more respect." Thenceforth, she projects a different character toward her partner, eliciting different behavior from him, and thus altering the stimuli that influence her own future self-construction.

In sum, a key assumption of the homunculus perspective is that the phenomenal self has causal force; it directly affects the physical world, specifically, via its interfacing with the body/brain's action production system (as is discussed later in more detail). Again, this does not mean that there is an actual "inner man" inside of each of our heads, deciding what to do; instead, it means that the constructed sense of self, in the act of relating itself to percepts, images, and memories, has powerful influence on subsequent actions. At each consecutive moment, the lived character within the unfolding story does what it thinks is necessary to forward its organism's values and interests.

The Homunculus and the Cartesian Theater

The postulation of a psychological homunculus raises many difficult questions in the philosophy of consciousness, issues that have been hotly debated for decades. I next consider the homunculus question in light of a prominent modern representative, namely, Daniel Dennett's (1991) well-known "multiple drafts" theory of consciousness, a theory that in some ways opposes the idea of a homunculus. Specifically, Dennett argues against the idea of an internal "stage" or "theater" within the brain, which a mental observer watches from some seat within a gallery. He referred to this as "Cartesian dualism," an idea originally formulated by Descartes (summarized in the dictum "I think, therefore I am") and that insidiously persists within scientific theorizing to the present day.

The problem, says Dennett, is that there is no physical location in the brain where such an observer could sit and, more generally, no single place in the brain where "everything comes together." Furthermore, there seems to be no meta-monitoring function to which all information is passed, or that centrally collates experience. Here are Dennett's own words on this topic:

> Once a localized, specialized "observation" has been made, the information content thus fixed does not have to be sent somewhere else to be re-discriminated by some "master" discriminator. In other words, it does not lead to a re-presentation of the already discriminated feature for the benefit of the audience in the Cartesian Theater. (Dennett, 1992)

In short, Dennett is saying that the homunculus is, in principle, *not* locatable in the brain. As discussed earlier, if this is true, it considerably detracts from the homunculus construct's appeal and consilience potential.

How does consciousness work, according to Dennett? Via "multiple drafts," as the organism's state is continually updated by a clamoring array of processes distributed across the brain. In addition, there is no single or "final" stream of consciousness. Dennett's own words are again worth quoting:

> The stream of contents is only rather like a narrative because of its multiplicity; at any point in time there are multiple "drafts" of narrative fragments at various stages of "editing" in various places in the brain.... Most importantly, the Multiple Drafts model avoids the tempting mistake of supposing that there must be a single narrative (the "final" or "published" draft) that is canonical—that represents the actual stream of consciousness of the subject, whether or not the experimenter (or even the subject) can gain access to it.

Notably, Dennett's position on the "I" is essentially the same as that of William James. James (1890/1950) claimed that there is no "immaterial substance" underlying the stream of consciousness (i.e., no objective homunculus). Instead, James argued that feelings of personal unity and behavioral coherence are provided by the fact that as each new "I" (or draft) comes into existence, it takes possession of the thoughts and feelings of the "I" before it. Again, from this perspective, the self's sense of being a tangible, stable entity is likely illusory. However, James went somewhat farther than Dennett, by assuming that the "I" process or "selfing function" (McAdams, 1998) may have significant functional utility for humans, nonetheless. Rather than considering this functional possibility, Dennett instead seems to assume that the matter is closed—in other words, once it becomes impossible to map the experience of singular consciousness on a particular brain region, there is no need to think further about the "self" and its potential causal effects. Instead, he described people, somewhat facetiously, as "zombies" and "robots."

How do Dennett's (1991) assertions relate to my own model? First, I agree with Dennett that there is likely no single objective place in the brain where consciousness happens, or where the homunculus sits. Instead, the "selfing" process is likely widely distributed, just as Dennett claims. Still, this does not necessarily mean that the homunculus is unreal, ineffectual, or chaotic. I suggest that the self process can become singular (or at least function in a singular way), precisely because it thinks of itself as singular. In other words, the fact that the narrative self believes that it is real can give it significant effects on material reality, even if the self (i.e., the ghost in the machine) is not really what it thinks it is. To use an analogy, the "I" may work like a placebo—it can have effects, but only as long as people believe in the reality of the effect! Indeed, this may be why "believing in oneself" and "being oneself" are so important, and also why the sense of self-efficacy (Bandura, 1997) and self-appropriation (Allport, 1937) are so important.

How would the selfing process (McAdams, 1998) be represented in the brain? As Dennett suggests, it is likely to be widely distributed, perhaps skipping around to different regions of the brain as different "drafts" of reality come into prominence. Indeed, rather than being locatable at one place, the homunculus may instead be instantiated as particular emergent *sequences* or *patterns* of activation occurring across the brain, which are irreducible to the supporting neuronal events (see chap. 2). Such patterns might emerge most prominently during times when the organism is functioning most effectively or coherently, or evidencing the most effective self-regulation. Indeed, there is already some empirical support for this idea: For example, effective self-regulation is often characterized by a pattern of recurring or frequent activation within the left frontal lobe within the brain, in alternation with activation in other parts of the brain (Prabhakaran, Narayanan, Zhao, & Gabrieli, 2000; Stuss & Levine, 2002).

Evolutionary Roots of the Self

What is the ultimate origin of the psychological homunculus? Is it a recently emergent historical phenomenon, a product of cultural evolution, as suggested by Baumeister's (1987) analysis? Or, is it perhaps an evolved cognitive adaptation, representing the human brain's ability to synthesize its many strands of activity into a reasonably coherent totality? Sedikides and Skowronski (1997) developed an argument for the latter perspective, arguing that the "symbolic self" was long ago selected for because it provides important survival and reproductive advantages. The symbolic self is in part built on the capacity to simulate others' mental states, and also to model the overall social world. It is also built on the capacity to simulate and insert an agentic "character" into this world, which is entrusted with bringing about the organism's preferences within the material world. Sedikides and Skowronski argued that such a function may have been the most efficient way to deal with the complexity of negotiating the social environment. In other words, rather than evolving hard-wired response mechanisms for every imaginable social situation, human brains may instead have evolved the ability to create a symbolic self and then live in its world, reacting from moment to moment to social cues and circumstances impossible to anticipate in advance.

What of the apparent contradiction between Sedikides and Skowronski's (1997) depiction of the self as an evolved adaptation acquired by *Homo sapiens* tens of thousands of years ago, and Baumeister's (1987) assertion that the self is a relatively recent phenomenon within history? I believe that the contradiction can be resolved if one specifies that there is an evolved ability and genetic predisposition to create and live inside of models of oneself, but that the resultant models can be more or less complex, depending on learning and social influence. In other words, the type of self models that people inhabit may differ within different historical epochs and different cultures, depending on the particular norms regarding selves that the infant encounters. In this view, the self is both evolved and historically conditioned, and thus, as Baumeister (1987) suggested, the "Western" self may indeed be a relatively recent phenomenon.

COMPARING THE HOMUNCULUS CONCEPT
TO OTHER "I" THEORIES

In this section I compare my assumptions regarding the psychological homunculus to other "I"-type theories within psychology, while keeping in mind Damasio's (1999) distinction between the proto, core, and extended selves. The goal is to further elaborate the homunculus construct, and to show that it is theoretically intelligible.

William James's Theory of the "I"

First, let us again further consider James's (1890/1950) distinction between the "I" and the "Me." James viewed the "I" as existing *only in the moment*. That is, the "I" is nothing but the momentary sense of subjectivity that accompanies each "Me" as it flows through consciousness. Because each "I" experience is immediately replaced by a new "I" when the next set of self-images comes along, James believed that it made no sense to speak of a persisting or stable "I." As noted earlier, James ascribed functional utility to the "I" despite its transience, contrary to Dennett's

(1991) assumption that the "I" does not exist or does nothing. However, his definition is definitely limited; in Damasio's terms, James restricted his definition of the "I" to the momentary core self, with no reference to the extended self and its longer term stories and agendas.

Psychosocial Theory and the "I"

Many later personality theorists did not accept James's contention that the "I" exists only in the moment. For example, Erikson (1963), Loevinger (1997), Blasi (1988), and other life-span and identity theorists argued that the sense of "I" can be much more pervasive and longer lasting, manifested as a sense of personal sameness and historical continuity that suffuses consciousness over time. In Damasio's terms, the temporally extended self can be present, perhaps on a near-permanent basis, within the consciousness of the core self. From this perspective, the stability of the homunculus may simply depend on the chronic accessibility of the particular mental contents that frame the self-projection. Does the person's current "stance" toward the world (his or her "I") refer only to the moment and its affordances, or, does it also contain activated longer term self-images and beliefs (i.e., "Me's")? Again, the admixture of the two aspects might vary across persons, or across times within the same person.

Blasi (1988) argued that the "essence of the I" is to be found in its stance toward a particular type of mental content—namely, intentional action. Specifically, fully intact selfhood involves identifying with oneself and one's acts, and also perceiving a unity that connects earlier and later acts. From this perspective, to be an integrated self is to feel that one's mental self is the cause of one's own behavior, both in the moment and viewed over time (deCharms, 1968). Blasi's perspective also implies that an important human capacity is the ability to firmly occupy one's stance—to take the intentional attitude that "this is who I am, and I am going to stand behind it." Notably, this important existential and personality-developmental issue does not appear to be addressable within Damasio's "proto/core/extended self" framework. It is considered further in the next subsection.

Self-Determination Theory and the "I"

Self-determination theory (SDT; Deci & Ryan, 1985, 1991, 2000) is another "I" theory and has focused considerable empirical attention on the question of whether or not the person feels a sense of identity with respect to his or her own actions. Specifically, SDT explores the processes by which people can become alienated from action, such that they do not "endorse their own behavior at the highest level of reflection" (see www.scp.rochester.edu/SDT/index.html). In particular, says SDT, the struggle for self-ownership is forwarded to the extent that social contexts are *autonomy-supportive,* that is, when interpersonal dynamics support people's ability to make choices and to constitute themselves in a way that seems natural in that context (discussed further in chap. 8). In this case, people are enabled to internalize or appropriate social norms, prescriptions, and beliefs, taking them and making them part of self-experience (i.e., "I'm that"). In contrast, when social environments or authorities are too controlling, coercive, or indifferent to subordinate's autonomy, then the subordinate's sense of self may be diminished and the internalization of social norms and values forestalled (i.e., "I'm not that."). In such cases, people's ability to constitute themselves as a coherent psychological character within a relatively benevolent social order may be weakened or inactivated.

In addition to interpersonal dynamics, intrapersonal dynamics also affect the ability to achieve identity between self and action. For example, SDT proposes that people with "externally control-oriented" personality styles habitually locate causality outside of themselves, as they seek out rules and constraints with which to conform (Deci & Ryan, 1985). That is, people with this personality style typically report that external factors, not they themselves, are the source of their behaviors. A person's level of felt autonomy (vs. felt controlledness) may also change over time, as a function of personality-developmental issues (Sheldon & Kasser, 2001). For example, as discussed in the previous chapter, the self-concordance model (Sheldon, 2002) assumes that people are naturally motivated to take greater ownership of their own personal goals, and to move beyond the feeling that their goals are determined by others (such as parents or peers). Some important differences between the current homunculus perspective and SDT's conception of the self are discussed later in the chapter.

Narrative Perspectives on the "I"

McAdams (1993) and other narrative researchers have provided another type of window on the "I," by studying "the stories people tell" about themselves. These approaches emphasize the active processes through which individuals construct and reconstruct their self stories, thereby providing interpretive contexts for their lives as a whole. Thus, narrative approaches tend to move beyond "Me" perspectives, which, again, tend to assume that people's self-concepts are relatively static and often externally derived. However, McAdams's (1993) model also succeeds in straddling the I/Me boundary, by addressing both the storyteller and the story. The "I" helps create its own longer term "Me's," in the process of narrating itself.

Of course, the storyteller cannot tell just any story—it encounters many constraints, not least among these the actual factual and material circumstances of the person's life. Another constraint is cultural: Stories tend to follow similar patterns that correspond to dominant myths and narrative rules within the individual's culture. For example, a common narrative theme within Westerners' life stories is that of redemption, following an early fall from grace (McAdams, Josselson, & Lieblich, 2001). Another constraint is social: People cannot tell stories about themselves that are too discrepant from others' stories about them, or else they may face ridicule and ostracism. Despite these constraints, it is important to point out that people have rather large degrees of freedom in how they tell their own stories. Stories can take strange plot twists, introducing radical shifts into an individual's subsequent patterns of behavior.

The current homunculus view is largely consistent with McAdams's autobiographically based account of self processes. However, I am focusing primarily on the self as the active and forward-looking intentional agent, projected into and updated within moment-to-moment experience, rather than as a retrospective story or narrative, derived from consideration of one's long-term personal history. Again, this momentary "I" has been largely ignored within social and personality psychology, because of the ontological difficulties it raises. Arguably, however, it is the most important self of all: not just because it is the stuff of our daily and momentary existence, but also, because it has its hands on the reins of the biocognitive machinery.

The "Self as a Theory" Theory

Another influential "I"-based theory of the self was provided by Epstein (1973). Epstein's theory of the self was that the self is a theory! In other words, the self is, literally, an explanatory and predictive conceptual structure that the person has developed about him or herself, through both inductive and deductive reasoning. Like all scientific theories, self theories are based on reasonable inferences from observed data, as people labor to make sense of themselves and their behavior. Also, self theories may be more or less clear, complex, coherent, and closed.

Notably, this perspective does not just define the self as a set of dry theoretical postulates—Epstein's model also encompasses the "active I," because he assumed that people are actively engaged in applying their self theories. Specifically, self theories are used to explain one's own prior actions and outcomes to oneself, and also to derive hypotheses about what one should do next. Furthermore, Epstein viewed people as actively engaged in elaborating and extending their self theories.

However, Epstein largely sidestepped an important question, namely, the extent to which people's theories provide correct (vs. incorrect) models of some underlying personal reality. In other words, is the person's self theory an accurate description of the thing it describes, or is it instead inaccurate and incomplete? Again, conventional social-cognitive theory has few ways to even approach such questions, because it has focused largely on mental representations (i.e., "Me's"), without considering that which is represented. From the cognitive perspective, cognitions are all there is, and thus, underlying personality sometimes gets short shrift. Although Epstein (1973) did mention that the empirical accuracy of a self theory is one indicator of the theory's adequacy, he discussed neither what accuracy means nor how it is to be judged.

What, then, are self theories theories of? Epstein's model implies a rather circular answer to this question, namely, that self theories are theories of the self. However, I believe that it is possible to give a more cogent definition: Self theories are theories of the underlying organism, in whose brain the cognitive simulation or mental homunculus is being run. As noted earlier, Damasio's view is also consistent with this idea, in that cognitively based core selves may be viewed as phenomenal representations of proto-selves, which exist prior to, and help ground, core selves. The idea is also consistent with Dennett's theory of multiple drafts, if we assume that any particular draft in consciousness is only a partial representation of the complete underlying state or set of drafts-in-process.

If self theories are theories about the organism that houses the self, then the accuracy question, raised earlier, can be rephrased: Is the lived self theory a *correct* theory of its own underlying organism? That is, is the self in touch with itself (i.e., with its organism)? Thus, this view assumes that there is "something in there," to which the constructed self may or may not correspond (T. D. Wilson, 2002). I believe that much of the time there is considerable correspondence, because of the organismic valuing process (OVP), which enables people to fairly directly access and assess their underlying condition (Rogers, 1964; discussed in chaps. 1 and 6). Again, however, people do not always have access to, or listen to, their OVP. How do people lose touch with the OVP? One important way is that they become overly invested in sustaining a particular "Me" that is inconsistent with, or threatened by, the subtle sensations and signals arising within the organism. The simulation does not match reality, but the simulation is preferred. As discussed in the previous chapter, felt insecurity is often behind such processes (Rogers, 1951).

Hopefully, in this section I have shown that although the idea of a homunculus has long been taboo in philosophical theory, it may yet be useful—if we can hold onto the idea that the homunculus can be significant and functional, with important effects on behavior and adaptation, despite being somewhat arbitrary and fictional, that is, not necessarily what it thinks it is. Hopefully I have also shown how the homunculus concept is somewhat different from but also integrative with respect to other conceptions of the subjective self or "I." Now we are ready to consider the possible functions of the homunculus in detail. This paves the way for consideration of optimal human being from the self level of analysis, at the end of the chapter.

FOUR FUNCTIONS OF THE HOMUNCULUS

To summarize so far, the self is an ongoing construction of the human mind, a shifting mental character being "run" within the organism's brain. Although the homunculus is in part a fictional construction, nevertheless it has real effects, largely because it believes it is real. Thus, it has an important role to play within the psychic economy. It is a "fiction with functions."

Four important functions of the homuncular character are considered next. The first three of these roughly correspond to Hart's (1988) three functions of the "I" (namely, providing the person with a sense of reality and continuity, providing the person with a sense of distinctiveness from others, and aiding in the person's volitional efforts). The fourth function discussed, that of deriving accurate information about the underlying organism, corresponds to Carl Rogers's (1964) conception of the organismic valuing process. As we show, the fourth function, when properly enacted, may be an important means by which homunculus selves can become *less* fictional.

Function 1: Terror Management

Part of the self's function is to enable the organism to feel a tangible and continuous sense of its own reality and permanence. Terror management theory (TMT; Greenberg, Pyszczynski, & Solomon, 1986; Greenberg et al., 1995) asserts that this is necessary, because of the ineradicable fear of death that we all face (TMT is also discussed in chap. 4, in the discussion of organismic security needs). People know that they must die, and it is the momentary homunculus's job to try to minimize or even repeal this fear. As one way of defending against the potentially crippling knowledge that their organism could cease to exist at any moment, people try to affirm their organism, in the only form they can know it—that is, they try to affirm the stability and integrity of the momentary psychological homunculus or current self-character that they feel themselves to be (Steele, 1999). Conversely, they resist and defend against suggestions that "who they now think they are" is unstable or incoherent.

Ultimately, of course, what the current self fears, dissolution, cannot be avoided. First, in a weaker sense, the momentary homunculus cannot help but be reconfigured and reconditioned over time, simply because events are often unpredictable and can have strong and nonanticipatable influences on people's situations and self processes. Again, in Damasio's (1999) terms, the homunculus arises in the process of cognitively relating the proto-self to objects of awareness; thus, changes in objects cannot help but affect the homunculus. Second, the impermanence of the homunculus is likely true in an even stronger sense; the stability and coherence of the physical organism certainly do not survive the dissolution of death, casting grave doubt on the long-term stability and coherence of the psychological homunculus. Indeed, it seems apparent that concepts of "soul" and "spirit" have arisen precisely because of the homunculus's yearning for a greater or more permanent reality for itself. The ghost in the machine desires transcorporeal solidity.

Nevertheless, TMT says that the organism's fear of these inevitabilities can be ameliorated, via the self's affirmation of its own values and integrity. By verifying their own presence, meaningfulness, and worthiness, people gain the ability to control the anxiety that might otherwise cripple them. This can occur preemptively, in that individuals can largely buffer themselves from the negative effects of death awareness by having generally high self-esteem. It can also occur via particular defensive mechanisms, in response to episodic death anxiety. For example, individuals tend to more strongly affirm their in-groups and denigrate out-groups, tend to cling more tightly to personal and cultural norms, and tend to turn more strongly to self-affirming attachment figures, after mortality has been made salient (Greenberg et al., 1995).

The perspective here is entirely consistent with TMT, and merely hopes to spell out, in phenomenological terms, what is often being defended by terror management strategies. Indeed, the notion of a "projected phenomenal character," which serves as the momentary representative of the organism as a whole, may help terror management theory to better explain certain types of effects. For example, why do death-primed people temporarily reject their ethnic identities after their ethnic group has been presented in a stigmatized way (Arndt, Greenberg, Schimel, Pyszczynski, & Solomon, 2002)? According to the current view, this occurs because the momentary homunculus may sometimes ignore or deny the extended self, that is, its own longer term commitments and self-identifications, in an attempt to maintain or bolster its self-esteem at that moment. This account is also consistent with other recent accounts of self-regulation failures, in which people put short-term mood-regulation goals ahead of longer term life goals (Rachlin, 2000; Tice, Bratslavsky, and Baumeister, 2001).

Given the inevitability of death and defense, is the subjective self's quest for solidity and permanence just a vain delusion? No—the homunculus can succeed in achieving considerable self-stability, via a variety of means. To the extent that individuals can regularize and regulate environmental input to avoid threats to their self-conceptions (e.g., by forming bonds with others who verify their self-conceptions over the long term; Swann, 2000), they can maintain the basic structure of extended self-memory, and thus of a particular self-aware homunculus, for many years. Also, to the extent that they can maintain their hold on a particular story, successfully accommodating events that do not fit that story (McAdams, 1993), people can succeed in maintaining a temporally extended homunculus. At the opposite end of the spectrum, of course, selves can also come and go from moment to moment, as in the case of multiple personality disorders or, to a lesser extent, in the cases of individuals suffering from highly unstable self-esteem (Kernis & Paradise, 2002). From my own perspective (and consistent with many other "I" theories), an effective homunculus is one that successively weaves these various strands into a reasonably integrated whole (Harter & Monsour, 1992), maintaining and elaborating its basic stance and structure in the process.

Function 2: Enhancing Social Interchange

Social interchange is greatly forwarded when social actors are able to project stable character into their social performances. Indeed, humans are acutely sensitive to character in others, an interest and skill that may represent an evolved adaptation (Tooby & Cosmides, 1992). Perceivers especially like and resonate to *integrated* social characters, because they seem trustworthy and authentic (Robinson, Johnson, & Shields, 1995), and because we care about these characters' views of our *own* character's success and meaningfulness (Laing, 1969). Furthermore, perceivers of coherent self-characters tend to behave in ways that retroactively *verify* the integrity/reality of the actor's projected character, further strengthening the stability and performance of the actor's self (Goffman, 1959; Swann, 2000).

This reasoning suggests that to the extent that actors can feel and fully appropriate their own momentary social character (Laing, 1969), they can better succeed in convincing others of the reality of that self, thus experiencing many positive social advantages and outcomes. This explains why it is so important to "just be oneself" when interacting with others. In contrast, when an actor's projected homunculus seems hesitant and/or uncertain of its own reality or efficacy, others are understandably slow or hesitant to acknowledge and support that self.

Function 3: Helping to Guide and Regulate the Action System

As discussed earlier in the chapter, one of the most important functions of the homunculus arises via its interface with the organism's action system. Indeed, the projected homunculus or "lived character" has a vital role to play in instigating and regulating action, both in the short term and in the long term.

First, momentary self-construals can at times transform a person's long-term behavior and outcomes; recall the earlier example of the woman who decided, "I don't deserve to be treated that way," and whose altered behavior toward her partner, following the realization, changed her relationship with him. Or consider her husband, whose regnant self detects twinges of guilt in his organism regarding the aggressive way he is treating his romantic partner. If he acknowledges and focuses on these feelings, he may suddenly see himself in a new way: as a thoughtless bully. Accordingly he may veer away from this unpleasant character, trying to instead become the "sensitive mate" with which he would prefer to identify.

As this example suggests, the process of investing global self-representations with significance may become particularly important when those self-images (i.e., "me as a sensitive mate") begin to serve as guiding goals or standards within the action system. Again, according to Carver and Scheier (1998), such global self-images can provide overall orienting goals for the system, directing how the organism invests its energy in day-to-day activity (Emmons, 1989). Stated differently, self-images can provide "principle" and "system-level" reference standards for the action system, standards against which people can compare their present situation or current self-images, in order to take action to reduce discrepancies been actual and desired self-images.

Markus and Ruvolo (1989) referred to such future-oriented self-images as "possible selves," which serve important long-term motivational and directive functions within individuals. Possible selves may be viewed as somewhat idealized versions of the present homunculus, characters that are projected into the future, rather that into the present. Because these future characters can represent or stand in for the organism just as can current characters, they may gain access to significant motivational energy and metabolic resources.

Function 4: Properly Representing the Underlying Organism

As the previous point illustrated, providing high-level standards for the action system is one of the most important functions of the self (Carver & Scheier, 1998). The fourth function of the homunculus discussed in this section goes one step further, however, by focusing on the issue of whether the self properly represents the underlying condition of the organism in which it is housed.

To illustrate the importance of this process and to show how it can go awry, consider the case discussed in chapters 3 and 6 of the medical student who was on his way to the library. Suppose that 5 years later he is nearing the end of medical school, and has just managed to secure the surgical residency he desired. Nevertheless, he is apprehensive, suspecting, via his earlier experiences of dissecting cadavers and treating bloody wounds, that by nature he is too squeamish to become a surgeon. Suppose he shrugs off these organismic clues that surgery may not be for him, and continues to pursue a profession he is unlikely to enjoy. At the same time, he also ignores talents and dispositions that are in reality most central to his personal endowments (such as relating to sick children).

Why does this happen? According to the current view, it is because the student clings to an outdated "I" that does not properly represent his organism. Again, the homunculus, as a simulation, has the freedom to fail to represent its own deeper condition, and thus it has the potential to cause its organism's "best potentials" to be squandered. In the process, it may also fail to obtain organismic need satisfaction (Rogers, 1951). Even worse, people may embark on courses of self-construction that take them ever further from others and from psychological need satisfaction, with malignant consequences.

Consider this extreme example: As I initially wrote these words, Timothy McVeigh, the Oklahoma City bomber, was soon to be executed for his crime. Certainly his actions did not serve his organism's interests, as public execution is hardly a desirable outcome for anyone's life! Yet McVeigh displayed no remorse for his crimes, to the public's consternation. Although his lack of remorse may have seemed surprising given the heinousness of his crime, it is not at all surprising when one considers the strength of McVeigh's terror management needs. McVeigh *had* to affirm the reality and importance of the self that chose his actions, or else he could not cope with the knowledge of his organism's impending termination. This is simply the first function of the homunculus that was described earlier. Two other functions of the homunculus were still there, also, in McVeigh's life: He had a social life in prison, even succeeding in finding points of relationship with Ted Kacyzynski, the Unabomber. Also, McVeigh's sense of self still guided his action system, as he actively managed his pre-executionary career, to affirm and validate the extremist who chose to bomb the Murray Federal Building.

Still, in McVeigh, it appears that the fourth function of the homunculus (properly representing the underlying organism, and obtaining psychological need-satisfaction) may have remained latent or inactive. I think it likely that McVeigh felt twinges of guilt, remorse, and self-doubt in the days leading to his execution. If he had attended to these subtle signals within his organismic (or proto) self, and perhaps had made some attempt at apology and reparation to the victims' families, then he might have died a much less lonely death.

What brings about the McVeigh types, that is, people who give full expression to the antisocial fantasies of a malign self? How do they go so far down such "evil" paths? Of course, this is a very difficult and complex question. My own perspective is that such people still desire experiences of autonomy, competence, and relatedness, given that these are universal needs within human nature. But presumably, they are not getting very much of these experiences—that is, they do not feel affirmed and connected, and likely also feel somewhat powerless and nonautonomous. What do they do? As discussed in the preceding chapter, in some such cases people may get "stuck," doing the only thing they know how to do, but doing it even harder. As they proceed further down a negative path they must of necessity ignore or suppress more and more of their organismic signals, thereafter making the doing of evil even more probable, in a vicious cycle. Having lost all access to the OVP, almost any set of alternative values may be adopted, including morally reprehensible ones. If such "blind agents" come under the sway of a violent ideology, watch out!

Notice the implicit assumptions I am making, consistent with those of liberal humanism and Rousseauean romanticism: that the human organism is itself "good," or at worst "benign," until it encounters overpowering or overly frustrating circumstances. In other words, people have natural curiosities, urges for social connection, and interests in bettering themselves and their situation, which will hold sway if allowed and supported. Thus, although the human organism certainly has the power to "go bad" if life contexts push it that way, people are otherwise oriented toward growth, connection, and integration. Whether this optimistic assumption is true or not is, of course, an empirical question. However, as noted in the preceding chapter, Sheldon and colleagues have now amassed considerable evidence supporting the idea of a positive, health-relevant bias within human nature, which leads people to move toward greater self-concordance and more intrinsic valuing over time (Sheldon, in press; Sheldon & Kasser, 2001; Sheldon, Arndt, & Houser-Marko, 2003). Other recent research within the recent "positive psychology" perspective has also supported such optimistic assumptions (Masten, 2001; Seligman, 2002).

Developmentally, how do selves lose touch with their organisms? Humanistic and psychodynamic theories provide an intriguing lead, proposing that self-alienation often occurs when people become too concerned with pleasing critical others (Harter, 1999; Laing, 1969). For example, Winnicott (1957) argued that the infant who does not receive "good enough mothering" may start to create a false self, in an attempt to secure sufficient maternal attention and affection. Rogers (1961) also discussed the problems that arise when important others only give contingent positive regard to developing young selves. According to these perspectives, then, regnant selves may sometimes be constructed too much on the basis of other's definitions, and not enough on the basis of internal experience. In such cases, the "self-updating process" may yield a biased or incomplete output.

Let us return to the case of the aspiring surgeon, at an even later point in time: 12 months after the previous example. It is late in the first year of his residency, and things are going poorly. He has recurring feelings of disgust and distaste, and struggles to adequately perform his duties. As a result he becomes discouraged, and wonders why he cannot live up to his family's (especially his father's) expectations. This only makes him feel worse. In compensation, he tries to pour more energy into work. However, this doesn't really help—even his successes fail to satisfy, because underneath, he feels like an imposter. He sleeps poorly, his relationships suffer, and he battles feelings of hopelessness and futility.

How can such a self get back in touch with its organism? By making the effort to consult and listen to its own OVP. Perhaps the surgical resident will take some time to think carefully about what really makes him happy—his true inclinations, talents, and feelings. He may remember the feelings of joy he sometimes felt while interacting with sick children on the ward, and the feeling of making an important contribution when he helped these children to get well. As a result he may shed the outdated "self as surgeon" image, and adopt a new view of himself (i.e., "self as pediatrician") that better represents his actual experience and potentials. Thenceforth, his action system might commence taking him toward a more satisfying possible future.

I believe such changes can occur quite readily, because again, the OVP is an innate part of the human endowment (Rogers, 1964). However, Rogers also viewed the ability to make use of this endowment as a *skill,* which can be more or less well developed. Individuals must learn to recognize the significance of the fleeting thoughts, subtle impressions, complex emotions, and bodily tensions that occur within themselves (Gendlin, 1978; T. D. Wilson, 2002). This can be difficult, especially when those perceptions are inconsistent with an insecure regnant self, which is striving to maintain itself against the threat of dissolution (the first function of the homunculus). In the case of the medical resident, the "surgeon self" may be hanging on for dear life!

THE PSYCHOLOGICAL HOMUNCULUS
AND OPTIMAL HUMAN BEING

Basic Considerations

What is optimal human being, viewed from the perspective of the "self" level of analysis (i.e., the top level within Fig. 3.3, which itself expands on the personality level in Fig. 2.1)? There are various implications that can be drawn from the preceding discussion. Let us begin with the assumption that the self is in fact a projected character, a mental simulation—the means by which the organism represents its own state to itself and also constructs itself in relation to that state. What is the "best" kind of character to have, in these terms?

One answer concerns the four functions just discussed. First, the optimal homunculus would be one that derives a reasonable sense of continuity and permanence for itself, in part by coping successfully with death fear, and in part by finding and affirming central values and commitments (Steele, 1999). Presumably in this case, the person would be able to create and maintain a positive emotional state and sense of psychological well-being. Second, the optimal homunculus would be one that successfully projected itself to other people. Presumably in this case, the person would derive experiences of relatedness and also enjoy the advantages of social cooperation (discussed in the next chapter). Third, the optimal homunculus would be one that successfully pursued ideal goals or possible self-images, helping to bring its own longer term ambitions and possible selves into being. Presumably in this case, the person would move steadily toward better circumstances and opportunities (or increased negentropy, in the language of chap. 2). Finally, the optimal homunculus would be one that accurately included and represented the processes occurring within its organism, such that its volitional decisions would be fully informed by the relevant implicit information. Presumably, in this case, the person would be most likely to satisfy organismic psychological needs, such as those for security, competence, relatedness, autonomy, and self-esteem (as discussed in chap. 4). What is the best way to be, overall? From the "four functions" view, a person would thrive to the greatest extent when he or she was simultaneously fulfilling all four of the functions described.

More Complex Considerations

In this subsection I attend more carefully to the relationship between the homunculus and the organism, as this is an issue with great potential for confusion. It is also the issue with greatest relevance for the question of what it means to "be oneself," to "get in touch with oneself," and to "be true to oneself," issues that folk wisdom suggests may be particularly important for the question of optimal human being.

As one example of how the distinction between self and organism may be blurred, consider self-determination theory's account (Deci & Ryan, 1991). Although SDT defines the self as the active core of the person, just as I do, and emphasizes the importance of organismic needs and growth impulses, just as I do, SDT may conflate the self and the organism. Specifically, SDT treats the self as the unequivocally "good" part of the person, that is, as the impulse toward growth and integration itself, which can be suppressed or inhibited by social contexts. In this view, there is either self (when autonomous or self-determined motivation is present) or not-self (when controlled or nonautonomous motivation is present; Deci, 2003). However, my own view is that the self is almost always present, except in cases of severe schizophrenia, dissociation, or identity disorder. Everybody has a self, or, in Damasio's terms, a projected momentary homunculus that represents the organism, whether or not that self feels autonomous or controlled, and whether or not that self is "good" or "bad." In other words, it is not that many people exist "without selves"—instead, many people exist with "selves that are out of touch with organisms," or selves that do not conduce to organismic need satisfaction.

Although the self/organism distinction may seem subtle, it opens the way to acknowledge that there is a self in attendance within everyone, even if that self is deluded or disturbed. In addition, this distinction offers a way to make sense of phrases such as "get in touch with yourself"—what the phrase means is, "get in touch with your organism." Also, it offers a way to recognize that malign selves can exist (such as McVeigh), in which something is clearly wrong—in assuming that the self is "good," the SDT perspective would have to maintain that McVeigh had no sense of self. However, this was clearly not the case, as interviews with McVeigh revealed (Michel & Herbeck, 2001). Finally, the self/organism distinction opens up an interesting way of thinking about the struggle between "good" and "evil." As discussed earlier in the chapter, it may not be the *self* (located at the top of Fig. 3.3) that contains the positive tendencies and growth impulses, but rather, the *organism* that contains them (located at the bottom of Fig. 3.3). These universal features of positive human nature exist "before and beneath" the self, and hopefully, the psychological homunculus can learn to contact and express them (given supportive conditions).

The discussion of self-to-organism matching suggests that ideally, the homunculus would also be in tune with, or well represent, the middle two levels of personality listed in Fig. 3.3: traits/temperament (Level 2) and goals/intentions (Level 3). In terms of the example mentioned at the end of chapter 6, optimally, a woman's sense of self (i.e., as a convivial, talkative person) would match her genetically based personality traits (i.e., of extraversion and sociability). In addition, ideally, her sense of self would also match her goals and intentions (i.e., her strivings for frequent social contact and connection).

With which level of personality is it most important for the self to be consistent? In chapter 6 I suggested that it is most important for goals to match organismic needs, and the same suggestion can be made here: that it is most important for the self to be consistent with organism and organismic needs. In this case the person might still experience considerable satisfaction and well-being, even when his or her lived self is inconsistent with his or her traits or his or her goals. In fact, self–organism matches may be especially beneficial when the person's traits and goals are themselves inconsistent with organismic needs; in this case, the homunculus may provide an important top-down means of taking action to produce positive change in the person's traits and goals (consistent with the third function of the homunculus). For example, a highly introverted woman who typically strives to avoid social contact might benefit if she becomes convinced that she is a person with something to contribute after all; this might initiate much positive growth and change in her life. A complete discussion of the "level-matching idea" is provided in chapter 10 and gives overarching consideration to the nature of optimal human being.

In sum, I believe that the homunculus perspective outlined in this chapter has many positive features. First, it helps with the mind–body problem, by acknowledging that although the mind has no existence independent of the body, the mind's self-construals (fictional as they may be) have potentially large causal influence on the body, by virtue of the emergent self's top-down influence on the organism's action system and temporal destiny (Carver & Scheier, 1998; Sperry, 1993). Homunculus theory also helps with the I/Me problem, by proposing that "I's" and "Me's" are different facets of an ongoing self-regulatory dialectic that in part involves the generation and appropriation of new "Me's" by the regnant "I." In addition, the theory helps with the conflict between social constructivist and more agentic perspectives on the self, by admitting all of the insights of the constructionists, while asserting that the actions of the self—situated, gendered, acculturated, and contingent as they may be—nevertheless have real and important consequences for the organism in which the self is embedded. These consequences can be empirically studied, and the patterns underlying them detected. Furthermore, the theory helps to resolve the conflict between the Cartesian theater and Dennett's multiple-drafts model. There is no theater, but the drafts think that there is, and this itself makes the difference. Finally, the theory helps to resolve the conundrum posed by the expression "just be yourself." In the current model, to "be oneself" is to align one's mental self-projection with one's goals, traits, and emerging experiences. Perhaps most importantly, it is to align oneself with positive human nature and the organismic needs.

Obviously, however, the self does not exist in a vacuum. We live in a matrix with other selves, on whom we are radically dependent. This brings us to the necessity of considering yet a higher level of analysis in trying to understand optimal human being: that of social interaction.

8 Social and Group Interaction: Game and Role Theory Perspectives

In this chapter, I consider directly the obvious fact that many if not most human activities are situated within a social context. In other words, we do not just behave to satisfy our organismic needs, express our traits, and achieve our personal goals; we also act to communicate or share feelings with others, to enact or follow social norms, and to facilitate the functioning of our groups and social organizations. Indeed, human behavior is profoundly conditioned by the social context, and no understanding of scientific consilience can be complete without considering the social interaction level of analysis in some detail (see Fig. 2.1). Thus, one aim of this chapter is to canvass some important concepts at this level of analysis, and to try to show that effects of this level are irreducible to effects at lower levels of analysis, such as neurobiology, cognition, and personality. Of course, the primary aim is to examine the nature of optimal human being from the social interaction perspective.

The social interaction level of analysis encompasses a huge literature, including role theory, intergroup theory, relationship theory, social dilemma theory, social identity theory, and much of classic social psychological theory. Of necessity my review of this literature is quite selective, focusing on two realms I believe may be particularly relevant to optimal human being: evolutionary game theory and social role theory. I briefly defend this choice of theories next.

The game-theory perspective affords insights into the social adaptability or evolvability of various strategies for negotiating interdependent outcomes. Thus, this perspective enables us to evaluate how well different social philosophies work for those who employ them. For example, is it best to cooperate or compete, in a situation in which one might be exploited? From the eudaemonist and organismic perspectives, surely optimal human being involves cooperative and emotionally satisfying interactions between people. But how could we call trusting, cooperative, or group-centered behavior "optimal" if it ran counter to the individual's own best interests, so that he or she consistently got fewer resources than others? One goal of this chapter is evaluate the support for an optimistic perspective on human social nature, namely, that humans are by nature predominantly cooperative and other oriented. I try to show that this is true, and indeed, that it is only to be expected from a game-theory perspective.

Social-role theory affords insights into the specific processes by which individuals interface with groups, taking on particular group functions and accommodating to social norms and role expectations more generally. It takes into account both individuals' private experiences (of their role identities, obligations, duties, etc.) and their objective place and function within larger groups (such as family, friendship, and work groups). Thus, role theory may help us to understand the nature of optimal integration between the self level of analysis and the hierarchically adjacent social interaction level of analysis (see Figs. 2.1 and 3.3). In particular, we consider the ways by which individuals may fully internalize their social roles, so that they feel a sense of self-expression as they enact them, thereby enacting them effectively. We also discuss the best means for authorities to help subordinates to internalize their roles, so that things go better for all.

THE EVOLUTIONARY GAME THEORY PERSPECTIVE ON SOCIAL INTERACTION

Overview

Evolutionary game theory provides a compelling means of considering individual behavior in its social context, given its focus on how different types of interpersonal decisions lead to different types of outcomes for those involved. This is a crucial issue from the evolutionary perspective, which typically views individuals as competing with one another for scarce resources—both material (i.e., territory, housing, luxury items) and social (i.e., status, affection, services). Those behavioral strategies that best serve to maximize resource acquisition and thus survival and reproductive outcomes should be selected for, such that the genes coding for those strategies increase in frequency in the population over time.

Evolutionary game theory is built around social dilemma concepts (Axelrod, 1984). Social dilemmas are situations in which individuals' outcomes are dependent on other individuals' actions and choices as well as on their own actions and choices. The classic social dilemma is the prisoner's dilemma (Poundstone, 1992). Two men, coconspirators in a crime, are questioned separately by the district attorney. If both keep quiet, they know that the minimal evidence against them will lead to minimal sentences for each of them. But what if one of the men cuts a deal, confessing to the district attorney in exchange for immunity? In this case the confessor will go scot-free, and the other man, who tries to cooperate by refusing to confess, will bear the brunt of the crime. Given this, can either man afford to take the risk of cooperating, especially in the face of the temptation to "defect" and perhaps get away clean oneself? Maybe so, given that if both men confess (i.e., defect), then things will turn out worse for both of them than if neither had confessed. This is the dilemma.

There is no a priori way to know which choice (cooperation or defection) one should make, because it depends so heavily on what the other person does. Evolutionary game theory attempts to mathematically model the various possible strategies and decision rules, in order to understand which strategies and approaches lead to the best outcomes, in which situations. In principle, the most effective strategies are also the ones that should have evolved, and that should thus be manifest within human psychology.

The optimal strategy to play within social dilemmas might vary depending on a wide variety of factors. One factor is the number of other players involved: In addition to two-person prisoner's dilemma games (PDGs) there are also multiple-person prisoner's dilemmas (N-PDGs), in which individual payoffs depend on the decisions of several people, not just one other person (Liebrand, 1984). An additional factor is the payoff matrix: In any type of dilemma there are a large number of possible payoff matrices, which determine how much each participant receives for a particular paired outcome. For example, does mutual defection lead to the worst outcome for each, or to the second worst outcome? How large is the numerical value representing the "temptation to defect," or the value representing the "sucker's payoff" that results when a person is exploited (Pruitt & Kimmel, 1977)? Yet another factor influencing strategy is the wide variety of social-contextual conditions that can surround the game. For example, is there a sanctioning system in place to penalize noncooperation (Yamagishi, 1986)? Can the protagonists communicate with each other (Jorgenson & Papciak, 1980)? Still another factor is that games can vary widely in their length. For example, is it a one-shot dilemma that is over after the first choice, or is it an iterated dilemma that goes on for many trials, such that participants have the opportunity to respond to and adapt to each other (Komorita & Parks, 1995)? Finally, there are also multiple types of dilemmas besides prisoner's dilemmas. I next briefly discuss two other types of dilemma, as they reappear later in the discussion.

One important type of social dilemma is the resource dilemma, in which individuals have the opportunity to draw from a common community pool. Resource dilemmas are multiperson dilemmas, in which the temptation is to take more than one's fair share of the commons. This can happen because of greed (the desire to get something for nothing), fear (that others will exploit the resource, so one should "get while the getting's good"), or both (Bruins, Liebrand, & Wilke, 1989). Unfortunately, the more individuals pursue this overacquisitive strategy, the more quickly the resource collapses, leading to what Hardin (1968) referred to as "the tragedy of the commons." Indeed, it may be that the 21st century will see the playing out of a global tragedy of the commons, driven by increasing population pressure and the worldwide belief that material success is essential for "the good life" (Biel & Garling, 1995; Kasser, 2002).

Related to the resource dilemma is the public goods dilemma, in which the problem is to get people to contribute to a public good, rather than keeping people from abusing it (Komorita & Parks, 1994). For example, when we suffer an accident, we all hope that there is blood available in the community blood bank. But do we donate blood? Often not—instead, we yield to the temptation not to contribute (i.e., we defect). Similarly, public radio requires the support of public pledges. However, calling up to give away one's money "for nothing" can be a difficult act to justify! Thus, public goods dilemmas may be particularly difficult to solve, because they require people to take intentional, and somewhat costly, action (Brewer & Kramer, 1986).

The Problem of Cooperation

As these examples illustrate, cooperation is a "nondominant strategy" within many social dilemmas (Rapoport & Chammah, 1965). Thus, although it has many potential benefits, it is somewhat unstable, that is, difficult to bring about and maintain. To illustrate, consider a standard prisoner's dilemma payoff matrix, presented in Fig. 8.1. In one sense, one should always choose defection (the dominant strategy), because one will always do better by defecting than cooper-

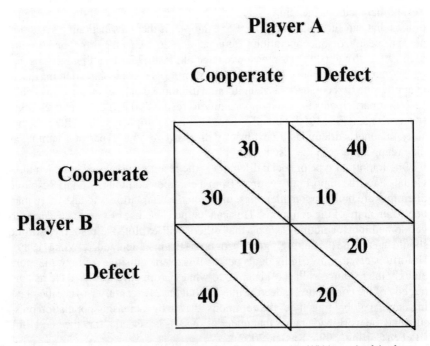

FIG. 8.1. A standard two-person prisoner's dilemma matrix. Within each of the four cells, numbers below the diagonals represent B's outcome, and numbers above the diagonal represent A's outcome.

ating, whatever the opponent's choice. If one chooses defection while one's opponent cooperates, one receives 40, versus the 30 one would have received if one had instead cooperated in that circumstance. If one chooses defection while one's opponent defects, one receives 20, versus the 10 one would have received if one had instead cooperated. It is only when we compare the two outcomes of mutual cooperation (30, 30) and mutual defection (20, 20) that the potential advantage of cooperating becomes clear.

The Human Disposition to Cooperate

Because cooperation is a nondominant strategy, and because of the assumption of individual self-interest made by traditional evolutionary theory, it was long thought that genes coding for cooperative behavior would have a disadvantage in the evolutionary arms race (Axelrod, 1984). However, late-century developments in evolutionary theory began to make a clearer place for cooperative behavior. One fundamental advance, made surprisingly recently, was inclusive fitness or kin selection theory (Hamilton, 1964). Taking a gene-centered view, Hamilton recognized that cooperative behavior might evolve because it benefits one's relatives, even if it occurs at some cost to oneself. Thus, although a honeybee may die after using her sting to defend the hive, or a sentry animal may die after alerting her kin to danger (because she also attracts the predator's attention to herself), these behaviors could still be selected for because, overall, they benefit copies of the genes of those who perform them.

Could cooperative behavior evolve even in the case where the actors are not related to each other? Reciprocal altruism theory (Trivers, 1971) showed that it could. A gene or complex of genes that prompted individuals to help another in need, at some small personal cost but with a potential large benefit for the other, could be very adaptive—if that other would do the same for you, were the situations reversed. In other words, cooperating with others might be advantageous to a person if the cooperation was reciprocated at a future time, when one could in turn derive large benefit from aid. However, this is a big if! Indeed, the problem of preventing "free riders," those who take the benefit without paying the cost, is one of the most perennial within game theory.

Still, it seems apparent that humans are strong reciprocal altruists, with a significant disposition to cooperate despite the risks of nonreciprocation (Trivers, 1971). We have social welfare agencies, international relief organizations, charitable foundations, and many less formal supports for the disadvantaged, who are typically unrelated to their benefactors. Providing empirical support for the proposition that humans are dispositionally inclined to take the risk of cooperation, Caporael, Dawes, Orbell, and Van de Kragt (1989) showed that people would cooperate at surprisingly high rates in one-shot prisoner's dilemmas, despite the fact that defection is the "most rational" strategy in such situations. Perhaps an optimistic perspective regarding the positive social nature of human beings is warranted after all.

Cheater-Detection as a Second Cooperation-Relevant Disposition

How might we further support the proposition that humans are fundamentally cooperative and other oriented? One way is to seek evidence of further adaptations that should also be present within human nature if the cooperative proposition is correct. One such candidate is obvious: We should have a cheater-detection mechanism, that is, a sensitivity to the possibility of being exploited by others who might take undue advantage of our efforts and charity. Indeed, as discussed in chapter 4, Cosmides (1989) provided rather convincing evidence for this proposition, in research using the Wason selection task. Cosmides argued that a cheater-detection feature had to evolve, once humans went down the path of reciprocal altruism—this is the only way the cooperative strategy could have worked. Laboratory research on social dilemmas further confirms the "cheater sensitivity" idea: Even dispositional cooperators will readily shift to defection when they encounter opponents who consistently defect (Kelley & Stahelski, 1970). The importance of social reputation also supports the idea that humans are alert cheater-detectors—once one is known as an exploiter or as being untrustworthy, it is very difficult to win one's way back into others' good graces (D. S. Wilson et al., 2000).

Axelrod's Tournaments

To summarize so far, it appears that there are at least two features of human nature relevant to bringing about mutual cooperation: first, an initial disposition to cooperate, when possible; and second, a disposition to detect and punish cheaters, who exploit the first disposition. This idea that reciprocal altruism and cheater-detection are linked evolved social strategies is perhaps best supported in Axelrod's (1984) well-known computer simulation tournaments, which compared the functional efficacy of a wide variety of strategies for playing iterated two-person prisoner's dilemmas. Axelrod invited leading game theorists from around the world to submit strategies or algorithms for making decisions in a round-robin tournament, in which each submitted strategy would be pit for 200 rounds against each other submitted strategy. The strategy that accumulated the most points, averaging across all of its opponents, would be the winner. Widely varying strategies were submitted, most of them focused on outfoxing or achieving some type of competitive advantage over the generic opponent.

Surprisingly, the strategy that won the tournament was the simplest, and the one that sought no advantage whatsoever: "tit-for-tat." The classic tit-for-tat strategy involves starting with cooperation, and then doing whatever your opponent did on the last move. If the opponent defected last time, you defect now. If the opponent cooperated last time, you cooperate now. Although the tit-for-tat strategy never won a match against another strategy (in fact, the best it can do is tie), it scored the most points overall (and won the tournament) by maximizing the mutual cooperation (CC) outcome across all matches. In contrast, the other strategies more often got caught in the "DD lock," a situation in which both protagonists are defecting and cannot seem to escape this mutually detrimental state of affairs.

What was the source of tit-for-tat's advantage? In his 1984 book *The Evolution of Cooperation,* Axelrod ascribed beneficial three features to the strategy: First, it was "nice," meaning that it cooperated on the first move (another variant of tit-for-tat, which defected on the first move, did not fare as well). Second, it was "punitive," meaning that it did not tolerate the other's defection. If the opponent defects, tit-for-tat always defects immediately, in retaliation, as it were. Third, tit-for-tat was "forgiving," meaning that it immediately returns to cooperation after its opponent returns to cooperation.

In terms of the two cooperative-relevant dispositions just discussed, "niceness" is analogous to the human disposition to seek reciprocal altruism (i.e., mutually beneficial relations), and "punitiveness" is analogous to the disposition toward cheater-detection, a characteristic without which cooperation cannot be maintained. However, Axelrod's results further suggest that "forgiveness" may be a third necessary precondition for reciprocal altruism to evolve—a disposition that allows mutually beneficial cooperation to be reinstated, following inevitable breakdowns in cooperation.

Still, it is apparent that mutual cooperation remains ever unstable and uncertain, given the ever-present temptation to cheat, and the necessity of overcoming one another's lapses in this regard. Exacerbating the problem is the fact that there is typically considerable randomness or "noise" in both decision communication and strategy deployment (Kraines & Kraines, 1995), the fact that defection is often undetectable, especially in large-group situations (in which social loafing and free-riding become significant problems; Komorita & Parks, 1995), and the fact that sanctioning systems are often applied in a biased or inconsistent matter (such that an upper class exempts itself from the rules, thereby exploiting an underclass). In what other ways might the risks be mitigated, such that cooperation becomes a more viable strategy? And, correspondingly, what other features might we look for within human nature to support the proposition that humans are fundamentally cooperative creatures?

The Group Selection Concept

Further possibilities for cooperative risk mitigation are suggested by the concept of "group selection," which is the idea that natural selection might sometimes occur at the level of groups, rather than at the level of individuals. The group selection concept has long been controversial in evolutionary biology, because early proponents sometimes assumed that it means that animals evolved to sacrifice themselves "for the good of the group" (or species; Wynne-Edwards, 1962). However, more recent theorizing, based on the concept of the selfish gene (Dawkins, 1976), indicated that such a disposition could not evolve—that is, we should never see animals sacrificing themselves for no return on the investment. Another reason for scientific reluctance to accept the group selection concept, I believe, is reductionist resistance to the idea that holistic factors (i.e., the group in which one is nested) have irreducible influence on human behavior and outcomes.

David Sloan Wilson and his colleagues (Sober & Wilson, 1998; Wilson & Sober, 1994) advocated a less extreme view of group selection, in which animals derive distinct individual benefits from being encompassed within cooperative groups, benefits that can sometimes be enough to counterbalance the risk of being overly cooperative within such groups. According to Wilson, in order to see group selection at work, it is essential to decompose individual outcomes into the part resultant from intragroup processes, and the part resultant from intergroup processes. To fail to do so is to make the "averaging fallacy," in which individual outcomes are completely attributed to individual-level (and typically within-group) processes. When the averaging fallacy is made, the advantages of competition and defection may be overestimated, and the advantages of cooperative group membership underestimated (Sober & Wilson, 1998).

In order to illustrate this point more clearly, it is necessary to reconsider hierarchical or multilevel statistical models (first discussed in chap. 2). Again, in such models, a particular person's outcomes are determined by factors at more than one level of analysis. Variation in individual outcomes may be partitioned into two independent sources: that resultant from within-group processes and dynamics (the lower level), and that resultant from between-group processes and dynamics (the upper level). There can be different effects or patterns of effects at each level of analysis, which must be considered jointly in order to understand the final outcome. Reiterating the example discussed in chapter 2, elementary students' outcomes are not determined simply by their individual characteristics (such as their own intelligence), but also by the characteristics of the class in which they are nested (such as the teacher's instructional philosophy). Research in a wide variety of fields, over the last 20 years, has confirmed the importance of considering such "group composition effects" (Bryk & Raudenbush, 1992).

Sheldon and McGregor (2000) recently reported two-level data supportive of Sober and Wilson's (1998) group selection model, in a laboratory study of the tragedy of the commons. Participants were first placed into groups of four, based on their scores on the Aspirations Index, a measure of intrinsic versus extrinsic valuing (Kasser & Ryan, 1993, 1996; discussed in chap. 6). Some groups consisted of four participants with predominantly intrinsic and prosocial values (i.e., community, intimacy, growth); some groups consisted of four participants with predominantly extrinsic and self-serving values (i.e., money, fame, beauty); and some groups consisted of two of each type. Participants made repeated bids concerning a group resource, specifically a forest. The forest replenished at a 10% rate, and each group continued bidding until their forest was gone. Sheldon and McGregor (2000) hoped to show that "nice groups finish first," by showing that intrinsic groups received the largest score in the resource dilemma. In other words, despite their self-restraint, they should perhaps score better because they benefit from the replenishment of the forest over time.

Hierarchical linear modeling revealed support for this initial idea, but also suggested a more complex picture. Specifically, individual value scores had contradictory influence on individual harvest totals, at within-group and between-group levels of analysis. Group members who were more intrinsic than their groupmates harvested less than their groupmates, and thus did worse, within groups. However, members of groups that were more intrinsic than the other groups harvested more, because of their group's aggregate ability to preserve the resource. Overall, intrinsic individuals did no better or worse than extrinsic individuals, because the within- and between-group effects essentially canceled out.

Thus, it appears that the aggregate (and real-life) outcome for dispositional cooperators is crucially dependent on a particular social-contextual factor: the extent to which cooperators are concentrated within groups, such that would-be exploiters are excluded from their midst. Without such a context, cooperators are at a significant disadvantage. Notice that this fact again supports the hierarchical pluralism perspective discussed in chapter 2, which says that factors at the social interaction level of analysis can have higher level effects that are irreducible to lower level factors. This perspective also highlights one potentially important reason for the slow endorsement of the group selection idea by the biological community: reductionist resistance to the idea of higher level processes, that is, higher level selection.

The Problem of Group Assortation

Notably, in the Sheldon and McGregor (2000) study, those high in intrinsic value orientation were concentrated together by *experimental assignment* (as were those high in extrinsic value orientation). Could intrinsic types achieve such an assortative arrangement on their own? This would seem to be an essential ability for cooperators to have, in order for cooperation to be a stable and viable strategy. Indeed, given the enduring vulnerability of cooperators, such an ability might viewed as a *fourth* cooperation-relevant adaptation, in addition to the three already discussed (reciprocal altruism, cheater detection, and the willingness to forgive). Finding such an ability would further support the optimistic idea that humans have a species-typical disposition toward cooperation and positive sociality.

Sheldon, Sheldon, and Osbaldiston (2000) addressed the self-assortation question by inviting college students to play an *n*-person prisoner's dilemma game for movie ticket prizes (which went to the top 15% of game scorers). Participants completed questionnaires in which they listed three friends, to whom the researchers also sent questionnaires. All participants' (extrinsic vs. intrinsic) values were assessed, including both primary participants and secondary (primary participant-selected) participants. Then an N-PDG was presented. Participants and their friends constituted self-selected groups, whose outcomes were pooled over five rounds of bidding, in order to determine each individual's total outcome. Figure 8.2 presents the payoff matrix that was employed to determine each person's score on each round.

First, Sheldon, Sheldon, and Osbaldiston (2000) demonstrated, via intraclass correlational analysis, that significant value-based assortation had occurred during group formation; specifically, participants with intrinsic values tended to select other intrinsic participants for their groups, and vice versa for participants with more

If all four choose C: **Each gets 8**

If 3 choose C and 1 chooses D: **Cs get 6, D gets 11**

If 2 choose C and 2 choose D: **Cs get 4, Ds get 9**

If 1 chooses C and 3 choose D: **C gets 2, Ds get 7**

If all four choose D: **Each gets 5**

FIG. 8.2.   N-Person prisoner's dilemma matrix used by Sheldon, Sheldon, and Osbaldiston (2000).

extrinsic values. Such heterogeneity at the group level is an important precondition for group selection to occur (Sober & Wilson, 1998)—if groups do not differ then there can be no advantage in belonging to one group rather than another. Apparently, those with prosocial values can indeed successfully assort with one another.

Second, Sheldon, Sheldon, and Osbaldiston (2000) showed that intrinsic values had a significant positive effect on participant game scores at the between-groups level of analysis, and a significant negative effect on game score at the within-group level of analysis, replicating the finding of Sheldon and McGregor (2000). That is, once again, groups with more intrinsic individuals did better, but more intrinsic individuals did worse within groups. Because of these largely canceling effects, intrinsic individuals fared no worse than extrinsic individuals, on average. Although this may not sound impressive, it was actually quite striking given the intrinsic types' much greater vulnerability to exploitation. By aggregating themselves into groups prior to the game, they managed to completely mitigate their disadvantage. Indeed, if group-level heterogeneity (i.e., the intraclass correlation) had been even larger, reflecting even greater value-based assortation, then the intrinsic types would have achieved a clear victory. Sheldon, Sheldon, and Osbaldiston (2000) suggested that the correlation might have been larger if the primary participants had been aware of the game at the time they chose secondary participants.

Notably, D. S. Wilson's contemporary group selection model can be viewed as "just another way of doing the math" for traditional reciprocal altruism theory (Pinker, 2002). Perhaps the primary advantage of the group selection perspective is that it enables a clear distinction to be made between intergroup and intragroup effects, and for independent consideration (and prediction) of the effects of these two different levels of analysis. Using this framework, researchers may be less apt to make the "averaging fallacy," in which individual outcomes are assumed to result primarily from within-group processes. In addition, the group selection perspective allows for consideration of the dynamic relation between the two levels of analysis. How bad does the within-group free rider problem have to get, before the between-group advantage derived from cooperation disappears? This question involves comparing the size of main effects at two different levels of analysis. Or, in what types of group is a particular personality trait (such as Machiavellianism) most advantageous for the individual, and in what type of group is it less advantageous? This question involves evaluating whether there are cross-level interactions between individual traits and group traits. Evaluating these types of effect is an important task for any multilevel perspective on optimal human being.

To conclude this section, we have been considering what features of human nature should be present if humans are fundamentally prosocial and cooperative, as we might like to believe. Several relevant features have been observed: Humans are prone to cooperate, even when this is an "irrational" thing to do (i.e., in one-shot dilemmas). But in compensation, we are also very sensitive to cheaters. However, most of us are reasonably forgiving as well, always hoping to arrive at a more congenial state of affairs. Finally, we have an ability to preassociate with others who will cooperate with us, reducing the risk of cooperative social strategies. These features suggest that human nature may be fundamentally cooperative after all.

OPTIMAL HUMAN BEING FROM A GAME-THEORY PERSPECTIVE

Rather than postponing discussion of optimal human being as seen from the game-theory perspective until the end of the chapter, I consider it here, while the preceding concepts are fresh and in order to further illustrate the game-theory perspective on human nature. Afterward, in the latter part of the chapter, I turn to the social role perspective.

Playing Tit-for-Tat

What is optimal human being, from the perspective of evolutionary game theory? That is, what approach to social dilemmas yields the most resources? The fact that tit-for-tat won Axelrod's (1984) tournament indicates that the "optimal way to be" involves doing what it takes to cooperate with as many people as one can. Specifically, by being "nice," "punitive," and "forgiving," one maximizes other's cooperation with oneself, and thus one's own long-term individual outcomes and resources. Indeed, we might take these three features of tit-for-tat as foundational prescriptions for optimal human being at the social interaction level of analysis.

Should Tit-for-Tat Sometimes Be Exploitative?

However, the picture is also more complicated than this. From a strictly resource-acquisition standpoint, the ideal strategy may be "tit-for-tat plus a provision to defect repeatedly when the opponent permits it," because this strategy should score more points than simple tit-for-tat. Concretely, this would mean that someone playing the tit-for-tat strategy should throw in a defection every now and then, to see if one has perhaps has met a "patsy." If the other person lets one get away with it, then one should milk the situation for all it is worth. This reasoning suggests that a fourth possible recommendation for optimal social being, derivable from the game-theory perspective, might be to "exploit others whenever possible." Clearly, such a conclusion would not be consistent with my claim that humans are fundamentally cooperative and other oriented!

To illustrate the potential importance of being "willing to exploit," let us return to the findings of Sheldon and McGregor (2000) and Sheldon, Sheldon, and Osbaldiston (2000). Figure 8.3 shows how individuals' game scores in Sheldon and McGregor (2000) varied as a function of both the type of group in which the person was nested (extrinsic or intrinsic?) and the participants' relative intrinsic value standing within his or her group (less than average, or more than average?). Which participants achieved the highest scores of all in this study? The answer: those nested within relatively intrinsic groups, but who had relatively more extrinsic values compared to their groupmates. In this case they received both the between-group benefit that comes from being matched with self-restrained groupmates and the within-group benefit that comes from out-harvesting (or out-defecting on) one's groupmates. Again, does this mean that the "optimal way

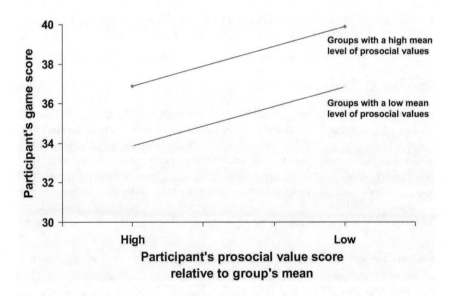

FIG. 8.3.   Relationship between extrinsic value orientation and cumulative harvest as a function of both group membership and relative standing within groups. Reprinted from *Human Nature 11:4,* p. 398. Copyright © 2000 by Walter de Gruyter, Inc. Published by Aldine de Gruyter, Hawthorne, NY.

to be," at the social interaction level of analysis, includes being willing to exploit vulnerable others?

The Long-Term Nonviability of Exploitative Strategies

I suggest that the answer to the question is "No," because of the significant problems associated with exploitative strategies in the long run. Once other group members realize that a person is harvesting more than others, or defecting more often, they may begin punishing or sanctioning that person, or might even expel the person from the group altogether. Furthermore, the exploiter's problems may not end after he or she is expelled from a group: Word of such events often travels to other groups, which as a result may be more reluctant to accept that person. Thus, he or she may end up without any group-level benefits at all. These reputational considerations suggest that the material benefits of exploiting one's cooperative groupmates may not last in the long term. Indeed, this would be expected, given the aforementioned likelihood that all humans, including cooperators, possess cheater-detection mechanisms and a willingness to punish exploiters.

The Emotional Costs of Exploitation

In addition, there are other considerations for optimal human being besides mere resource acquisition. Indeed, very few life philosophies assert that resource acquisition is the ultimate route to happiness and personal thriving—instead, most philosophies assert that materialism and status seeking are harmful for optimal personality development. The wisdom of this idea is supported by the negative association between strong extrinsic valuing and psychological well-being, discussed in chapter 6—those who concentrate too much on wealth, looks, and status (all implying competition and temptations to exploitation) tend to pay a price in happiness, and eventually in physical health (Kasser, 2002). Again, Kasser (2002) suggested that this negative association occurs in large part because status-based and materialistic ambitions lead to failure of relatedness need satisfaction. It is difficult to connect authentically with another person if one is bent on using the person as a stepping-stone to a self-serving goal!

Within social dilemma contexts, exploitative behaviors might lead to relatedness or belongingness need deprivation for several reasons. First, those who undermine cooperating groups know (at some level) that they are taking advantage of the others, a fact likely to induce implicit guilt and shame and a disconnection from others. Second, when others suspect or find out what the exploiter is doing, they may react with hostility or disgust, even if they do not go so far as to exclude the person altogether. This would further detract from belongingness need satisfaction, and also from self-esteem, according to sociometer theory (Leary & Baumeister, 2000). Thus, although competitors may achieve (at least short-term) material gain, they may pay a price in psychosocial integration and psychological well-being.

Still, why should evolution "care" about people's well-being and happiness? After all, survival and reproduction are the drivers of evolution, not happiness and bliss—if being miserable produced greater survival and reproductive benefits, we would all be miserable! In this light, the fact that we are not all miserable—indeed, that the majority of people around the world instead report being reasonably happy (Myers, 2000)—is suggestive. In particular, it suggests that the causes of evolutionary success (i.e., sustained cooperation; Axelrod, 1984) are also causes of psychological well-being and happiness. Perhaps there is not so much conflict between evolved human nature and individual happiness, after all (Buss, 2000).

The Roots of Exploitative Dispositions

If exploitation is indeed an inadvisable strategy, then why do some people follow it? In other words, what are the roots of overly competitive, extrinsic, or exploitative interpersonal orientations? As discussed in chapter 7, a prominent candidate is psychological insecurity, resultant when environments and relationships are fundamentally unstable and inconsistent. Consistent with this idea, Kasser, Ryan, Zax, and Sameroff (1995) showed that children of cold, controlling parents, or children raised in insecure or dangerous neighborhoods, are more likely to develop extrinsic values. Focusing on dispositions directly relevant to behavior in social dilemmas, Van Lange, De Bruin, Otten, and Joireman (1997) showed that competitive value orientations are associated with insecure attachment styles.

Of course, competitive or extrinsic orientations may sometimes be appropriate, within negative circumstances—one must be prepared to retaliate in defense against exploiters, and to perhaps battle for one's share of the resources when they are overly scarce. The potential problem with dispositional competitiveness comes later on, when circumstances change for the better. By this time the competitor may not be able to reform, feeling that life has handed him or her a "bum deal," that it is a dog-eat-dog world, and that he or she is deserving of compensation and special rewards. Indeed, asymmetries of this type are typically observed, such that competitors typically do not switch to cooperation against cooperators, although cooperators will switch to competition against competitors—competitors seem to be more rigid and inflexible, unable to accommodate to benign circumstances (Kelley & Stahelski, 1970). In attachment theory terms, competitors may have developed a negative "internal working model" regarding others' trustworthiness (Van Lange et al., 1997), which impedes their social relations in the present. In ego-developmental terms, competitors may exist in a state of "arrested development," unable to adapt their strategy and style to the current social context (Ryan, 1995).

Mealey's (1995) evolutionary analysis of sociopathy, the pathological tendency to exploit and dehumanize others, is consistent with the idea that exploitative dispositions are primarily environmentally based. Mealey distinguished between "primary" sociopathy, in which a person's antisocial disposition is based on genetic factors, and "secondary" sociopathy, in which a person's antisocial disposition is based on a negative rearing environment. Mealey showed that primary sociopathy is quite rare (occurring in perhaps 2% of all cases of sociopathy); the vast majority of antisocial pathologies result from the person's early negative experiences in life, which have persistent negative influences. She further argued that the genetically based cases do not represent an evolved adaptation, but rather reflect genetic anomalies or transcription errors. If this is true, it again suggests that humans evolved to be reciprocal altruists, a tendency that should predominate unless cooperation is untenable. Mealey's analysis also supports my suggestion that if such situations generally characterize a person's childhood environment, then the person will have considerable difficulty adapting to more positive circumstances, should these arise.

Still, there is also some reason for optimism regarding dispositional competitors' potential to shift toward more cooperative strategies as a result of life experience. As one example, Sheldon (1999b) conducted repeated prisoner's dilemma tournaments, 1 month apart, in which all participants faced a tit-for-tat strategy during the first session, and participants were randomly paired against other participants in the second session. Sheldon showed that those with competitive dispositions evidenced the largest shift toward greater cooperation during the second session, after having faced the "punitive" tit-for-tat in the first session; that is, they had accommodated their strategy to the fact that exploiting the opponent was not feasible. It appears that dispositional competitors, and perhaps even sociopaths, retain the potential to reform to a more positive style of social interaction. Indeed, this is what we would expect, given the optimistic proposition that cooperation and positive sociality are fundamental characteristics of human nature.

To conclude this section, we have been considering whether optimal human being at the social interaction level of analysis entails playing the tit-for-tat strategy with an additional provision, of being willing to exploit others when conditions permit. However, the considerations discussed lead to the conclusion that the "optimal way to be," from a social game-theory perspective, is instead to play a nonexploitative version of tit-for-tat. This fourth game-theory prescription will allow one to maximize one's resource acquisition in the long term, and also to satisfy one's need for relatedness and belongingness.

When Cooperation Fails

What if those around are not willing to cooperate, no matter how cooperative, forgiving, and nonexploitative one is? In other words, might a search for cooperation and high-quality social experience actually be maladaptive in such circumstances? Perhaps in some social contexts, positive social goals should be abandoned in favor of goals that serve more of a damage control function. For example, a child in an uncaring or abusive home, or a wife in a violent marriage, or a teenager in a hostile school environment, might be best served by refusing to allow him- or herself to be exploited by abusers—that is, by remaining combative and continuing to defect for as long as necessary. Supporting this idea, tit-for-tat will defect consistently when the other person continues defecting—waiting for the other to make an "overture."

However, this points to a potential problem with the conventional tit-for-tat strategy, not yet considered: that tit-for-tat has no provision for making an "overture" itself. Thus, if tit-for-tat finds itself paired against a generally cooperative strategy that also has no overture-making provision, then the two parties may find themselves stuck for good in the suboptimal DD lock. This suggests that tit-for-tat strategies that periodically make cooperative efforts during times of strife might fare best overall (see Wu & Axelrod, 1995, for supportive data). This observation also points to a potential limitation of the socioemotional strategy of being resolutely hostile in negative circumstances—namely, that one may miss opportunities to transform the situation. In sum, "making overtures," at least on occasion, might be viewed as a fifth game-theoretical prescription for optimal human being, along with being cooperative, punitive, forgiving, and non-exploitative. This idea is considered further in the chapter summary.

THE SOCIAL ROLE PERSPECTIVE ON SOCIAL INTERACTION

Let us shift focus, away from the evolutionary game theory perspective, to a different brand of theory that is perhaps equally relevant to the issue of social adaptation: social role theory. Role theory addresses the ways in which individuals adopt specialized functions within society, a process that influences many important social outcomes, such as which individuals interact (i.e., a teacher and a student; an employee and a manager; a teammate and another teammate), how they interact (i.e., as equals or in subordinate/superordinate power relationships), and what results from their interaction (i.e., learning, producing, playing). In particular, social role theory considers the social processes that induce individuals to occupy various social roles, performing the behaviors prescribed for those roles. Indeed, as discussed in chapter 2, some social and sociological perspectives assert that human behavior is largely determined by normative role prescriptions, which supply rules and expectations for those who play the role (Kincaid, 1997). Such role prescriptions may be viewed as causal factors embedded at the social and cultural level of analysis, which, again, have irreducible holistic influence on human behavior.

Optimal Human Being According to Role Theory

There are many more role-theory concepts that could be discussed, as several books have been written on the topic (Biddle, 1979; Deasy, 1964). However, I proceed on from the brief introduction just given to consider the nature of optimal human being from this point of view. In the process, a variety of issues in role theory are illustrated.

What is optimal human being, from the perspective of traditional social role theory? Actually, this question is somewhat deemphasized within such perspectives, because they focus more on optimal social being, that is, the smooth functioning of society. However, a first prescription for optimal (individual) human being derivable from the role perspective would probably be: "Play one's roles to the best of one's ability, so that both personal and social benefits accrue." In other words, workers should work, fathers should father, mentors should mentor, and coaches should coach, all to the best of their ability.

The Question of Person–Role Fit

Traditional role theory focuses primarily on the contextual or life-span factors that prompt people to adopt particular roles in particular situations or at particular times (Biddle, 1979). Again, this reflects the typical sociological assumption discussed in chapter 2, that the primary determinants of behavior reside at this higher level of analysis. As a result, role theory has given less attention to the personality level of analysis and the question of how personality influences which roles a person occupies. This appears to be an important question, because, after all, people have some choice about what roles they embrace or resist. Some adults willingly become parents, and others avoid this role; some adults willingly become spouses, and others avoid this role. Given this freedom of choice, the question becomes: Has the person chosen the "right" roles for him- or herself? What if he or she is trying too hard to be something he or she is not? What if this attempted interface between the person's personality and the social world is the wrong interface? The claim that person–role fit matters is similar to the claim made in chapter 6, that self-concordance (person–goal fit) matters (Sheldon, 2002).

Person–role fit has been considered extensively in the counseling, personnel selection, and industrial–organizational literature, where it is conceptualized as person–vocation fit or person–job fit (Holland, 1985; Kristoff, 1996). How should employees select jobs, and how should employers select employees for particular jobs, so that the demands of the job are best met? Although this research supports the general proposition that person–role fit matters, its narrow focus on vocational choice limits its relevance for the question of optimal human being. When one turns to the personality literature, one finds that surprisingly little research has attempted to connect traditional personality constructs with social role theories; also, surprisingly little research has considered how personality–role fit influences the quality of a person's life (but see Roberts & Donahue, 1994). Thus, I now consider some of my own work in this area, which begins to explore these issues.

Sheldon, Ryan, Rawsthorne, and Ilardi (1997) examined the question of person–role fit in detail, in a study of the within-subject variations in the Big Five traits that occur across different roles within people's lives (these five traits were discussed in chap. 5). Participants rated themselves on each trait (openness, extraversion, neuroticism, agreeableness, and conscientiousness), separately within each of the five roles of student, friend, employee, child, and romantic partner. They also rated their sense of satisfaction in each role, and the extent to which they feel stressed in each role. Finally, they rated how authentic or personally expressive they feel when playing each role, which served as a measure of person–role fit.

Sheldon et al. (1997) discovered that on average, people manifest different levels of the Big Five traits in different roles (i.e., more neuroticism in the student role, less agreeableness in the child role, and so on). This further supports a general claim of this book, that human behavior and personality are irreducibly influenced by higher level or more holistic factors, in this case, by one's social role context. Sheldon et al. also found that some roles are more satisfying than others; for example, participants did not enjoy the "employee" role, given that the jobs available to college students tend to be menial and low-paying, but they did enjoy the "romantic partner" role, in which presumably their relatedness needs were met. Finally, Sheldon et al. found that the relationship between role occupation and satisfaction depended on how authentic students felt in each role. For example, those who felt more authentic in the employee role reported ample satisfaction in that role, and those who felt inauthentic in the romantic partner role reported reduced satisfaction within that role. In other words, role-playing is not as well embraced or enjoyed when the demands of the role do not seem to fit one's personality.

Bettencourt and Sheldon (2001) further demonstrated the importance of person–role fit, in several studies. Their Study 5, an experimental study, provided the strongest evidence. Participants were randomly assigned to play one of five roles during a group discussion exercise: Idea person (who brainstormed approaches to the topic), devil's advocate (who criticized the idea person's ideas), moderator (who sought common ground between the latter two), secretary (who recorded the group's final answer to the question), and announcer (who spoke the group's conclusion to the class as a whole). Two months before the exercise, participants had rated themselves on 20 trait terms. Before receiving their assignment to a role, participants rated the importance of each of the 20 trait terms to each of the five roles that had been described. "Person–role fit" was operationalized as the extent to which the person's earlier self-rated trait strengths matched the role-requirements (as rated both by the participant him- or herself, and by the class as a whole). As hypothesized, Bettencourt and Sheldon (2001) showed that both measures of person–role fit predicted better performance in the role, and better mood while playing the role. In short, people liked playing the role better, and performed it better, if it fit their personalities. Thus, "choose roles that fit one's personality" appears to be a second possible prescription for optimal human being, derivable from a role theory perspective.

The Importance of Role Internalization

In short, it appears that before accepting a role, a person should think carefully about whether the role is appropriate for his or her dispositions, talents, and inclinations. Unfortunately, in some cases people cannot know the answer to these questions in advance. For example, a person starting a new job, a person starting a new relationship, or a person contemplating parenthood may simply not have the experience necessary to make a fully informed judgment. In other cases, one may have little choice about adopting a role, as in the case of unplanned parenthood. In both cases, a crucial factor influencing the person's success in the new role is likely to be the quality of his or her motivation to occupy the role. Can the person engage in the role fully and authentically, despite any underlying uncertainty about the self-appropriateness of the role? In Sartre's (1965) terms, can the person enact the role with "good faith," so that he or she has the best chance of benefiting from his or her efforts? This question reflects the possibility discussed in chapter 1, that a certain "intentional attitude," or way of living and being, may be characteristic of optimal human being (discussed further in chap. 10). It also suggests a third prescription for optimal human being that is derivable from the social role perspective, in addition to "play your roles well" and "choose personally appropriate roles"—namely, "if you have to play a role that does not fit you, do your best to internalize and own it anyway."

Role internalization is influenced by at least two factors. One is personality and personal maturity. For example, those with greater ego development, higher agreeableness, or greater autonomy orientation are more likely to responsibly enact a new role or role obligation (Sheldon et al., 1997). In terms of psychosocial theory, they are more likely to develop an "achieved identity" (Marcia, 2002) with respect to the role. In contrast, those at less advanced stages of ego development, with lower trait agreeableness, or with a greater tendency to feel controlled by external forces may be less able to authentically engage in a new role. In terms of psychosocial theory, they are more likely to feel "diffused" identity with respect to the new role, perhaps because they are unable to outgrow their "foreclosure" on older, outdated roles.

A second relevant factor influencing role internalization concerns the social environment, and its level of supportiveness. What social-contextual factors promote individuals' internalization of roles and role prescriptions, such that when these factors are present, nearly anyone might move toward greater ownership of the roles involved? Self-determination theory (SDT) has made clear claims regarding this issue, and has also provided considerable relevant empirical data (see Ryan & Stiller, 1991). Specifically, autonomy support is of critical importance, according to SDT. Especially when there is an unequal balance of power, it is important for authorities (i.e., teachers, coaches, bosses, parents) to promote a subordinate's sense of freely choosing to engage in the behavior. In this case, subordinates can come to feel that they are the cause of the behavior (rather than the situation or the authority being the cause), thus taking maximal responsibility for the behaviors and roles they are being asked to adopt.

The practice of autonomy support has at least three important facets (Deci, Eghrari, Patrick, & Leone, 1994; Sheldon, Williams, & Joiner, 2003). First, authorities should provide subordinates with as many choices as possible. For example, a teacher hoping to encourage students to take responsibility for various classroom functions might allow each student to select the role he or she wants to play. Second, authorities should take subordinates' perspectives when an unpleasant or aversive role is being promoted, or when choice cannot be provided. For example, a manager, hoping to encourage an employee to take over a tedious administrative chore, might say, "Susan, I need you to stay on top of updating this database for me. Believe me, I know how you may feel about this—I once had to do it myself!" Third, authorities should provide a meaningful rationale when an unpleasant or aversive role is being promoted (i.e., "But I no longer have the time, and will need to trust somebody else to do it. Just remember how important this job is to the organization"). When subordinates feel that their right to choose is being respected, then they tend to internalize the role or duty into their sense of self, a desirable appropriative process in which the social influence and the self levels of analysis come into harmony (Deci & Ryan, 1991). This in turn leads to responsible role enactment, which in turn leads to further benefits, including enhanced role competence (Bettencourt & Sheldon, 2001).

The foregoing discussion leads to articulation of a fourth possible principle for optimizing human being, as seen from the perspective of social role theory; in addition to performing one's own roles as well as possible, selecting roles that fit one's personality, and doing one's best to internalize necessary roles that may not fit one's personality, one should also "treat others in ways that help them internalize their roles."

SUMMARIZING: OPTIMAL HUMAN BEING
AT THE SOCIAL INTERACTION LEVEL OF ANALYSIS

In sum, several broad conclusions can be drawn from this chapter concerning "the optimal way to be" with respect to others and the social surround. The game theory perspective, discussed in the first part of the chapter, suggested five central prescriptions for optimal human being at this level of analysis. First, cooperate whenever one can; thus, one will gain the many benefits of reciprocal altruism. Second, do one's best to detect and punish defectors. Thus, one will avoid some of the drawbacks of the cooperative strategy. Third, remain open to the possibility that defectors have reformed, that is, be ready to forgive them; thus, one will gain an ability to reinstate cooperation when the other takes the initiative to do so. Again, these three characteristics, taken together, constitute the tit-for-tat strategy. However, the considerations discussed later in the chapter suggested two further recommendations as well. Fourth, be prepared to make overtures toward cooperation, at times when mutual defection reigns. In this case one will achieve a benefit not afforded by simple tit-for-tat, namely, the ability to overcome a potentially cooperative other's unwillingness to make overtures himself. Fifth, avoid the temptation to exploit those who will permit it, because ultimately it will come back to haunt one (either in terms of undermining one's resource acquisition after others catch on, or in terms of undermining one's need satisfaction and well-being, or both). In addition, a sixth potential prescription, derived from the group selection studies cited earlier, might be to try to intentionally associate yourself with others who you believe will cooperate with you (Sober & Wilson, 1998).

The social role perspective, discussed in the second part of the chapter, suggests four prescriptions for optimal human being at the social interaction level of analysis. First, play your roles to the best of your ability. On average, this will tend to bring both personal and social benefits. Second, seek out roles or functions that suit your personality traits and characteristics. In this way, social context and individual personality (the seventh and eighth levels in Fig. 2.1) will achieve a harmonious resolution. Third, if you must adopt roles that do not suit you well (i.e., if an introvert feels the need to speak for a community organization, knowing that only he or she has the necessary knowledge), then do your best to internalize that role, to make it part of your sense of self anyway. In Sartre's (1965) terms, you will thus gain the benefits that come from acting "in good faith." Fourth, if you are trying to motivate others to take on roles, be sure to remember to support their autonomy. This will best support their internalization of the role, and their ability to achieve harmony between their sense of self and the social context. In this way, benefits will be maximized for all.

Conclusion

This concludes my discussion of optimal human being at the social interaction level of analysis (Level 8 in Fig. 2.1), as seen from the perspective of game theory and role theory. Of course, the influence of social processes on individual behavior does not stop here; dyads and groups are always nested within particular cultures, with their unique histories, shared ideas, and common practices. Such cultural factors doubtless have many holistic or top-down effects on the course of social interactions and also on the personalities nested within those interactions. Thus, chapter 9 proceeds to consider this final level of analysis within Fig. 2.1.

9

The Cultural Level of Analysis: Memes, Genes, and Other Themes

In this chapter I consider the cultural level of analysis and its influence on human behavior. This is also a huge field, worthy of a book (or many books) in itself. Thus again, of necessity, I confine myself to just a few important issues. First, I consider some definitions of culture, pointing out recent trends to define it in terms of socially transmitted mental contents and cognitive processes, rather than as particular social traditions or patterns of social behavior. Next, I consider the epistemological status of the cultural level of analysis. Does culture have its own unique sphere of influence, or might its effects instead be reducible to effects of lower levels of analysis, such as genetic constitution, cognitive process, individual personality, or social interaction (see Fig. 2.1)? By considering the relationship between cultural evolution and genetic evolution, I try to show that culture, located at the top of the Fig. 2.1 hierarchy, has legitimate causal status. Next, I consider some important dimensions of cultural difference, in particular, the distinction between individualism and collectivism. I try to demonstrate the adaptive advantages and disadvantages of each of these cultural modes for its members, using a game-theory perspective. After having laid this groundwork, in the last part of the chapter I consider the question of optimal human being as seen from the cultural perspective. How does the "optimal human" relate and contribute to his or her culture, at the same time that he or she is fundamentally influenced by it? Also, is there such a thing as optimal *cultural* being? If so, what characterizes it?

DEFINING CULTURE

An early definition of culture was "that complex whole which includes knowledge, belief, art, morals, custom and any other capabilities and habits acquired by

164

man as a member of society" (Tylor, 1889, p. 1). Although this definition is admirably inclusive, it contains few hints as to the likely mechanisms and processes of culture and enculturation, and also suggests that almost any human behavior might be labeled as culture. Thus, within the past 30 years, "ideational" theories of culture have come to predominate (Durham, 1991), which narrow the definition by focusing on culture as information that is both stored within and transmitted between human brains. For example, Geertz (1973) defined culture as "an historically transmitted pattern of meanings embodied in symbols, a system of inherited conceptions expressed in symbolic forms by means of which men communicate, perpetuate, and develop their knowledge about and attitudes towards life" (p. 89). More recently, D'Andrade (1995) defined culture as "learned systems of meaning, communicated by means of natural language and other symbols" (p. 116). Thus, consistent with the cognitive revolution discussed earlier in this book, most cultural anthropologists now assume that culture is best understood in terms of specifiable cognitive contents, rules and processes that are shared by large groups of individuals. Understanding these rules will help us to understand both the interpersonal behavior of individuals within cultures (as influenced by norms, manners, customs) and the institutions and material products of cultures (i.e., governments, inventions, and gross national product, GNP).

THE LEGITIMACY OF THE CULTURAL LEVEL OF ANALYSIS

One appeal of ideational approaches is that they make culture more mental and representational, providing degrees of freedom for asserting that culture is more than the deterministic result of genes, environment, and history. Mental representations can be incredibly diverse. Indeed, the human imagination may have few inherent limits, as illustrated by the continued outpouring of written fiction and technological innovation in the world today. If new ideas or practices would have been impossible to predict in advance (i.e., Einstein's theory of relativity, as discussed in chapter 2), then surely they must involve "more than biology" (Ehrlich, 2000). A further advantage of this definition of culture is that it allowed anthropologists to align themselves with the "standard social science model." Again, this paradigm assumes that humans are blank slates (Pinker, 2002), largely programmed by the social and cultural surround. The potential appeal of such top-down assumptions for anthropologists should be obvious, as they help secure for the field an important place at the scientific table.

Although adopting a cognitively oriented definition of culture solved several problems for cultural anthropologists, this approach also created perils for the field. Perhaps the most obvious one is that culture might be reduced, ultimately, to the principles of cognitive psychology. Maybe the endless diversity of culture results from nothing more than the action of a few simple mental mechanisms (such as imitation, transfer, and generalization), such that if one had exact knowledge of the environmental and historical input to those mechanisms, one might predict a new culture's later shape with a fair degree of certainty. Indeed, the primary aim of the field of evolutionary cognitive psychology (Tooby & Cosmides, 1992) is to identify such a set of fundamental mental mechanisms and processes, encoded into the genes by natural selection, many of which are directly relevant to sociality and the generation of culture (see chap. 4). If such genetically determined mechanisms exist, then perhaps a science of culture is not needed after all. In the words of Durham (1991), "Is it genuinely appropriate and/or necessary for us to distinguish between genes and culture as two different kinds of influence on human diversity? What, after all, is to be gained by this distinction?"(p. 33).

Cultural Evolution

To better illustrate the conundrum, let us consider the science of cultural evolution. One important question for this science is that of how cultures evolve over time, adapting to both their physical environments and to other cultures, in order to both maintain their integrity and extend their complexity. In other words, how do various types of technological, historical, and environmental change influence the course of cultural development? Such ethnographic and behavioral–ecological approaches use the word "evolution" primarily as a stand-in for "positive change," and typically do not try to consider the influence of biological evolution (Smith, 2000). However, another important question for theories of cultural evolution is that of how genetic evolution and cultural evolution relate to each other. Are genetic evolution and cultural evolution completely distinct and independent temporal processes, or is cultural evolution perhaps "nothing but" an expression of genetic evolution? Also, how do cultural changes relate to changes in the human gene pool, and conversely, how do changes in the gene pool influence culture?

Next I consider some important issues and debates within the field of cultural evolution, because they bear so directly on the issue of whether culture is a distinct and irreducible level of analysis for understanding human behavior.

The Social Brain Hypothesis

Perhaps the most predominant starting point for modern cultural evolutionists is the "social brain" hypothesis. Proposed surprisingly recently by Humphrey (in 1976, but widely anticipated earlier), this is the idea that human brain evolution was driven primarily by the increasingly complex demands of cooperative group living (Alexander, 1990; Caporael, 1997), rather than by purely ecological and environmental demands.

Before considering the social brain hypothesis in detail, first, some background. It appears that sometime in the past 100,000 years *Homo sapiens* reached a new level of functioning, a level that provided tremendous benefits for the average individual (Alexander, 1990). In relatively short order humans developed sophisticated new tools, hunting practices, and living arrangements; these in turn led to the Neolithic revolution, in which humans developed art, religion, the calendar, agriculture, and commerce; and these in turn led to the development of the scientific method, with its capacity to attack large-scale problems logically and systematically, deriving new technologies in the process. Together, these changes made possible a huge population explosion within the human species, an explosion that continues today (Diamond, 1997). The rapidity of these changes on the geological time scale is especially notable given that *Homo erectus*, our immediate precursor, used the same crude stone tools for more than a million years with no signs of improvement over time.

What accounts for this first "cognitive revolution" in human history? Many are of the opinion that this first revolution was a *cultural* revolution, driven by the emergence of cooperative group functioning at a level never before seen (Bingham, 1999). Such functioning was characterized by extensive reciprocal altruism and sharing, complex role specialization and division of labor, and flexible coordination of group activity by leaders and interacting subgroups. As a result, humans working together could solve many more adaptive problems than they could by working alone. Another way to view the revolution is in terms of the much larger online cognitive capabilities that became available to individuals because of their interactions with others. Indeed, humans might literally be said to have developed a "group minding" capacity—enabled by increasingly sophisticated language, complex thoughts could flow between brains as well as within them, and group minds could produce emergent solutions and products that could not have been created by any subset of the brains within the group. Yet a third way to view the shift is that individuals acquired access to a much larger knowledge base. Recall Geertz's definition of culture as "a system of inherited conceptions expressed in symbolic forms by means of which men communicate, perpetuate, and develop their knowledge about and attitudes towards life" (1973, p. 89). As this definition implies, culture provides for transgenerational retention of new information and innovation, so that succeeding generations do not have to keep "reinventing the wheel." In short, culture making, that is, the ability to take part in a spatially and temporally extended group mind, may be the very means by which humans have achieved such ecological dominance today.

The social brain hypothesis itself is based on the assumption that, as cooperative group functioning became an ever more effective survival tool, it became ever more important for human individuals to be able to function effectively to the social matrix (Alexander, 1990; Caporael, 1997). Material existence became relatively easy, as long as the person was a reasonably competent member of a reasonably competent group. However, in order to gain access to these benefits, the person had to be able to remain in good graces with the group. Better yet, the person might increase his or her share of the group benefits over time, by enhancing his or her relative status within the group. The social brain hypothesis assumes that contingencies such as these created strong selection pressures on humans, which led to the evolution of the large suite of sociocognitive skills and abilities that now characterize the human mind.

What are these abilities? Some relatively basic components of the social brain would seem to include the ability to reliably distinguish other group members, to remember each group member's relative rank within the group, and to remember one's history of interaction and communication with each group member. More complex abilities include keeping track of one's current relations with many others and managing each relationship in distinctive fashion; balancing and trading off these relationships against each other, when necessary; and appeasing and reconciling with others with whom one has had a falling out. In addition, humans learned to play a wide variety of social roles (parent, child, student, leader, worker, etc.), and to flexibly shift between different roles as a function of shifting social and task dynamics. Even more complex abilities may include that of being able to create a psychological self, that is, a theory of who one is "behind" one's roles (Sedikides & Skowronski, 1997), so that one inhabits a coherent character within the social world (see chap. 7). In addition, the social brain has apparently evolved the ability to create "theories of mind," that is, to form representations of other's selves and mental states (Geary, 1998). These representations can then be taken into account in one's own decision-making (e.g., "If I say x, but he interprets it as y, then he'll say z back, and I'll need to say q."). Many of these abilities have already been discussed, in the chapter 4 consideration of universal social-cognitive mechanisms.

Another aspect of the social brain likely evolved in accordance with the game-theoretical considerations discussed in the previous chapter. In any cooperative living situation it is necessary to develop abilities such that one is not exploited within one's group. In other words, one needs to be able to discern whether one is contributing more than one's fair share to the group, and conversely, whether there are "free riders," people who are benefiting without paying the cost. Such social dilemma-related skills, already discussed in earlier chapters, may include detecting cheating or bad faith, conducting negotiations with others, engaging in tactical deception of others, and forming temporary and long-term coalitions and alliances with others (see Caporael et al., in press, for a recent review).

Highlighting the potential importance of such game-theoretical issues for the social brain, Bingham (1999) recently forwarded a general theory of cultural evolution based entirely on the concept of "coalition enforcement." Specifically, Bingham proposed that *Homo sapiens* has achieved its ecological pinnacle in large part because group members learned to cooperate with each other in meting out punishment to those who threaten the group or threaten its functioning. This practice spread out the risks for any one person of taking action against exploiters or interlopers, greatly enhancing groups' ability to maintain and police themselves. Indeed, Bingham argued that the evolution of coalition enforcement can account for many later positive developments, including the evolution of sophisticated language and symbolic thought. Although he may overstate the case for the hypothesis, nevertheless, it is an intriguing one.

In sum, the social brain hypothesis presumes that the primary selective environment for humans became the social (and cultural) environment, rather than the natural or physical environment, and that the contemporary human brain powerfully reflects this shift. As a result there occurred a rapid evolutionary spiral or autocatalytic process, in which the new opportunities afforded by cooperative group functioning produced intense selection pressure for brains that could contribute to the process, as well as cope with the many problems that came with it. Of course, it is difficult to say which would come first in such a process—the evolution of new brain capacities that then afforded the development of culture, or the development of culture that then created selection pressure for the social brain. Probably both were occurring simultaneously, and indeed, such positive feedback processes may be the very hallmark of the rapid evolutionary spiral mentioned earlier (Alexander, 1990).

Notice that the social brain hypothesis leaves the ultimate causal status of the cultural level of analysis somewhat in doubt. After all, in this view, the social brain is an evolved set of adaptations, ultimately based on physico-cognitive processes encoded within the genes. Perhaps if we thoroughly understood the social brain, then we would no longer need to consider cultural-level processes and effects in order to predict individual behavior. Thus, once again, it may be that ethnography and traditional cultural anthropology focus their theoretical imaginations on too high a level of analysis, compared to the parsimony that might be achieved from a more reductionistic perspective. Indeed, some sociobiological and evolutionary psychological theorists subscribe precisely to this view (see Flinn, 1996, or Smith, 2000, for relevant discussion).

Memetic Evolution

One recent theoretical development that might help to combat this unsettling possibility and thereby afford a secure place for the cultural level of analysis within Fig. 2.1 is that of *memetic evolution*. Ironically, this idea was first proposed by Richard Dawkins (1976), one of the most reductionistically inclined evolutionary theorists. The idea is that ideas or units of meaning (memes) compete for dominance in the cultural mind in the same way that genes compete for dominance within the population gene pool (although no intentionality is necessary in either case). New ideas, beliefs, and practices can "flash" through a society, taking up residence in nearly every mind contained within the society, while simultaneously other ideas, beliefs, or practices may die out, because of their failure to capture enough minds. In addition, memes can outlast particular human lifetimes, persisting to influence generation after generation. Examples of cultural memes include particular musical melodies, scientific theories, religious rituals, and political ideologies.

As implied earlier, proponents of this view typically draw a close functional analogy between genetic evolution and memetic evolution. Thus, just as with genes, processes of selection are said to operate on memes, determining which ones best survive and expand their influence over time. Memes propagate by "colonizing" individual minds, which bear them until they are able to reproduce themselves within other minds; this is similar to the case with genes, which propagate by creating physical bodies, which bear them until they are able to reproduce themselves within other bodies. Also, memes tend to thrive when they become linked to larger "meme-plexes" or ideologies (Blackmore, 1999), just as genes tend to thrive when they become linked to larger complexes of genes. Furthermore, just as is the case with genes, some kinds of memes are better adapted for survival than others. For example, particularly effective memes may be ones that both emphasize the sacred and unvarying nature of the meme (i.e., the Ten Commandments), and call for their holder to actively seek new converts to the meme (i.e., evangelical religion; Atran, 2002). In this case the colonizing meme can both conserve its essential form over long periods of time and prompt its holders to actively try to spread it to new minds.

Despite the functional analogy to natural selection, most proponents of meme theory argue that memetic evolution takes place largely independently of genetic evolution—that is, that the destiny of particular memes is determined by cultural selection, not natural selection. In other words, "dual inheritance" is occurring, such that cultural and genetic evolution proceed on separate courses (Boyd & Richerson, 1985). Other theorists go even further, arguing that memetic evolution has largely supplanted genetic evolution as the primary shaper of human destiny (Blackmore, 1999). Because memetic (cultural) evolution takes place at a much swifter a rate than genetic evolution, genetic evolution may have been rendered largely irrelevant or impotent. Some even argue that *Homo sapiens* will not resume its genetic evolution until it learns to produce such evolution intentionally, through our growing knowledge of genetic engineering. In this scenario, memetic evolution (in the form of the evolving science of molecular biology) might eventually become the most important cause of genetic evolution, rather than perhaps being merely an effect or result of genetic evolution (Aunger, 2002).

Despite the intuitive appeal and fascination of the concept of memetic evolution, there are more critics of the idea than there are proponents. This is because meme theory faces significant problems, including how to identify distinct memes as units of analysis (quite difficult, compared to the ease of identifying distinct genes); how to justify the idea that memes operate unconstrained by the genes and bodies on which they depend (surely memes could not thrive if they were maladaptive for the minds, bodies, and genes that housed them); and how to handle the fact that memes are so easily altered during the process of transmission (anyone who has played the game of "telephone," in which a message whispered from person to person inevitably becomes more distorted with every act of transmission, will understand this problem of signal degradation). Further difficulties are introduced by the fact that memes are necessarily causally secondary to physical brains (i.e., without brains, memes could not exist), whereas genes are necessarily causally primary to brains (i.e., without genes, brains could not exist). Thus, according to Atran (2002), the concept of memes may at best supply an appealing metaphor or heuristic, rather than a rigorous scientific theory. Certainly, he says, those seeking a secure scientific foundation for culture as an irreducible influence on human behavior should be wary of pinning too much on the idea.

Still, even if meme theory ultimately fails, the foundational place of culture seems relatively secure. Few contemporary scientists adhere to "sociobiological reductionism," in which all cultural variations can be boiled down to the action of inherited mental mechanisms. Instead, most human scientists take an interactionist perspective, in which the propensities and proclivities inherent in the human mind are moderated by the unique environmental context, historical trends, and developing traditions within a particular region, to produce regional variations in behavior (Flinn, 1996). As discussed in chapter 4, for example, there was probably no way to predict in advance the character of Chinese, Bantu, or American culture from simple knowledge of basic human nature; these unique cultural traditions took much time to develop, through extended social interaction and "group-minding," occurring within geographically isolated groups. In terms of Fig. 2.1, emergent processes occur at the cultural level of analysis, processes that cannot be themselves explained by any other level of analysis, even though they are necessarily built on the lower levels.

CONFORMIST TRANSMISSION, PSYCHOLOGICAL SELECTION, AND INDIVIDUAL AUTONOMY AS FOUNDATIONS OF CULTURE

To summarize, the social brain hypothesis assumes that humans evolved cognitive capabilities for living and negotiating with others, capabilities that both support the creation of culture and are necessary for living within cultures. Indeed, the social brain hypothesis has become the foundational or core assumption for many anthropologists and human scientists. In this section, I consider which features of the social brain are most important or essential for understanding how cultures expand and elaborate themselves. In other words, what are the most crucial mechanisms that enable the creation, transmission, and preservation of cultural knowledge and beliefs?

Conformist Transmission

One important candidate mechanism is *conformist transmission,* the focus of Boyd and Richerson's (1985) influential model of cultural evolution. These authors begin with the observation that different cultural groups can evidence very different beliefs and practices, even though they may live near each other and encounter essentially the same physical environment. The Pennsylvania Amish are a good example of a group that maintains large differences between itself and neighboring groups. Boyd and Richerson's model explains such phenomena via the simple idea that human brains evolved a bias to preferentially imitate the cultural traits that are most predominant in the local population. This idea relies on two assumptions: that humans easily learn new behaviors simply by observing what others are doing (Flinn, 1996), and that they are most likely to learn the new behaviors that they see the most other people doing. Boyd and Richerson (1985) used game-theoretical models and simulations to show that this simple mechanism could account for the preservation of cultural differences, in part by inhibiting individuals from adopting new ideas and practices imported by cultural out-group members.

Boyd and Richerson's conformist transmission theory may do a good job of explaining how norms, rules, and other memes are propagated and maintained over time within groups, such that the group maintains its distinctiveness relative to other groups. However, the theory does not do such a good job of explaining where the group memes came from in the first place. As we know, many if not all new cultural ideas and practices originally arise in individual minds, prior to their broader propagation (Csikszentmihalyi, 1993). It is difficult to reconcile the theory of conformist transmission with this necessity for individual creativity, given that conformity and creativity typically "don't mix" (Amabile, 1996; Sheldon, 1999a). Also, the theory has difficulty explaining cases when cultures do import innovations from other cultures, rather than clinging tightly to their own prior norms. In short, conformist transmission seems to be primarily a conservative process, which is based on resistance to new and uncommon ideas and practices.

In order to address the question of where new cultural practices come from, I believe it necessary to consider other levels of analysis not usually considered by cultural evolutionists—specifically, the level of self, and the level of personality. In particular, I suggest that the process by which individuals integrate and internalize the cultural information they encounter is of critical importance for creativity and innovation. People do not just passively imitate the actions of their neighbors; they also think about those actions, grapple with them, and at times try to revise them. In other words, humans have a desire to constitute themselves as somewhat autonomous agents within the cultural milieu, deciding what practices they understand, agree with, and accept, and also, what practices they oppose and might like to change. Because of this process, the cultural group mind is in a sense "born anew" within each new individual and generation.

Psychological Selection

Inghilleri (1999) provided a revealing analysis of this person-level contribution to the cultural process, which he termed *psychological selection* (in contrast to natural selection and cultural selection, discussed earlier). Individuals engage in psychological selection by focusing attention differentially on the contents of their consciousness, such that they gravitate toward some ideas and practices, and ignore others. Inghilleri considered a variety of factors that influence psychological selection, that is, the person's endorsing of or attention to a particular belief, technology, or religious practice. These factors include whether the practice is easy, whether it gives one influence over others, whether it promotes one's sense of connection with others, and so on. Most important of all, said Inghilleri, may be people's attempts to find and follow intrinsic motivations, that is, to pursue activities and themes that are inherently interesting and engaging for them (Deci & Ryan, 1985). Given that intrinsic motivation is so strongly associated with creativity (see Amabile, 1996, for a review), the latter process in particular may help to explain how cultural innovations and changes arise.

Inghilleri's (1999) analysis suggests that we cannot understand cultural evolution (defined in the first way mentioned earlier, as positive change within a culture) without considering the processes by which people constitute themselves in relation to their cultures. In other words, a purely top-down analysis of cultural givens will not do; person-level factors must be considered, and hierarchical pluralism is necessary. The final output (individual behavior and cultural change) is a function of both the cultural givens and the person's experience of those givens.

Individual Autonomy and Psychological Selection

To address the question of how people take in and creatively modify existing cultural beliefs and practices (i.e., how psychological selection occurs), I believe it is particularly useful to consider a personality-level factor already discussed in Chapter 4, namely, the organismic need for autonomy. Again, self-determination theory (Deci & Ryan, 1985, 2000) defines the need for autonomy as a universal or species-typical aspect of human beings. Deci and Ryan (2000) argued that one important benefit of this need is that it motivates individuals to at times gain distance from the group mind, enabling them to freshly encounter cultural givens. Another benefit of the search for psychological autonomy is that autonomy is typically associated with cognitive flexibility and knowledge integration (Ryan, 1995). Perhaps as a result of this, autonomy in personality is substantially associated with trait intrinsic motivation and creativity (Sheldon, 1995).

If personal autonomy is so important for individual creativity and also cultural innovation, then it seems that a very important determinant of a culture's long-term viability may be the extent to which it supports its citizen's right to choose for themselves which aspects of the culture to endorse and develop. When this occurs people may be best able to internalize the ideas and practices of previous generations, while at the same time transforming them in positive ways. In contrast, cultures that are overly controlling or rigid may ultimately fail to persuade their citizens to internalize predominant cultural beliefs and prescriptions and, by choking off an important source of innovation, may also fail to adapt successfully to the changes around them (Sternberg & Lubart, 1995). If this is true, it again illustrates the importance of autonomy support, discussed in chapter 8—paradoxically, by giving their charges the freedom to make their own choices, authorities may best support both the transmission and the positive evolution of the culture they represent (Amabile, 1996; Sheldon, Elliot, Ryan, Chirkov, Kim, Wu, Demir, & Sun, 2004).

IMPORTANT DIFFERENCES BETWEEN CULTURES: INDIVIDUALISM VERSUS COLLECTIVISM

In this section we leave behind general questions concerning the relationship of cultural and genetic evolution and how cultural evolution proceeds, instead turning to consider some fundamental differences between cultures, as evidenced in the psychologies of their proponents. This brings us to the realm of cross-cultural psychology, which concerns itself with characterizing different kinds of cultures, and cataloguing their effects on the minds of those contained within them (Triandis, 2001). There are many cultural differences on which theorists might focus, including whether the culture is "tight" or "loose," whether the culture is "vertically" or "horizontally" oriented, and whether it is "complex" or "simple" (Matsumoto, 2001). However, the most commonly studied dimension focused on by cross-cultural psychologists is the distinction between individualism and collectivism. This is a very broad distinction, which is sometimes applied too broadly and indiscriminately (Triandis, 2001). Nevertheless, the distinction is very useful for considering "big picture" issues concerning cultural differences. In addition, the individualism/collectivism distinction may help us apply the game-theoretical perspective on optimal human functioning, developed in the last chapter, to the question of optimal cultural functioning.

I first discuss some cardinal features of the collectivist mentality, by contrasting it with the individualist mentality. Within collectivist cultures, individuals tend to define themselves as interdependent with other individuals, rather than defining themselves as independent of others (as in individualist cultures; Markus et al., 1996). Collectivists are typically more concerned with the needs and concerns of their groups, rather than with their own personal needs and concerns, separate from groups (Triandis, 1995). They are typically more focused on social norms and traditions as determinants of their behavior, rather than internal attitudes and beliefs (Suh, Diener, Oishi, & Triandis, 1998). Also, they are typically more concerned with communal relationships, in which enhancing bonds with and benefits for others is a priority, rather than with contractual relationships, in which personal benefit is the primary goal (Mills & Clark, 1982). Also, collectivists tend to have just a few "in-groups," to which they are deeply bound over time, rather than having many in-groups to which they feel only superficially related and which they will readily leave (as in individualist cultures; Sugimoto, 1998). Those within collectivist cultures tend to be more conforming, even with clearly incorrect group judgments (as shown using the Asch experimental paradigm), and are more willing to sacrifice their personal interests when these seem to be in conflict with group interests (Bond & Smith, 1996).

It is important to note that not all persons within collectivist cultures display the characteristics listed earlier, just as not all persons within individualist cultures display the converse characteristics; there is considerable variation within cultures, in addition to the average propensities already described. Also, most individuals within either type of culture are able to make use of either set of assumptions or "cultural tools," depending on the context (Triandis, 2001). Because of this, Triandis (1995) suggested that the distinction between individualism and collectivism should be confined to a between-culture level of analysis, whereas a distinction between idiocentrism (self-centeredness) versus allocentrism (other-orientedness) should instead be made at a between-person level of analysis. Conceptually, however, idiocentrism maps well on individualism and allocentrism maps well on collectivism, and thus I continue to use the individualism/collectivism terminology.

Examples of collectivist cultures include Asian societies such as South Korea, China, and Japan; Russia; and also many African, Eastern European, and Latin American societies. Examples of individualist cultures include the United States, Australia, Scandinavia, and New Zealand, and also most Western European societies. Triandis (2001) noted that collectivism is common within traditional societies and agricultural societies, in which cooperation is highly functional, and in relatively homogeneous societies, in which population density is high. In contrast, individualism is common within affluent societies, especially societies at the geographical intersection of many cultural traditions; it is also high among the upper classes and professionals within any society. Again, however, it is important to keep in mind that the individualism/collectivism dichotomy is likely too simple—for example, there are obviously many important differences between North Korea, Uganda, and Mexico, although they are all classified as collectivist cultures.

Adaptive Implications of Individualism and Collectivism

Cross-cultural psychology has to date been little concerned with evolutionary issues, and with the adaptive implications of different cultural styles for the individuals contained within the cultures in question. However, I believe this is an important issue, as it speaks to the link between genetic and cultural evolution, and also provides tools for understanding the (positive or negative) relations between adjacent cultural groups. Thus, I venture some speculations concerning this issue in the next subsection, using the game-theoretical perspectives developed in chapter 8. Indeed, it seems that individualism and collectivism may have very important adaptive implications for individual humans, to such an extent such that these two cultural syndromes may themselves be viewed as evolved features of the human social brain. Either syndrome might be activated and developed within a particular child, purely as a function of the cultural context into which the child is born (again, the cultural level of analysis has irreducible holistic effects for explaining a particular person's behavior). I next consider the possible adaptive benefits of the two styles, beginning with collectivism.

Adaptive Advantages of Collectivism

One obvious potential benefit of cultural collectivism is that it maximizes within-group cooperation while minimizing the problem of free riders (and again, some view the emergence of such group cooperation as the primary agent of human evolutionary change; Alexander, 1990, Bingham, 1999). For example, there is evidence that those within collectivist societies are less prone to "social loafing," in which n people working together exert less effort than the same n people working alone (Earley, 1989). Also, members of collectivist cultures are more likely to be classifiable as "cooperators" (with the trait of trying to maximize joint outcomes) and less likely to be classifiable as "competitors" (with the trait of trying to maximize own outcomes, relative to others; Parks & Vu, 1994). Indeed, many of the characteristics of collectivism discussed earlier (i.e., considering group needs ahead of individual needs, defining the self in terms of group memberships rather than personal attributes, staying within close-knit groups over the long term rather than moving between different groups, and being willing to conform to obviously incorrect group norms) can be viewed as adaptations that promote in-group cooperation, while simultaneously minimizing the problem of free riders. In addition, it seems likely that Boyd and Richerson's (1985) model of conformist transmission, discussed earlier, is most applicable within collectivist societies; in such societies group norms and practices would be maximally conserved over time, because individuals in such societies base their behavior primarily on what the group (i.e., most other people) is doing.

This line of thinking can also explain the finding that collectivists tend to prefer group-based compensation practices, whereas individualists tend to prefer individual rewards (Earley & Gibson, 1998), and the finding that collectivists prefer equality in exchange relationships (in which all receive the same, regardless of performance), whereas individualists prefer equity in exchange relationships (in which individual performance is the basis for allocation; Leung, 1997). In short, it appears that collectivists stake their future on group-level performance, rather than on their own performance within the group. As a result, their groups may function with maximal cohesiveness, and with minimal internal conflict.

Importantly, however, collectivists are not nicer to everybody; in fact, they typically evidence stronger in-group/out-group biases than do individualists (Triandis, 1972). Within collectivist cultures, persons viewed as nongroup members are often treated with indifference or even hostility (Triandis, 2001), whereas in individualist societies, in-group and out-group members are treated much more equally. Recall Bingham's (1999) coalition-enforcement hypothesis, according to which human brain evolution was driven by groups' increasing ability to band together to punish cheaters and interlopers; it appears that collectivist cultures may take maximal advantage of this adaptation, by emphasizing the distinction between in-group (those to be treated well) and out-group (those to be treated less well).

The tendency toward strong in-group/out-group biases within collectivist cultures is also consistent with the group-selection perspective discussed in chapter 8. Again, contemporary group-selection theory asserts that group membership can become an important influence on individual adaptation when there is strong homogeneity within groups, and at the same time, strong heterogeneity between groups (Sober & Wilson, 1998). Strong in-group (vs. out-group) biases seem to be precisely the kind of mechanism that would evolve via group-selection, as such biases would tend to maximize within-group homogeneity and between-group heterogeneity, while also preventing the admixture of new individuals into the group (which would mitigate these differences). More generally, cultural collectivism itself may be viewed as a complex mental syndrome that evolved by group selection, just as religiosity and spirituality may have evolved by group selection (D. S. Wilson, 2002).

The potential relevance of group selection theory for understanding the adaptive benefits of collectivism is further illustrated by considering "Simpson's paradox," which illustrates the primary basis for many types of group selection (Simpson, 1951). The paradox is this: A trait can increase in frequency in the overall population, even as it decreases in frequency within particular groups. Why? Because groups containing much of the trait grow more rapidly (relative to other groups) than people containing much of the trait disappear (relative to other group members). In other words, the expanding between-group effect trumps the counteracting within-group effect, leading to increasing frequency of the trait in the aggregate population. To use a more concrete example: The disposition to trust and cooperate with others would put individuals at a disadvantage relative to nearby others who do not possess this trait, such that the trait becomes scarcer over time within a particular group. However the trait might still spread in the population, if groups containing much of this trait did very well compared to groups containing less of the trait.

This idea might be applied to explain the successfulness of collectivism in the world today, as evidenced by the large and densely packed populations seen within many collectivist cultures such as India, China, and Japan. In these cases the collectivist mentality seems to have afforded the means for very many individuals to be supported, by living in close conjunction with one another, with maximal cooperation and minimal conflict (Triandis, 2001). In a sense, such societies more thoroughly "domesticate" their citizens, creating much within-group homogeneity so that they can live in concentrated groups without conflict (Livingston, 1994). As a result, collectivist genes (if there be such a thing) may be more frequent in the human gene pool than individualist genes.

However, recall that collectivists also tend to demonstrate stronger in-group bias and out-group hostility than do individualists. This suggests that the collectivist approach may have problems when there is too much heterogeneity within the culture, that is, "too many out-groups." In this case, the collectivist mentality may be vulnerable to intense intergroup conflict and internecine warfare. This suggestion is consistent with the observation that many if not most of the world's wars occur in places where there are strong ethnic divisions nested within generally collectivist nations (i.e., the Bosnians and the Serbs in Croatia, or the Shiites and the Sunnis in Iraq).

To summarize this section, the collectivist mentality may be viewed as one aspect of the social brain, an aspect that can provide significant benefits for most individuals within societies that emphasize it. Collectivism promotes group cooperation as well as social virtues such as compassion and sharing (at least with in-group members), and collectivist cultures are likely to be quite stable, because of the dynamics of conformist transmission. Collectivism likely evolved by the mechanism of group selection, which links individual destinies to group-level outcomes. However, collectivism may be less functional when there are multiple racial or ethnic groups contained within a society, in which case intergroup conflict may predominate. Another possible disadvantage is that by deemphasizing psychological selection and individual autonomy, collectivist cultures may suffer in their inability to generate innovations and to adapt to changes that threaten existing traditions and norms (Sternberg & Lubart, 1995).

Adaptative Advantages of Individualism

In contrast, individualism may provide a different suite of advantages and disadvantages. By emphasizing personal attitudes, needs, and preferences over the needs and preferences of the group, individualism may more directly support individual striving and self-enhancement. Given that individuals are functionally closer to their own genes than are the groups in which they are nested, this may confer significant evolutionary benefits. Also, given that creativity and innovation are more encouraged in individualist cultures (Sternberg & Lubart, 1995), people's ability to adapt flexibly to changing local circumstances may be heightened within such cultures. Also, those within individualist cultures may benefit on average because of the greater rate of innovation within their societies, and because of their societies' abilities to both accept and lead the technical revolutions occurring in the region and in the world.

Of course, there are also potential disadvantages of individualism. These may include the reduced connection with others that is fostered in such cultures, and the greater incidence of depression (Seligman, 1990); the overemphasis on materialistic and extrinsic strivings within such cultures (Kasser, 2002); and also the reduced "social capital" in such cultures (Putnam, 2000), that is, the lower amounts of community feeling, volunteerism, and institutional cohesiveness found within the society. In addition, the emphasis on personal achievement and status and the reduced emphasis on group performance and acceptance likely encourage more cheating and free-riding within individualist cultures, undermining the group-level benefits that might ensue to individuals as a result of cooperative group functioning (Wilson & Sober, 1994). Finally, to a greater extent than in collectivist cultures, individualist cultures may "leave behind" those with the least ability and the most need. It was probably no accident that the concept of social Darwinism and the practice of eugenics, both of which advocate the "culling" of the less accomplished from the gene pool, arose in highly industrialized, individualistic cultures.

OPTIMAL HUMAN BEING AT THE CULTURAL LEVEL OF ANALYSIS

This concludes my tour of some major issues and debates within cultural anthropology, evolutionary psychology, and cross-cultural psychology. In particular, I have focused on issues relevant to establishing and understanding the irreducible effects of the cultural level of analysis on individual human behavior—cultures reflect unique history and developed traditions, and provide the prior foundation on which psychological selection acts. I have also considered the dynamic relations between genes, personalities, and cultures, showing that each has unique effects on individual human behavior and adaptation (see Fig. 2.1). In this final section I will revisit some of these ideas, to consider the nature of optimal human being as seen from a cultural perspective.

Person–Culture Fit as Optimal Adaptation

Perhaps the most obvious starting place is to say that optimal human being at the cultural level of analysis involves successful adaptation to one's culture, whatever its particular traditions. Each culture provides predominant norms or prescriptions for proper behavior, and those who best follow these prescriptions are likely to be best off, in many different ways (with some exceptions, considered later). Within individualist cultures, in which outcomes are based primarily on equity and one's unique accomplishments, successfully adapting to one's culture may entail developing one's personal talents and skills to a maximal extent. In this way one receives many personal rewards—both material, in terms of receiving many opportunities and possession, and psychological, in terms of receiving much status and self-esteem. Within collectivist cultures, in which outcomes are based more on equality and one's contribution to group thriving, this may entail developing one's ability to relate to and cooperate with others to a maximal extent. In this way one also receives many personal rewards—both material, in terms of group-based opportunities and possessions, and psychological, also in terms of status and self-esteem (Sedikides, Gaertner, & Toguchi, 2003).

How does one successfully adapt to one's culture, whatever its particular orientation? Consistent with the earlier discussion of personality-level effects on cultural evolution and with the chapter 8 discussion of role ownership, an important consideration would seem to be one's ability to internalize the culture's norms and practices, such that they become a part of one's sense of self (Chirkov, Ryan, Kim, & Kaplan, 2003). In this way one may follow the dictates of the culture, while at the same time maintaining a sense of personal autonomy in one's behavior. As demonstrated by research in the self-determination theory tradition, such felt autonomy seems to be crucial for understanding and predicting optimal flexibility, persistence, creativity, and performance (see Deci & Ryan, 2000, for a review).

Countercultural Activity as Optimal Adaptation

What about cultural practices that are difficult or even impossible for individuals to internalize? In terms of the chapter 8 focus on person–role fit, what about when the roles or behaviors imparted the culture are incompatible with the person's needs or personality? Here, we must necessarily move our discussion of optimal human being to a higher level, namely, to consider optimal cultural being. It is clear that some cultural practices are less "healthy" and desirable than others. For example, the practice of clitorectomy, found in 28 different African cultures, is a difficult one for parents to fully internalize, as it involves intentionally mutilating their own daughters and crippling their ability to fully enjoy sexual relations (Kouba & Muasher, 1985). Similarly, the practice of systematically exterminating Jews, found in mid-20th-century German culture, was distressing to many if not most of the Germans who were forced to participate in it (Hamerow, 1997).

Another reason why some cultural practices may be highly problematic for the individual is that they run counter to survival and reproduction, the ultimate currencies of genetic evolution. For example, a cultural practice of committing mass suicide on certain momentous occasions would seem to be a significant drain on the genes of those who conformed to it, such that to the extent the practice has genetic inputs, it would tend to disappear over time. Similarly, it may be that the long-term destruction of the biosphere which is being occasioned by Western economic practices will eventually have significant negative effects on the human population as a whole. This returns us to an issue discussed earlier, that memetic evolution could not be expected to occur completely independently of genetic evolution, as some meme theory proponents assert. Memes (and cultural practices) are doubtless constrained somewhat by their usefulness (or harmfulness) for the genes of those whose minds they colonize.

These two considerations lead to a caveat to my first suggested prescription, that optimal human being at the cultural level of analysis involves successfully adapting to one's culture, whatever its particular beliefs and practices. Instead, optimal human being and optimal adaptation may sometimes require resisting or taking action against norms and roles that are personally aversive or noninternalizable. Although this can have harmful consequences for resistant individuals, such acts of "civil disobedience" can have very beneficial consequences for other individuals within the culture, and for the culture itself in the long term. This line of reasoning implies that "adaptive benefit" needs to be defined very carefully—beneficial to whom?—that is, for the behaving individual, or for other culture members who reap rewards from his or her behavior? Beneficial at what time scale?—that is, in the short term, in which it may be very harmful, or the long term, in which the individual may receive large benefits?

The idea that individuals may sometimes sacrifice their self-interests to the ultimate advantage of their culture returns us to the question of how cultural evolution in the first sense (i.e., defined as positive change over time) occurs. As suggested by the foregoing, large-scale changes may often depend on the actions of particular individuals who resist, redefine, or revolutionize the predominant beliefs and traditions that they find. For example, Galileo's celestial observations helped create the overthrow of the Ptolomaic worldview, paving the way for modern science and technology. However, he paid a high price, living under house arrest for the last part of his life. Surely he was not adapting effectively to his culture; on the other hand, his efforts helped his culture to achieve greater effectiveness and adaptation in the long term. Of course, even as individuals such as Galileo suffer material, social, and physical harm at the hands of resistant cultural institutions, they may also benefit in other more subtle ways, as they follow intrinsic motivations toward greater meaning and personal growth (Inghilleri, 1999). Again, it would be very difficult to compute the individual cost–benefit trade-offs implied by this analysis, although it should in principle be feasible. The main point here, again, is that at times, countercultural activity may be optimal for the individual and perhaps for his society. Chapter 10 considers in more detail the question of when this is likely to be the case.

Optimal Intercultural Being

Finally, let us take the concept of "optimal cultural being" even further, to consider how cultures best relate to other cultures. In other words, we might perhaps add one more level to Fig. 2.1, which could be labeled the "cross-cultural" or even the "planetary" level of analysis. I believe this tenth level of analysis might supply important explanatory power for understanding individual behavior and outcomes. Obviously, intercultural processes negatively affect countless individuals, as evidenced by the long history of national strife and warfare that has plagued the human race. However, intercultural relations also have important positive implications for individuals, as evidenced by the long history of technological diffusion between cultural groups that has allowed for the tremendous expansion of the human population.

What is the most optimal outcome, at the level of intercultural relations? Perhaps most simply, that conflict between cultures is minimized, while the spread of adaptive new ideas and practices between cultures is maximized. It is likely that the economic success of European and Western culture is due to the latter process; Europe is located at the "crossroads" of many different cultures and trading routes, and has greatly benefited from the resulting infusions of knowledge and technology (Diamond, 1997). Indeed, intercultural diffusion may be a necessity for cultures simply to maintain themselves at a given level. For example, the first colonists of Tasmania arrived with fire, boomerangs, axes with handles, canoes, and the ability to fish. Over time they lost all of these abilities, such that when Tasmania was discovered by Europeans, Tasmanians were the most primitive people in recorded history. Diamond (1997) speculated that this regression might have occurred for a variety of reasons, including the depletion of key natural resources, the simultaneous loss of many skilled artisans in some disaster, or the emergence of taboos or proscriptions that break the chain of intergenerational transmission. Due to Tasmania's geographic isolation, these losses could not be rectified through later encounters with other cultures that still possessed these technologies. In short, cultures that have no relations at all with other cultures may be doomed to a "downward spiral."

As a final speculation on the question of optimal intercultural relations, let us consider the relation of individualism and collectivism in the world today. Obviously, there is an uneasy balance. Most individualist cultures are thriving economically, at least at the present time (if not in the future, when overburdened resources may collapse). In contrast, although some collectivist cultures are doing well (Hong Kong, Costa Rica, South Korea) others are not doing well at all (Africa, the Middle East). In the latter cases we often see strong emotions, as members of poor but traditionalist cultures feel both envious at what they are lacking, and angry that the thriving cultures seem to have so little respect for their cultural beliefs and traditions (or memes).

It seems clear that the world will slowly convert to a more individualist economic system, assuming that global networking, technological diffusion, and dissemination of western media and perspectives continue. Ideally, however, the best aspects of the collectivist mentality, namely, self-discipline and deep caring and loyalty for one's family and groups, can also be integrated into the emerging "planetary mind." I believe this can happen only to the extent that the worst aspects of collectivism, such as the tendency toward out-group hostility and the resistance to innovation, are leavened or tempered. Hopefully, the worst aspects of individualism, namely, the tendencies toward greed, exploitation, and self-centeredness, can also be left behind.

10 Optimal Human Being and Optimal Human Science: Summary Prescriptions

In this final chapter I attempt to bring the ideas in this book together, to form a reasonably coherent whole. First, I review and summarize the recommendations for optimal human being already suggested in earlier chapters. As I hope this book has demonstrated, there are a wide variety of potential prescriptions that can be derived simply by examining current scientific knowledge within each succeeding level of analysis. Next, I return to the more abstract perspective on optimal human being suggested in chapter 1, that it involves achieving harmony or integration between all of the different levels of one's life. I conclude that there are important limitations to the idea, such that interlevel integration is not enough—content (i.e., "that which is to be integrated") must also be considered. Based on this discussion, I suggest that obtaining organismic need satisfaction may provide the most general and invariant prescription for optimal human being, because the evolved psychological needs have already been tailored to solve problems of both within-level content and between-level integration. Finally, I attempt to apply some of the foregoing ideas to the case of the human sciences, as a group. Can the question of how to achieve harmony and integration within an individual life be extended to the question of how to achieve harmony and integration between the human sciences? In what ways might the recommendations regarding these two questions converge?

REVIEWING AND SUMMARIZING: OPTIMAL HUMAN BEING AT EACH LEVEL OF ANALYSIS

In briefly reviewing the most promising perspectives on optimal human being already suggested, I begin with the level of organismic foundations, or species-typical human nature (the bottom level of Fig. 3.3), and work my way up. I state these conclusions as "prescriptions," that one might try to follow in order to approach a more optimal state of being. However, I do not mean to imply that people "should" do these things; of course, it is their choice. Figure 10.1 provides a summary of the prescriptions at each level, beginning with the organismic foundations level.

The Organismic Foundation Level of Analysis

Recall that in chapter 4 we examined four types of human universal: physical needs, social-cognitive mechanisms, psychological needs, and sociocultural practices. From this perspective, the prescriptions for optimal human being might be as follows. First, "satisfy one's basic bodily needs." It is hard to think of much else when one is cold, hungry, and tired (Oishi, Diener, Lucas, & Suh, 1999)! Second, "develop one's innate social-cognitive abilities," such as abilities to detect exploitation, to model other's states of mind, to recognize and express the basic human

I. Organismic Foundations

1. Satisfy your basic bodily needs.

2. Develop and calibrate your innate social-cognitive abilities.

3. Satisfy your psychological needs in the process of living.

4. Help create a society that expresses social-cognitive universals (i.e., spiritual

communion, dancing, music-making, athletic competition, joking).

II. Personality Traits

5. Try to develop more positive personality traits, such as agreeableness, openness,

extraversion, and conscientiousness.

6. Change your activities and behaviors, rather than your external circumstances, to

get to the top end of your potential happiness range.

III. Goals and Intentions

7. Set and pursue goals, as effectively as possible.

8. Develop greater systemic coherence in your action system.

9. Pursue intrinsic more than extrinsic goals.

10. Pursue goals for self-concordant more than non-concordant reasons.

FIG. 10.1.   Prescriptions for optimal human being derived in chapters 4–9.

(continued on next page)

IV. The Self-Homunculus

11. Construct and maintain a coherent life-story.

12. Successfully project your self-character to other selves.

13. Successfully organize and regulate your intentional life.

14. Live in a self that correctly represents its organism and traits ("be in touch with yourself").

V. Social Interactions

15. Be nice in new situations.

16. Punish those who exploit this practice.

17. Forgive them when they return to cooperation.

18. Make occasional overtures when you are fighting with someone.

19. Avoid exploiting those who seem to tolerate it.

20. Choose associates who will support you and cooperate with you.

21. Perform your social roles as well as possible.

22. Choose and enter social roles that best fit your personality dispositions.

23. Do your best to internalize ill-fitting roles, making them part of yourself.

24. Be autonomy-supportive when encouraging others to adopt social roles.

VI. Culture

25. Adapt to one's culture's norms and prescriptions.

26. Go against the societal grain when it seems necessary.

27. Draw from both individualist and collectivist mentalities, as needed.

FIG. 10.1. *(continued)*

emotions, to learn language, and to distinguish between in-group and out-group members. Perhaps more importantly, properly calibrate these mechanisms to the particular environment one actually encounters (Buss, 2001), so that one most effectively applies the potentials embedded in one's inherent human nature in service of positive adaptation. Third, one might try to "satisfy one's psychological needs in the process of living"—needs such as autonomy, competence, relatedness, security, and self-esteem (Ryan, 1995; Sheldon et al., 2001). As suggested earlier, this third prescription may be particularly important, and thus it will receive further consideration later in the chapter. Fourth, one might "help create a society that expresses sociocultural universals," such as spiritual communion, dancing, music making, athletic competition, and joking (Brown, 1991). Such activities certainly seem to be an important part of "the good life" (Seligman, 2002), even if many people, or their societies, do not partake of all of them.

The Personality Trait Level of Analysis

The level of personality traits and temperament (chap. 5) also suggested a variety of possible prescriptions for optimal human being. We considered and rejected the idea that one should strive to be true to one's traits, whatever they are; after all, some traits, such as high neuroticism or low agreeableness, are less conducive to adaptation and well-being than others. Of course, it is undoubtedly true that selecting activities that match one's basic temperament and traits will be beneficial in some circumstances and for some traits. The general point, however, is that some personality dispositions and tendencies may require countering, not bolstering (as was the case for Allison's exaggerated emotional reactivity, discussed in chap. 5). We also considered the idea that optimal human being involves selecting activities that compensate for one's baseline arousal level, either raising or depressing one from that chronic level, in the direction of moderation and optimality (Eysenck, 1990). However, this idea was rejected also; although proper arousal regulation may also have benefits, arousal regulation seems too simplistic and noninclusive with respect to the world of meaning (eudaemonia) to serve as an all-purpose recommendation (Apter, 2001).

Two other prescriptions were considered and endorsed in chapter 5. The first was that one "try to develop more positive personality traits," especially traits associated with well-being and adaptation such as extraversion, conscientiousness, openness, and agreeableness. Conversely, one might strive to decrease one's levels of less adaptive traits, such as neuroticism. Although all of these traits have substantial heritabilities, still, people have considerable latitude to change in their traits, both relative to others (as illustrated by the fact that the typical long-term test–retest coefficients for the Big Five traits are substantial but not huge), and in absolute terms (as illustrated by the fact that mean-level change toward positive traits and away from problematic traits may be normative over the life span; Costa et al., 2000; Robins et al., 2001).

The second prescription endorsed in chapter 5 was "change your activities and behaviors, rather than your external circumstances, to get to the top end of your potential happiness range." This conclusion emerged from the chapter 5 consideration of whether it is possible to permanently increase one's happiness, given that happiness may be just as heritable as major personality traits (Lykken & Tellegen, 1996). Lyubomirsky, Sheldon, and Schkade (in press) argued that permanent increases in happiness are indeed possible, but only if one makes life changes that yield and continue to yield positive new experiences. Furthermore, it matters what kind of change is made: Sheldon and Lyubomirsky (2004) showed that merely changing one's external circumstances may be less effective, because changed circumstances quickly become the status quo, such that one begins to fail to notice them. In contrast, adopting new activities can continue to bring rewards and fresh experiences, enabling one to stay in the top end of the potential range of happiness for people of one's temperamental type.

The Goals and Intentions Level of Analysis

The "change your activities, not your circumstances" idea leads naturally to the recommendations of chapter 6, which directly addressed goals and intentional activity. Most generally, "set and pursue goals, as effectively as possible." Again, this does not mean that one has to be an obsessive list-maker, as goals need not be conscious or explicit (Emmons, 1989)—rather, one's behavior should be organized in such a way as to continually reduce discrepancies between present states and desired future objectives. According to Carver and Scheier's (1990, 1998) control theory, such steady forward motion leads to frequent positive affect, as well as successful adaptation and psychological development. The control theory perspective also leads to second prescription of chapter 6 for optimal human being: "strive to develop greater systemic coherence within one's action system." For example, ideally, one would develop many skills and competencies; use and apply them at the appropriate times in service of goals; set goals that minimally conflict with the other goals in one's system; and set approach, more so than avoidance, goals. In this case, one will maximize one's forward progress and the process of "negentropy creation."

Chapter 6 also provided recommendations for optimal human being based on organismic considerations of optimality. From this perspective, not all progress is beneficial (Kasser & Ryan, 2001; Sheldon & Kasser, 1998), because not all successful behaviors successfully satisfy organismic needs. In Sheldon and Kasser's (1998) data, attaining extrinsic goals involving money, beauty, and status left participants no better off than before, whereas attaining intrinsic goals involving intimacy, community, and personal growth led participants to enhanced well-being. Similarly, Sheldon and Elliot (1999) showed that pursuing goals for self-concordant reasons, because one enjoys and fully identifies with the goals, predicted greater need satisfaction and well-being than did pursuing goals for nonconcordant reasons, because of environmental pressures and/or internal compulsions.

Again, recent research suggests that both these factors, i.e., both the contents of goals and the reasons behind goals (i.e., the "what" and the "why" of motivation), have independent main effects on psychological well-being (Sheldon, Ryan, Kasser, & Deci, in press). Thus, those pursuing intrinsic goals for self-concordant reasons tend to be happiest, whereas those pursuing intrinsic goals for non-concordant reasons and those pursuing extrinsic goals for self-concordant reasons tend to be in the middle of the distribution, whereas those pursuing extrinsic goals for nonconcordant reasons evidence the lowest levels of happiness and satisfaction. Based on these findings, two distinct organismically based goal prescriptions can be suggested: "pursue intrinsic more than extrinsic goals" and "pursue goals for self-concordant more than nonconcordant reasons."

The Self Level of Analysis

Chapter 7, concerning the "self" level of personality, also suggested some possible prescriptions for optimal human being. These prescriptions focused on the four functions of the self-homunculus that were discussed in that chapter. First, the optimal self is one that achieves a reasonable degree of stability and continuity, via construction of a coherent life story (or temporally extended self, in Damasio's (1999) terms). In this way, people can handle existential insecurity and mitigate the fear of death. Second, the optimal self is one that successfully projects its character to other selves during the course of social interaction. It is difficult to imagine a person fully thriving if his or her self is not recognized, valued, and appreciated by others. Third, the optimal self is one that successfully organizes and regulates the person's behavior, in part by providing global or "system-level" standards for the functioning of the action system (Carver & Scheier, 1981). In this way, the gap between present selves and desired future selves is continually reduced. Fourth, the optimal self is one that successfully mirrors and represents the processes occurring "deeper" within the personality system. Again, the self may be viewed as a lived simulation of the total organism, which can be more or less accurate with respect to the person's actual feelings, needs, and interests (Damasio, 1999). Ideally, people will be "in touch with themselves," "true to themselves," and so on—that is, the self-simulation will accurately model the underlying totality.

The Social Interaction Level of Analysis

Chapter 8, which focused on the social interaction level of analysis, provided prescriptions for optimal human being based on game theory and role theory. From a game-theory perspective, people might seek to establish sustained cooperative relations with others, by being "nice" in new situations, by "punishing" those who exploit this practice, and by "forgiving" those punished, after they return to cooperation (Axelrod, 1984). In addition, it appears it may be more optimal if people are willing to make overtures on occasion when mutually damaging competition reigns, and if they avoid exploiting those who seem to tolerate it. Finally, the group-selection perspective suggests that people may do best when they intentionally associate with others who they believe will be cooperative and nonexploitative

(Sober & Wilson, 1998). When people follow these six prescriptions they are likely to do well both in an economic sense, by avoiding detrimental competition, and in a psychological sense, by satisfying needs for relatedness and belongingness.

Four prescriptions were derived from the role-theory perspective. First, one might try to perform one's roles as well as possible. Second, one might try to choose social roles that best fit one's personality and dispositions (Bettencourt & Sheldon, 2001), just as one might try to identify personal goals that are concordant with these underlying personality features (Sheldon, 2002). Of course, we do not always have a choice about the roles we play. This leads to the third role-theory prescription, namely, that one do one's best to internalize such roles and make them a part of one's self. In so doing, one maximizes one's chances of personally benefiting from one's role-playing, and also, of benefiting others. Fourth, when encouraging others to adopt social roles, one might try to be as autonomy-support-ive as possible, so that these others have the best chance of internalizing the roles into their own sense of self. By these means, the gap between the self level of anal-ysis and the social interaction level of analysis is best closed, as is the gap between self and other selves.

The Cultural Level of Analysis

From the cultural level of analysis (chap. 9), optimal human being involves adapt-ing successfully to one's culture, whatever its norms and prescriptions. In this way, one achieves many benefits, both economic and interpersonal. However, we also examined the likelihood that countercultural activity may at times be most benefi-cial. Those whose goals and objectives express strongly held countercultural iden-tifications or fascinating but socially unsupported intrinsic motivations may still derive considerable meaning and enjoyment, even though they are going "against the societal grain." We also saw that some individuals who cross the grain pay sig-nificant costs, as in the examples of Galileo and the many other people throughout history who have sacrificed their freedom or their lives in the attempt to develop new ideas or to rectify wrongs that they perceive in their society. Still, their cul-tures (and thus their own descendants) may benefit in the long run from their ac-tions, as their cultures evolve and develop in generally beneficial directions. Thus, "psychological selection," the process by which individuals pay attention to and sometimes contest particular elements of the culture (Inghilleri, 1999), can have important implications for both individual and cultural thriving.

A final culturally based prescription for optimal human being, derived from the discussion of the adaptive advantages and disadvantages of individualism and collectivism in chapter 9, might be as follows: "Try to draw from both indi-vidualist and collectivist mentalities, as needed." Again, the collectivistic and in-dividualistic approaches to social life may be viewed as two different modes or strategies that every person contains to some extent, whatever his or her culture (Buss, 2001; Triandis, 2001). Thus, ideally, one can manifest both the self-disci-pline and deep loyalty for one's family and groups that are characteristic of positive collectivism, and the attention to internal information and creative impulses that are characteristic of positive individualism, while at the same time avoiding the in-group favoritism and closed-mindedness that can characterize collectivism, as well as the self-centeredness and tendencies toward greed and exploitation that can characterize individualism.

The foregoing discussion considered a variety of promising prescriptions for optimal human being. Although many of these ideas are not new or startling, hopefully they are now better grounded, due to our consideration of the state of the art at each level of human science. Of course, there are doubtless other prescriptions that could be derived at each level of analysis, from other literatures not discussed in this book. However, I believe that the set of 27 prescriptions summarized in Fig. 10.1 is reasonably comprehensive, as well as reasonably well grounded in a scientific sense.

MORE GENERAL PRESCRIPTIONS
FOR OPTIMAL HUMAN BEING?

In this section I return to the important question first posed in chapter 1: Is it possible to derive a more abstract, and perhaps content free, conception of optimal human being? A conception that concerns positive interrelations between levels of analysis, rather than particular approaches, states, or strategies within a level of analysis? In other words, given that people simultaneously exist at every level of analysis discussed in this book, might it be possible to define optimal human being in terms of some optimal configuration or set of arrangements between the different spheres of a person's life, such that the aggregate harmony or integration between the different levels is empirically maximized? Such a definition might circumvent or sidestep the political and value-laden issues involved in trying to say what particular philosophies, goals, or cultural styles are optimal within a level of analysis. From this kind of "systemic" perspective (Sheldon & Kasser, 1995), perhaps it does not matter what kinds of traits, goals, selves, social relations, and cultural matrix a person has, as long as all the pieces fit together in a consistent whole.

Optimal Human Being as Top-Down Regulation

One approach to the inter-level integration question is suggested by Carver and Scheier's (1981, 1998) control theory model. As discussed in chapters 2 and 6, control theory is holistic and teleological, assuming that things go best when stable and high-level goals within a person's action system provide top-down organization of lower level functioning. In this case, the person is "vertically coherent" (Sheldon & Kasser, 1995). Can the concepts of top-down regulation and vertical coherence be extended from the hierarchical action system, depicted in Fig. 3.1, to apply to the more general causal hierarchy of human behavior, depicted in Fig. 2.1? For example, might it be best if the highest levels of influence within the causal hierarchy were also the ones that most organize and control one's behavior?

Notice that the Fig. 3.1 hierarchy stops at the self level of analysis (i.e., the top level of personality in Fig. 3.3)—that is, it does not extend beyond the personality level of analysis, as depicted in Fig. 2.1. However, one might extend Carver and Scheier's top-down regulation idea upward from personality, to the two highest levels presented in Fig. 2.1 and discussed in chapters 8 and 9: social interaction and culture. In terms of the concept of vertical coherence, people may serve as skills or capabilities that effectively reduce discrepancies between present social and/or cultural states (whatever they are), and more desirable social and cultural states that are possible within the future. From this perspective, optimal human being might involve having an action system that maximally serves positive social interactions with others, or that serves the society or culture as a whole.

One problem with this suggestion is that the source of the higher level goals or standards that a person might serve is somewhat unclear. Whose goals, residing in which brain? At the social interaction level of analysis, one might impute the general social goal of "maximizing cooperative functioning," based on the evolutionary analyses offered in chapters 8 and 9. From this perspective, optimal human being might involve having a self that, in fulfilling the third function of the homunculus (projecting character to others), maximizes others' desire to cooperate with oneself. Still, this might not be the actual goal or intention being pursued by the person, rendering the leap from personal goal system to social system problematic. At the cultural level of analysis, the goals or standards that a self may serve are even murkier; cultures are complex and multifaceted, containing many possible goals and prescriptions. A further problem with the suggestion that optimal human being involves serving cultural goals arises in considering countercultural activity, which may be disapproved of by most within the culture. Again, some norms, traditions, or practices may be problematic or inconsistent with the person's personality, needs, and dispositions, in which case the person might be better off resisting or rebelling against those predominant cultural goals (Inghilleri, 1999).

Despite the complexities and ambiguities that emerge when extending control theory to the two highest levels of analysis within Fig. 2.1, I believe that the general prescription has merit; optimal human being is at least somewhat more likely when people "try to serve something beyond themselves," that is, social and cultural goals (Myers, 2000). In other words, people are well advised to try to connect themselves to the larger systems in which they are embedded—more often than not, such holistic impulses (Sheldon & Schmuck, 2001) bring significant rewards, both economic and emotional. Of course, it is also important to try to understand the cases in which they do not.

A somewhat weaker conception of interlevel integration may be supplied by simply positing that there should be consistency between lower and higher levels of the person, if not discrepancy-reducing functionalities. In this view, optimal human being involves minimizing conflict between organism, traits, goals, selves, other people's selves, and one's culture, without necessarily entailing that each level should effectively serve higher levels above it. For example, a person's personality trait of introversion may be largely irrelevant to his goal of raising his family, to his sense of himself as a good father, to his ability to form close relationships with others, or to his ability to contribute to the culture at large. However, as long as the trait does not actively conflict with these factors, then it would at least be consistent with them.

Still, even here, we encounter the possibility that circumstances at a given level of analysis may themselves be nonoptimal, entailing that one would be better off resisting or seeking to change those circumstances, rather than seeking to accommodate them or make oneself consistent with them. Indeed, the ability to take the initiative to rectify negative circumstances (such as having an abusive relationship partner) may be one of the most important functions of the action system (Sheldon, 2002). As another example of this function, the ability to take action against deficiencies within one's culture may at times be a very important requirement for optimal human being (as was discussed earlier in this chapter). Thus, although interlevel consistency may also be beneficial more often than not, it is not always beneficial.

The Necessity of Considering Content

In short, it may be impossible to avoid consideration of a level's "content" in defining optimal human being. Contents (i.e., the particular qualities, themes, or circumstances found at a given level of analysis) vary, and some contents may be less beneficial than others, no matter how well they are put together with other parts of the person. Again, however, once content comes into the mix a host of problems arise, involving value judgments, cultural relativism, and political correctness (see chap. 1). For example, the earlier discussed claim that extrinsic goals are problematic for well-being (Kasser & Ryan, 1993, 1996) has received considerable criticism (Carver & Baird, 1998; Srivastava, Locke, & Bartol, 2001), in part because of other scientists' objections to the implied value judgment. Who is to say that "materialism is bad," for all people and all circumstances?

Fortunately, the relation of content to optimal human being is ultimately an empirical question. That is, researchers at any level of analysis might postulate that certain conditions, contexts, or circumstances are better or more health promoting than others, and then test these ideas using defensible measures of well-being or optimal functioning, while also ruling out plausible alternative explanations. Thus, for example, Sheldon, Ryan, Kasser, and Deci (2004) showed that extrinsic goal content indeed has negative effects on well-being, even when one controls for other salient factors that covary with extrinsic goals, such as the person's underlying motives. Does this mean that extrinsic goal pursuits are always "bad"? Perhaps not—again, it is an empirical question, and we need high-quality data to ascertain the exact main effects of various circumstances at different levels of analysis on optimal human being, and the extent to which these main effects are moderated by other factors.

Organismic Needs as an Invariant Foundation?

To summarize, interlevel integration may not always be beneficial, because contents vary within particular levels, and not all contents are beneficial. Thus, for example, it may do one little good to develop a lifestyle that panders to one's negative traits, or to tailor one's goals to an inaccurate or limiting self-theory, or to conform unquestioningly to a corrupt group or society.

However, there is one level of analysis at which content is thought *not* to vary; that of organismic or species-typical psychological needs (Level 1 in Fig. 3.3). As discussed in chapter 4, self-determination theory (Deci & Ryan, 2000) claims that all humans need experiences of autonomy, competence, and relatedness in order to thrive, no matter what their culture, circumstances, contexts, and conditions. Again, there is fairly good empirical support for these three psychological needs, along with some indication that needs for security and self-esteem should perhaps be added to the basic set (Kasser, 2002; Sedikides et al., 2003; Sheldon et al., 2001).

Perhaps, then, "behave so as to satisfy one's species-typical psychological needs" is the broadest and most invariant recommendation for achieving optimal human being? Consider: Those meeting the need for security are likely achieving necessary prerequisites for optimal human being—they are able to contemplate and select from many present possibilities, and also, they have the luxury of planning the longer term future. Those who are also feeling autonomy and intrinsic motivation are likely expressing their values, developing their talents and interests, and enjoying their experiences. Those who are also feeling a sense of relatedness and belongingness with others are likely connecting and cooperating with other selves; that is, they are effectively bridging the personality and social interaction levels of analysis. Those who are also feeling a sense of competence and self-esteem are likely succeeding in their various endeavors, and are also receiving positive esteem from others (Leary & Baumeister, 2000). Indeed, it is hard to imagine a scenario in which someone experiencing much security, autonomy, competence, self-esteem, and relatedness would be failing to thrive, either personally or in terms of aiding the thriving of others.

However, one caveat is in order before concluding that "maximizing need satisfaction" is the best route to optimal human being—namely, that a person might have a high general need satisfaction score but still not be thriving, because his or her system is configured in a way such that one particular need is being largely unmet. For example, an aggressive and highly successful businessman may feel very much autonomy, security, competence, and self-esteem. However, if his way of life produces almost no relatedness need satisfaction (i.e., he is alienated from his wife, children, and coworkers), then he still might not thrive, despite having a high satisfaction score overall. As another example, an indentured servant might feel much competence, relatedness, security, and self-esteem, but feel very little sense of autonomy, preventing her from truly thriving. This reasoning suggests that the balance of need satisfaction, as well as the overall amount of satisfaction, may be important. To date there has been little research on this topic.

Notice that this purely needs-based conception of optimal human being focuses on only one level of analysis (Level 1 in Fig. 3.3), rather than focusing on integration between many levels of analysis, the issue that began this section of the chapter. However, I believe this single-level focus may be justified, given the assumption that the psychological needs evolved because they helped humans solve adaptive problems of many different kinds (Deci & Ryan, 2000). In other words, the evolutionary and universal foundations of personality may already have been tailored to handle problems at every level of analysis ranging from personality to social to cultural, and also to handle the problem of resolving conflict between the different levels. Thus, obtaining much need satisfaction may be a shorthand route to optimal human being as described by many of the theories discussed in this book (Ryan, 1995).

Integration of the Top Three Levels of Personality in Relation to Need Satisfaction

In sum, it appears that organismic need satisfaction may provide the most important avenue for understanding and approaching optimal human being, because the needs are invariant aspects of human nature, are directly relevant to personal thriving, and may provide a shortcut to satisfying many of the different criteria for optimal human being discussed in chapters 4–9. But how does one best satisfy the needs?

I first consider this question by returning to the issue of interlevel integration, specifically, by considering the vertical connections between the three higher levels of personality (traits, goals, and selves; see Fig. 3.3). Again, these are the three levels at which people are thought to vary, and thus it is useful to consider how variations at particular levels, in combination with variations at other levels, relate to positive outcomes. What configurations best predict satisfaction of the universal needs, located at the lowest level of personality? In addition to further illuminating the relations between the four major levels of personality, this inquiry may give some ideas about how interlevel integration interacts with content to influence optimal human being. I next consider each of the three higher levels of personality in turn, both as a resource that influences functioning at the other two levels and as an outcome that is influenced by functioning at the other two levels.

Let's start at the level of personality traits (Level 2 in Fig. 3.3), and consider the trait-as-resources issue. Should one's traits help one's goals and one's selves (Levels 3 and 4)? Maybe, or maybe not—it depends on the contents at the two higher levels of analysis. For example, if the goals are highly extrinsic ones, or if the selves are inaccurate and limiting, then having traits that help those goals or selves may be problematic, ultimately, for organismic need satisfaction. More concretely: Suppose that the medical resident's trait of strong conscientiousness helps with his surgeon goal, and indeed has been the main thing keeping him going toward this nonconcordant goal. In this case, his trait of conscientiousness may actually be working against him (i.e., against need satisfaction), by delaying his abandonment of the goal. Or, suppose that he is high in the trait of agreeableness; this trait might also be working against him, by causing him to try for too long to accept the "self as surgeon" image that his father insists on.

Turning to the traits-as-outcomes issue: To what extent should trait functioning by helped and supported by goal functioning (Level 3) and self functioning (Level 4)? This also depends on content, in this case, the content of the trait. If the trait is generally positive and adaptive, then yes, goals should help the person express the trait, and also, selves should include and accept the trait. However, if the trait is maladaptive, then it may be best if the person sets goals to change the trait (as in the case of Allison, who has long striven to control her reactivity and disagreeableness), or if the person adopts possible self-images that counteract the trait (as in the case of Allison, who in her mid-30s began to see herself as a more emotionally stable person, which helped her to better contain her trait of neuroticism).

Now let's consider the issues from the perspective of Level 3, that of goals and intentions. Concerning the goals-as-resources question, and looking "down" from this level: Should goals be supportive of trait functioning (Level 2)? Again, it depends on the content of the trait. "Avoid contact with other people" might be an inappropriate goal for a person who is already too psychologically introverted. Looking "up": Should goals help people to develop their life stories and move toward desired future selves? Maybe, but goals should not always be consistent with selves, if the selves involved are inaccurate representations of the person as a whole (as was the case with the aspiring surgeon). In this case, vertical incoherence may be best, such that one's goals actually move one away from inappropriate selves, rather than toward them.

Turning to the goals-as-outcomes question: It may seem ideal if traits and selves support positive goal functioning, but again it depends on content—in this case, the content of the goals. Consistency may be less desirable if the goals are organismically problematic, in which case it may be better if the other levels work against those goals. As an example of the latter process, perhaps the medical resident will begin to develop a new image of himself as a pediatrician, speeding up his disengagement from the nonconcordant "surgeon" goal. Or, his trait of openness to experience might prompt him to seek out further opportunities for working with children, also supporting disengagement from the surgeon goal. In such cases, a lack of consistency within the personality system might actually help a person to achieve greater need satisfaction in the long run.

Finally, let's consider the issues from the perspective of Level 4, the self. This level may be most complex of all, because it mirrors and to some extent contains the other levels of personality below it. Beginning with the self-as-resource question: On the one hand, it may seem ideal for a person to identify his or her sense of self (at Level 4) with his or her goals (at Level 3), thereby deriving motivational resources for enacting the goals. But again, the desirability of this process may depend on the content of the goals—if the goals are highly extrinsic, then such identification may be problematic and may even slow the necessary rejection of those goals. Turning to whether there should be helpful relations between Level 4 (self) and Level 2 (traits), again, it depends. If it is a positive trait (i.e., high conscientiousness), then having a sense of self (i.e., as someone who upholds their commitments) that supports trait expression is likely to be beneficial. However, if it is a negative trait (i.e., high neuroticism), then having a sense of self that is consistent with the trait (i.e., as someone who will never be able to control her emotions) may be less beneficial, ultimately, for need satisfaction.

Turning to the self-as-outcome question: The reasoning is the same. In some cases it is doubtless desirable if traits and goals are consistent with self-level functioning, but this may be undesirable if the self-image is inaccurate or self-limiting. In this instance, it may be better if the person's traits and goals work against the current self, thereby speeding the formation of a new and more satisfying sense of self.

Figure 10.2 graphically summarizes the foregoing discussion, by again presenting the four levels of personality depicted in Fig. 3.3. As illustrated by the three solid lines, it is probably best if all three higher levels help produce psychological need satisfaction. As illustrated by the three dashed lines, the optimality of having

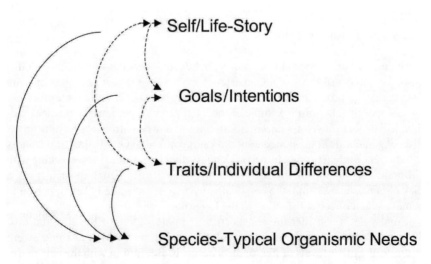

FIG. 10.2. Optimal arrangements between the four levels of personality. Solid lines refer to noncontingent relations and dashed lines refer to contingent relations. Arrows pointing at a level mean that the other level will at least be consistent with, or perhaps be functionally supportive of, the level pointed to.

consistency or positive functional relations between traits and goals, traits and selves, and goals and selves depends on the content at each of these levels of analysis—again, it may be more optimal in the long term if there are inconsistencies with respect to a particular level, if the elements at that level are themselves problematic (i.e., in the case of maladaptive traits, nonconcordant goals, and inaccurate selves). Although considerable data have been reported in this book that are consistent with these speculations, obviously much more work needs to be done.

Optimal Human Being as a Particular Intentional Attitude

The preceding section addressed the question of how to obtain organismic need satisfaction by considering the optimal configurations among the top three levels of personality. In this section I consider the question in a very different way, by asking: How should we live our lives, from the inside? That is, what kind of approach or general attitude should we take in our daily behavior, in order to derive satisfaction? This brings us back to an idea first discussed in chapter 1, that optimal human being may involve a certain intentional attitude or special "way of being" (Blasi, 1988; Maslow, 1971). What is this special intentional attitude?

One clue is provided by the chapter 6 discussion of two meanings of goal self-concordance—either that self-concordance involves having selected the "right" goals for oneself (emphasizing the decision phase of goal pursuit), or that it involves internalizing and endorsing one's goals, whatever they are (emphasizing the enactment phase of goal pursuit). I suggest that the second meaning of self-concordance is a strong candidate for the "optimal intentional attitude" to take toward self and world. In Sartre's (1965) terms, one is taking unshakable responsibility for one's choices, by consciously aligning one's sense of self with those choices. Indeed, feeling that one's self is in full agreement with the other levels of one's life may be of particular importance, because the self is the "window" through which one's life is made personal. The existentialist perspective suggests that such agreement is largely a matter of personal declaration.

However, what if one's goals and choices are incorrect or inappropriate? After all, we can never have perfect knowledge of circumstances, nor of the totality of our underlying state (Damasio, 1999; T. D. Wilson, 2002). Thus, it is almost certainly the case that people will sometimes assert ownership of the "wrong" goals. For example, they may mistakenly identify their sense of self with goals that are antithetical to their deeper talents and predispositions (as in the example of the aspiring surgeon, who might be better off trying to become a pediatrician).

On the other hand, what if the goal is not a mistake, and the aspiring surgeon really would thrive if he persisted in the goal, rather than changing in mid-course? Perhaps such a mid-course change would be indicative of bad faith or insufficient resolve, rather than indicative of self-liberation from an inappropriate goal. This raises an important question: How can one ever know that the decision to give up an important goal is truly appropriate and justified, rather than representing a loss of patience or a case of copping out when the going gets tough? If we are always "strangers to ourselves" (T. D. Wilson, 2002), then perhaps our choices can be no better than random. Worse yet, perhaps our choices are inevitably biased toward short-term, feel-good solutions, solutions that fail to address long-term problems.

The OVP as a Tool for Authentically Revising One's Choices

This brings us back to another foundational characteristic of the human personality, which may help to further ground the concept of optimal human being: namely, the organismic valuing process (OVP; see chaps. 1 and 6). Again, the organismic philosophical perspective (most thoroughly discussed at the end of chap. 4) makes positive assumptions about human nature, emphasizing humans' propensity to become more internally integrated over time. Consistent with this idea, the OVP concept proposes that humans have an innate ability to perceive the well-being and growth-relevant implications of their experiences and choices (Rogers, 1964). In other words, all people have the ability to be in touch with the health-sensing aspects of their organisms, although this inner sense may at times be ignored or obscured.

Although the OVP concept may seem overly optimistic, again, recent data provide considerable empirical support for it (Sheldon, 2003; Sheldon, Arndt, & Houser-Marko, 2003; Sheldon & Kasser, 2001). Indeed, it is only logical to expect that humans would have evolved an internal sensing capacity, as a necessary facet of self-regulation—no complex system can function well without being able to make self-adjustments based on accurate internal state information, and humans are no exception. Of course, people undoubtedly make foolish, "feel-good" choices that undermine the healthy functioning of the system. However, I believe it is only logical that overall, humans would have a slight bias toward healthy choices rather than feel-good choices, when circumstances permit—presumably, we evolved to maximize positive adaptation in the long run, not just positive experience in the short run.

If the OVP concept is correct, it implies that people can in principle sense the difference between (a) legitimately abandoning a goal that is no longer (or perhaps never was) appropriate for their personality and organism, and (b) illegitimately "copping out" on a goal simply because it is harder than one first imagined. In other words, we are not merely adrift in our decision making, with no compass or internal information concerning our true state to call on (Kasser & Sheldon, in press). From this perspective, the prescription for optimal human being becomes: Consult one's OVP when making goal choices, to try to determine what is best. After making the decision, embrace the goal as thoroughly as possible (i.e., intentionally align one's sense of self with the goal). However, remain open to the OVP, so that as new information comes in, one is able to recognize any emerging necessity to make changes. In this way, one can balance the twin imperatives of being and becoming (Kasser & Sheldon, in press), and maximally satisfy one's organismic needs and personality.

To illustrate, let us return to the example of the aspiring surgeon, and suppose that he finally recognized the subtle internal signals telling him that pediatrics might be a better choice for him. In addition, through careful reflection, he became more aware of the extent that his prior choices, and indeed his very preferences in life, had been dictated by his father. Thus, he was able to authentically abandon the surgeon goal, instead taking steps toward becoming a pediatric resident. It was a difficult and time-consuming process, requiring a large amount of self reorganization and considerable conflict with his father, but it was worth it: In the end, he got a long and satisfying career for himself, and countless children got dedicated care from a gifted physician.

FIVE META-PRESCRIPTIONS FOR OPTIMAL HUMAN BEING

The preceding section of the chapter evaluated the possibility of identifying more abstract conceptions of optimal human being. I next summarize the discussion by suggesting five "meta-prescriptions" for optimal human being. These five prescriptions do not focus on any particular level of analysis, but rather reflect a more general systems perspective on human thriving. Of course, there are other global prescriptions that might also be derived from other literatures and conceptual approaches; these five are simply the ones that emerged from the inquiry as framed in this book. Again, however, I believe they provide a reasonably comprehensive and scientifically grounded list.

The five meta-prescriptions are listed in Fig. 10.3; and are as follows:

1. Pursue higher level (social, cultural) goals—that is, attempt to align your personal action system with the action systems of others or of cultural institutions. In this way you will be expressing a healthy human impulse, namely, to integrate yourself into the larger systems in which you are embedded. Again, such an impulse is expectable and even necessary according to the organismic philosophical perspective, and following such holistic impulses is likely to bring many rewards (Sheldon & Schmuck, 2001).

2. Seek balanced need satisfaction—for example, do not sacrifice relatedness needs for security, competence, and self-esteem needs. In this way you will thrive at every level of your personal existence, not just at some levels.

3. Be prepared to work against parts of yourself that are nonconducive to need satisfaction. In this way you will be able to improve problematic aspects of yourself, rather than mindlessly accommodating to them. Notice that this prescription is analogous to the earlier culturally based prescription, namely, that one should be prepared to go against the cultural grain when necessary.

4. Take responsibility for your goal choices—only you can alter yourself and your life, and only if you follow through on your own initiatives with good faith. In this way, you will maximize your ability to create the future of your choice.

5. Finally, listen to your organismic valuing process—and be prepared to modify your choices when it seems necessary. In this way you will be able to appropriately update yourself and your goals, as a result of new learning. You will

1) Try to serve something beyond yourself, i.e., social and cultural goals.

2) Seek balanced need-satisfaction.

3) Be prepared to work against (or to try to modify) problematic aspects of yourself or your world.

4) Take responsibility for your goals and choices.

5) Listen to your organismic valuing process and be prepared to change your goals if it seems necessary.

FIG. 10.3.   Five "meta-prescriptions" for optimal human being.

also be in position to tell when the social and cultural goals you have adopted may be inappropriate or unworthy.

To illustrate these five meta-prescriptions more concretely, let us turn one last time to the medical resident. In the end, he committed himself to the social and cultural goal of helping children stay healthy, realizing that he had to focus on "more than himself" if he wanted to thrive. By making the change, he increased his own level of organismic need satisfaction, primarily by rectifying prior imbalances in autonomy and competence need satisfaction. To make the change, he had to work "against" himself for a time, so that the surgeon goal could be undermined. The fact that the process took so long suggests that the resident was indeed taking responsibility for his choices; he was acting with good faith, trying to follow the goal set earlier to its conclusion. Ultimately, however, his organismic valuing process helped him to recognize that his true vocation lay elsewhere. Fortunately for him (and for the world), he had the courage to act on this knowledge.

Notably, in using this example, I do not mean to focus overmuch on the issue of "deciding on a career." If the five meta-prescriptions just suggested are valid, then they should in principle apply to anyone, in any situation. Of course, it will take considerable new empirical research to thoroughly evaluate, and perhaps modify, these prescriptions. In particular, the concept and conditions of the organismic valuing process may require further clarification and elaboration.

OPTIMAL RELATIONS BETWEEN THE HUMAN SCIENCES

Let us now turn to final topic of this chapter—namely, can any of these ideas or prescriptions be used to illuminate the nature of optimal human science? Clearly, the analogy between optimal human being and optimal human science is an imperfect one. For one, there are different criteria for optimality within the two spheres: Within the individual sphere, organismic need satisfaction, enhanced personal functioning, and psychological well-being are arguably the basic objectives, whereas in the scientific sphere, integrated understanding and advancing technology are the basic objectives. Obviously, it makes little sense to suggest that optimal human science involves satisfying organismic needs, attending carefully to an OVP, or developing certain personality traits!

Still, the more abstract conceptions of vertical integration, discussed earlier in the chapter, may have relevance. In control theory terms, perhaps it is best if lower level sciences effectively serve the advancement of higher level ones. Indeed, this is what was implied by E. O. Wilson (1998), in his discussion of how medical science is served by advances in the basic physical sciences (discussed in chap. 2). Notice that this prescription has both reductionistic and holistic implications. First, it entails that problems at a higher level of analysis might be solved by advancing knowledge at more basic or elemental levels of analysis—here, the reductionist threat is that this new knowledge might make the higher levels of analysis unnecessary. But this prescription also entails that higher levels of analysis might help set the agenda for lower levels of analysis, to some extent regulating activity at the lower levels—here, the holistic benefit is that the higher level perspective might guide and make most useful the lower level perspectives.

Again, causality undoubtedly goes both ways—from the top down, and from the bottom up (as illustrated in Fig. 2.1 and by the "killer" example, discussed in chap. 2). Thus, I believe that a hierarchical pluralist perspective is probably best, in which each level of scientific analysis can potentially contribute to solving problems at each other level of analysis. In the case of bottom-up influence, lower level sciences can fill in the mechanisms by which higher level processes work, clarifying those higher level processes. For example, consideration of cellular neurobiology may illuminate basic cognitive processes, which can in turn illuminate the workings of personality, which can in turn illuminate different modes of social interaction, which can in turn illuminate the workings of particular cultures. In the case of top-down influence, higher levels of scientific analysis can help to set the agendas for lower level sciences, as discussed earlier; also, in terms of the multilevel model perspective developed in several places throughout this book, higher levels of scientific analysis may serve lower levels by revealing moderator effects, in which variations in higher level factors condition and channel the lower level effects. For example, type of cultural norm may moderate the effects of different social interaction strategies, which may in turn moderate the expression and satisfaction of psychological needs, which may in turn moderate the functioning of neurobiological systems, which may in turn moderate the functioning of even more elementary physical processes.

The preceding paragraphs concerned the "strong" form of interlevel integration, in which functional connections exist between different levels of analysis (Carver & Scheier, 1998). However, the weaker definition of interlevel integration discussed earlier, based on mere consistency between different levels, may also have relevance. Indeed, E. O. Wilson (1998) focused primarily on this goal, arguing that each scientific discipline is obligated to be cognizant of the relations of its concepts and findings to the concepts and findings at other levels of analysis. At the very least, knowledge from adjacent disciplines should serve as a constraint on theorizing within a particular discipline. In this way, a "seamless web" may be woven, in which each science plays its unique role within the total picture at the same time that it is acknowledged by, and is ultimately consistent with, the other sciences.

On what foundation should this web be woven? Interestingly, E. O. Wilson (2001) argued that a consilient account of human nature must ultimately be based on "epigenetic rules" for development, built into the human genome. In other words, human nature is not defined or determined by the genes themselves; rather, it is defined by the "inherited regularities of mental development" (p. 14) that are coded for by the genes. These "rules" are not autocratic, in the sense of predetermining final outcomes; instead, they provide mere channels or predispositions for information processing, which both bias and guide the organism in its movement through the environment and the life span. In this sense, they are like the universal sociocognitive mechanisms, discussed in chapter 4. Examples of such epigenetic rules provided by Wilson include human predispositions to read emotional expressions, to avoid incest, to bond with infants, to fear spiders, to make aesthetic judgments based on similar criteria worldwide, and so on.

Thus, Wilson believed, as I do, that an integrated account of human nature must ultimately be based on the species-typical or universal features built into human nature by natural selection (Level 1, in Fig. 3.3). In this chapter, in trying to develop a proper foundation for understanding optimal human being, I have focused on just such a category—specifically, universal psychological needs (rather than the universal sociocognitive mechanisms discussed by Wilson, which can also be located at Level 1 of Fig. 3.3). To borrow Wilson's terms, the psychological needs may be regarded as epigenetic rules to seek out and benefit from certain types of experiences and incentives in life, for example, experiences of autonomous volition, competent functioning, and secure relatedness. As we have seen, needs may provide a better foundation for considering optimal human being than do social cognitive mechanisms, because needs are most directly relevant to human thriving, and because they may provide a short-cut to integration between the many levels of analysis within the personal world.

In sum, to the extent that individual lives are constructed so as to satisfy the basic psychological needs embedded within human nature, then those lives may be "optimized." Similarly, to the extent that the various human sciences ground their inquiry on assumptions about basic human nature, they may achieve optimal scientific understanding. Thus, in the final analysis, the prescriptions for optimal human being and optimal human science may converge: Focus on satisfying (or understanding) the deepest propensities built within human nature, as these propensities will provide the key to the rest.

References

Alexander, R. (1990). *How did humans evolve? Reflections on the uniquely unique species.* Ann Arbor: Museum of Zoology, the University of Michigan.

Allport, G. (1937). *Personality: A psychological interpretation.* New York: Holt, Rinehart & Winston.

Allport, G. (1961). *Pattern and growth in personality.* New York: Holt, Rinehart, & Winston.

Allport, G., & Oddbert, H. (1936). Trait-names, a psychological study. *Psychological Monographs, 47,* (1, Whole No. 211).

Amabile, T. M. (1996). *Creativity in context: Update to "The social psychology of creativity."* Boulder, CO: Westview Press.

Apter, Michael J. (Ed.). (2001). *Motivational styles in everyday life: A guide to reversal theory.* Washington, DC : American Psychological Association.

Argyle, M. (1999). Causes and correlates of happiness. In D. Kahneman, E. Diener, & N. Schwarz (Eds.), *Well-being: The foundations of hedonic psychology* (pp. 353–373). New York: Russell Sage Foundation.

Arndt, J., & Greenberg, J. (1999). The effects of a self-esteem boost and mortality salience on responses to boost relevant and irrelevant worldview threats. *Personality & Social Psychology Bulletin, 25,* 1331–1341.

Arndt, J., Greenberg, J., Schimel, J., Pyszczynski, T., & Solomon, S. (2002). To belong or not to belong, that is the question: Terror management and identification with gender and ethnicity. *Journal of Personality & Social Psychology, 83,* 26–43.

Atran, S. (2001). The trouble with memes: Inference versus imitation in cultural creation. *Human Nature, 12,* 351–381.

Aunger, R. (2002). *The electric meme: A new theory of how we think.* New York: Free Press.

Axelrod, R. (1984). *The evolution of cooperation.* New York: Basic Books.

Baard, P., Deci, E. L., & Ryan, R. M. (in press). Autonomy-support, need-satisfaction, and employee performance in a work organization. *Journal of Applied Social Psychology.*

Baars, B. (1986). *The cognitive revolution in psychology.* New York: Guilford.

Bandura, A. (1997). *Self-efficacy: The exercise of control*. New York: Freeman.

Bardone, A. M., Vohs, K. D., Abramson, L. Y., Heatherton, T. F., & Joiner, T. E. (2000). The confluence of perfectionism, body dissatisfaction, and low self-esteem predicts bulimic symptoms: Clinical implications. *Behavior Therapy, 31,* 265–280.

Bargh, J. A., & Ferguson, M. J. (2000). Beyond behaviorism: On the automaticity of higher mental processes. *Psychological Bulletin, 126,* 925–945.

Bargh, J. A., Gollwitzer, P. M., Lee-Chai, A., Barndollar, K., & Troetschel, R. (2001). The automated will: Nonconscious activation and pursuit of behavioral goals. *Journal of Personality & Social Psychology, 81,* 1014–1027.

Barlow, C. (Ed.). (1991). *From Gaia to selfish genes: Selected writings in the life sciences.* Cambridge, MA: MIT Press.

Barlow, C. (1992). *From Gaia to selfish genes: Selected writings in the life sciences.* Boston: MIT Press.

Baumeister, R. F. (1987). How the self became a problem: A psychological review of historical research. *Journal of Personality & Social Psychology, 52,* 163–176.

Baumeister, R. (1986). *Identity: Cultural change and the struggle for self.* New York: Oxford University Press.

Baumeister, R. F., & Leary, M. R. (1995). The need to belong: Desire for interpersonal attachments as a fundamental human motivation. *Psychological Bulletin, 117,* 497–529.

Becker, E. (1973). *The denial of death.* New York: Free Press.

Benedict, R. (1934). *Patterns of culture.* Boston: Houghton Mifflin.

Bettencourt, B., & Sheldon, K. M. (2001). Social roles as vehicles for psychological need satisfaction within groups. *Journal of Personality and Social Psychology, 81,* 1131–1143.

Biddle, B. J. (1979). *Role theory: Expectations, identities, and behavior.* New York: Academic Press.

Biel, A., & Garling, T. (1995). The role of uncertainty in resource dilemmas. *Journal of Environmental Psychology, 15,* 221–233.

Bingham, P. (1999). Human uniqueness: A general theory. *Quarterly Review of Biology, 74,* 133–169.

Blackmore, S. (1999). *The meme machine.* Oxford: Oxford University Press.

Blasi, A. (1988). Identity and the development of the self. In D. K. Lapsley & F. C. Power (Eds.), *Self, ego, and identity: Integrative approaches* (pp. 226–242). New York: Springer-Verlag.

Bond, M., & Smith, P. (1996). Culture and conformity: A meta-analysis of studies using Asch's line judgment task. *Psychological Bulletin, 119,* 111–137.

Boyd, R., & Richerson, P. (1985). *Culture and evolutionary process.* Chicago: University of Chicago Press.

Brandon, R. N. (1996). *Concepts and methods in evolutionary biology.* New York: Cambridge University Press.

Brehm, J. W., & Self, E. A. (1989). The intensity of motivation. *Annual Review of Psychology, 40,* 109–131.

Brewer, M., & Kramer, R. (1986). Choice behavior in social dilemmas: Effects of social identity, group size, and decision framing. *Journal of Personality and Social Psychology, 50,* 543–549.

Brickman, P., Coates, D., & Janoff-Bulman, R. (1978). Lottery winners and accident victims: Is happiness relative? *Journal of Personality and Social Psychology, 36,* 917–927.

Briggs, S. (1989). The optimal level of measurement for personality constructs. In D. Buss & N. Cantor (Eds.), *Personality psychology: Recent trends and emerging directions* (pp. 246–260). New York: Springer-Verlag.

Brown, D. E. (1991). *Human universals.* Philadelphia: Temple University Press.

Brown, J. (1998). *The self.* Boston: McGraw-Hill.

Bruins, J. J., Liebrand, W. B., & Wilke, H. A. (1989). About the salience of fear and greed in social dilemmas. *European Journal of Social Psychology, 19,* 155–161.

Brunstein, J. (1993). Personal goals and subjective well-being: A longitudinal study. *Journal of Personality and Social Psychology, 65,* 1061–1070.

Bryk, A. & Raudenbush, S. (1992). *Hierarchical linear models for social and behavioral research: Applications and data analysis methods.* Newbury Park, CA: Sage.

Bullock, A., & Stallybrass, O. (Eds.). (1978). *The Harper dictionary of modern thought.* New York: Harper & Row.

Buss, A., & Plomin, R. (1984). *Temperament: Early developing personality traits.* Hillsdale, NJ: Lawrence Erlbaum Associates.

Buss, D. (1991). Evolutionary personality psychology. In M. Rosenzweig & L. Porter (Eds.), *Annual Review of Psychology* (pp. 459–491). Palo Alto, CA: Annual Reviews, Inc.

Buss, D. (1995). Evolutionary psychology: A new paradigm for psychological science. *Psychological Inquiry, 6,* 1–30.

Buss, D. (1997a). Evolutionary foundations of personality. In R. Hogan, J. Johnson, & S. Briggs (Eds.), *Handbook of personality psychology* (pp. 317–344). San Diego, CA: Academic Press.

Buss, D. M. (1998). The psychology of human mate selection: Exploring the complexity of the strategic repertoire. In C. Crawford & D. Krebs (Eds.), *Handbook of evolutionary psychology: Ideas, issues, and applications* (pp. 405–429). Mahwah, NJ: Lawrence Erlbaum Associates.

Buss, D. M. (2000). The evolution of happiness. *American Psychologist, 55*(1), 15–23.

Buss, D. (2001). Human nature and culture: An evolutionary psychological perspective. *Journal of Personality, 69,* 955–978.

Buss, D., & Craik, K. (1983). Act prediction and the conceptual analysis of personality scales: Indices of act density, bipolarity, and extensity. *Journal of Personality and Social Psychology, 45,* 1081–1095.

Buss, D. M., Larsen, R. J., Westen, D., & Semelroth, J. (1992). Sex differences in jealousy: Evolution, physiology, and psychology. *Psychological Science, 3,* 251–255.

Caporael, L. R. (1997). The evolution of truly social cognition: The core configurations model. *Personality & Social Psychology Review, 4,* 276–298.

Caporael, L. R., Dawes, R. M., Orbell, J. M., & Van de Kragt, A. J. (1989). Selfishness examined: Cooperation in the absence of egoistic incentives. *Behavioral & Brain Sciences, 12,* 683–739.

Caporael, L., Wilson, D.S., Hemelrijk, C., Kurzban, R., Orbell, J., & Sheldon, K. M. (in press). Groups from an evolutionary perspective. *Small Groups Research.*

Carver, C. S., & Baird, E. (1998). The American dream revisited: Is it what you want or why you want it that matters? *Psychological Science, 9,* 289–292.

Carver, C., & Scheier, M. (1981). *Attention and self-regulation: A control theory approach to human behavior.* New York: Springer-Verlag.

Carver, C. & Scheier, M. (1982). Control theory: A useful conceptual framework for personality, social, clinical, and health psychology. *Psychological Bulletin, 92,* 111–135.

Carver, C. S., & Scheier, M. F. (1990). Origins and functions of positive and negative affect: A control-process view. *Psychological Review, 97,* 19–35.

Carver, C., & Scheier, M. (1998). *On the self-regulation of behavior.* Cambridge, UK: Cambridge University Press.

Caspi, A. (1998). Personality development across the life course. In W. Damon (Ed.), *Handbook of child psychology, Vol. 3: Social, emotional, and personality development* (5th ed., pp. 311–388). New York: John Wiley & Sons.

Chirkov, V., Ryan, R. M., Kim, Y., & Kaplan, U. (2003). Differentiating autonomy from individualism and independence: A self-determination theory perspective on internalization of cultural orientations and well-being. *Journal of Personality & Social Psychology, 84,* 97–109.

Compton, W. C., Smith, M. L., Cornish, K. A., & Qualls, D. L. (1996). Factor structure of mental health measures. *Journal of Personality & Social Psychology, 71,* 406–413.

Cooley, C. (1902). *Human nature and the social order.* New York: Scribner.

Cosmides, L. (1989). The logic of social exchange: Has natural selection shaped how humans reason? Studies with the Wason selection task. *Cognition, 31,* 187–276.

Costa, P. T., Jr., McCrae, R. R., Martin, T. A., Oryol, V. E., Senin, I. G., Rukavishnikov, A. A., Shimonaka, Y., Nakazato, K., Gondo, Y., Takayama, M., Allik, J., Kallasmaa, T., & Realo, A. (2000). Personality development from adolescence through adulthood: Further cross-cultural comparisons of age differences. In V. Molfese & D. Molfese (Eds,), *Temperament and personality development across the life span* (pp. 235–252). Mahwah, NJ: Lawrence Erlbaum Associates.

Csikszentmihalyi, M. (1993). *The evolving self: A psychology for the third millennium.* New York: HarperCollins.

Csikszentmihalyi, M. (1997). *Finding flow: The psychology of engagement with everyday life.* New York: Basic Books.

Damasio, A. (1999). *The feeling of what happens: Body and emotion in the making of consciousness.* San Diego, CA: Harcourt.

D'Andrade, R. (1995). *The development of cognitive anthropology.* New York: Cambridge University Press.

Dawkins, R. (1976). *The selfish gene.* New York: Oxford University Press.

Dawkins, R. (1986). *The blind watchmaker.* New York: Norton.

Deasy, L. (1964). *Social role theory: Its component parts, and some applications.* Washington, DC: Catholic University of America Press.

deCharms, R. (1968). *Personal causation: The internal affective determinants of behavior.* New York: Academic Press.

Deci, E. L. (2003). Personal communication.

Deci, E. L., Eghrari, H., Patrick, B. C., & Leone, D. (1994). Facilitating internalization: The self-determination theory perspective. *Journal of Personality, 62,* 119–142.

Deci, E. L., & Ryan, R. M. (1985). *Intrinsic motivation and self-determination in human behavior.* New York: Plenum.

Deci, E. L., & Ryan, R. M. (1991). A motivational approach to self: Integration in personality. In R. Dienstbier (Ed.), *Nebraska symposium on motivation, Vol. 38, Perspectives on motivation* (pp. 237–288). Lincoln: University of Nebraska Press.

Deci, E. L., & Ryan, R. M. (2000). The "what" and "why" of goal pursuits: Human needs and the self-determination of behavior. *Psychological Inquiry, 11,* 227–268.

Deci, E. L., Ryan, R. M., Gagne, M., Leone, D. R., Usunov, J., & Kornazheva, B. P. (2001). Need satisfaction, motivation, and well-being in the work organizations of a former Eastern bloc country: A cross-cultural study of self-determination. *Personality and Social Psychology Bulletin, 27,* 930–942.

DeNeve, K. M., & Cooper, H. (1998). The happy personality: A meta-analysis of 137 personality traits and subjective well-being. *Psychological Bulletin, 124,* 197–229.

Dennett, D. (1992). Temporal anomalies of consciousness: Implications of the un-centered brain. In Y. Christen & P. S. Churchland (Eds.), *Neurophilosophy and Alzheimer's Disease*. Berlin: Springer-Verlag.

DeRaad, B., Perugini, M., Hrebickova, M., & Szarota, P. (1998). Lingua franca of personality: Taxonomies and structures based on the psycholexical approach. *Journal of Cross-Cultural Psychology, 29,* 212–232.

Diamond, J. (1997). *Guns, germs, and steel.* New York: W. W. Norton.

Diener, E. (1994). Assessing subjective well-being: Progress and opportunities. *Social Indicators Research, 31,* 103–157.

Diener, E., & Lucas, R. E. (1999). Personality and subjective well-being. In D. Kahneman, E. Diener, & N. Schwartz (Eds.), *Well-being: The foundations of hedonic psychology* (pp. 213–229). New York: Russell Sage.

Diener, E., & Suh, E. (Eds.). (2000). *Culture and subjective well-being.* Cambridge, MA: MIT Press.

Dunn, J., & Plomin, R. (1990). *Separate lives: Why siblings are so different.* New York: Basic Books.

Durham, W. H. (1991). *Coevolution: Genes, culture, and human diversity.* Stanford, CA: Stanford University Press.

Durkheim, E. (1938). *The rules of sociological method.* New York: The Free Press.

Earley, P. (1989). Social loafing and collectivism: A comparison of the U.S. and the People's Republic of China. *Administration Science Quarterly, 34,* 565–581.

Earley, P., & Gibson, C. (1998). Taking stock in our progress on individualism and collectivism: 100 Years of solidarity and community. *Journal of Management, 24,* 265–304.

Ehrlich, P. (2000). *Human natures: Genes, cultures, and the human prospect.* Washington, DC: Island Press.

Ekman, P. (1971). Universals and cultural differences in facial expressions of emotion. In J. R. Cole (Ed.), *Nebraska symposium on motivation* (Vol. 26, pp. 207–283). Lincoln: University of Nebraska Press.

Elliot, A. J., McGregor, H. A., & Thrash, T. M. (2002). The need for competence. In E. L. Deci & R. M. Ryan (Eds.), *Handbook of self-determination research.* (pp. 361–387). Rochester, NY: University of Rochester Press.

Elliot, A. J., & Sheldon, K. M. (1996). Avoidance achievement motivation: A personal goals analysis. *Journal of Personality and Social Psychology, 73,* 171–185.

Elliot, A. J., & Sheldon, K. M. (1998). Avoidance personal goals and the personality-illness relationship. *Journal of Personality and Social Psychology, 75,* 1282–1299.

Elliot, A. J., Sheldon, K. M., & Church, M. (1997). Avoidance personal goals and subjective well-being. *Personality and Social Psychology Bulletin, 23,* 915–927.

Emmons, R. A. (1989). The personal strivings approach to personality. In L.A. Pervin (Ed.), *Goal concepts in personality and social psychology* (pp. 87–126). Hillsdale, NJ: Lawrence Erlbaum Associates.

Emmons, R. A. (1992). Abstract versus concrete goals: Personal striving level, physical illness, and psychological well-being. *Journal of Personality & Social Psychology, 62,* 292–300.

Emmons, R. A., & King, L. (1988). Conflict among personal strivings: Immediate and long-term implications for psychological and physical well-being. *Journal of Personality and Social Psychology, 54,* 1040–1048.

Emmons, R. A., & King, L. A. (1989). Personal striving differentiation and affective reactivity. *Journal of Personality & Social Psychology, 56,* 478–484.

Emmons, R. A., King, L., & Sheldon, K. M. (1993). Goal conflict and the self-regulation of action. In D. Wegner & J. Pennebaker (Eds.), *Handbook of mental control* (pp. 528–551). Englewood Cliffs, NJ: Prentice Hall.

Epstein, S. (1973). The self-concept revisited: Or a theory of a theory. *American Psychologist, 28,* 404–416.

Epstein, S. (1979). The stability of behavior: 1. On predicting most of the people much of the time. *Journal of Personality and Social Psychology, 37,* 1097–1126.

Erikson, E. (1963). *Childhood and society.* New York: Norton.

Eysenck, H. (1973). *Eysenck on extraversion.* New York: John Wiley & Sons.

Eysenck, H. (1990). Biological dimensions of personality. In L. Pervin (Ed.), *Handbook of personality theory and research.* (pp. 244–276). New York: Guilford Press.

Fazio, R. H., & Olson, M. A. (2003). Implicit measures in social cognition research: Their meaning and uses. *Annual Review of Psychology, 54,* 297–327.

Fleeson, W. (2001). Toward a structure- and process-integrated view of personality: Traits as density distributions of states. *Journal of Personality & Social Psychology, 80,* 1011–1027.

Flinn, M. (1996). Culture and the evolution of social learning. *Evolution and Human Behavior, 18,* 23–67.

Ford, D. H., & Lerner, R. M. (1992). *Developmental systems theory : an integrative approach.* Newbury Park, CA: Sage.

Funder, D. C., & Ozer, D. J. (1983). Behavior as a function of the situation. *Journal of Personality & Social Psychology, 44,* 107–112.

Gaskins, R. W. (1999). "Adding legs to a snake": A reanalysis of motivation and the pursuit of happiness from a Zen Buddhist perspective. *Journal of Educational Psychology, 91,* 204–215.

Geary, D. C. (1998). *Male, female: The evolution of human sex differences.* Washington, DC: American Psychological Association.

Geary, D. C., & Huffman, K. J. (2002). Brain and cognitive evolution: Forms of modularity and functions of mind. *Psychological Bulletin, 128,* 667–698.

Geertz, C. (1973). *The interpretation of cultures: Selected essays.* New York: Basic Books.

Gendlin, E. T. (1978). *Focusing.* New York: Everest House.

Gergen, K. J. (1991). *The saturated self: Dilemmas of identity in contemporary life.* New York: Basic Books.

Glansdorff, P., & Prigogine, I. (1971). *Thermodynamic theory of structure, stability and fluctuations.* New York: Wiley.

Goebel, B. L., & Brown, D. R. (1981). Age differences in motivation related to Maslow's Need Hierarchy. *Developmental Psychology, 17,* 809–815.

Goffman, E. (1959). *The presentation of self in everyday life.* Garden City, NY: Doubleday.

Goldberg, L. (1990). An alternative "description of personality": The Big-Five factor structure. *Journal of Personality and Social Psychology, 59,* 1216–1229.

Goldstein, K. (1939). *The organism.* New York: American Book Company.

Gollwitzer, P. M. (1990). Action phases and mind-sets. In E. T. Higgins & R. M. Sorrentino (Eds.), *Handbook of motivation and cognition,* (Vol. 2, pp. 53–92). New York: Guilford Press.

Gollwitzer, P. M. (1999). Implementation intentions: Strong effects of simple plans. *American Psychologist, 54,* 493–503.

Gould, S. J. (1984). This view of life. *Natural History, 93,* 24–33.

Greenberg, J., Pyszczynski, T., & Solomon, S. (1986). The causes and consequences of a need for self-esteem: A terror management theory. In R. F. Baumeister (Ed.), *Public self and private self* (pp. 189–212). New York: Springer-Verlag.

Greenberg, J., Pyszczynski, T., & Solomon, S. (1995). Toward a dual-motive depth psychology of self and social behavior. In M. Kernis (Ed.), *Efficacy, agency, and self-esteem* (pp. 73–99). New York: Plenum Press.

Greenwald, A. G. (1986). Self-knowledge and self-deception. *Przeglad Psychologiczny, 29,* 291–303.

Greenwald, A. G., Nosek, B. A., & Banaji, M. R. (2003). Understanding and using the Implicit Association Test: I. An improved scoring algorithm. *Journal of Personality & Social Psychology, 85,* 197–216.

Hamerow, T. S. (1997). *On the road to the wolf's lair: German resistance to Hitler.* Cambridge, MA: Harvard/Belknap Press.

Hamilton, W. (1964). The genetical evolution of social behavior I. *Journal of Theoretical Biology, 7,* 1–16.

Hardin, G. (1968). The tragedy of the commons. *Science, 162,* 1243–1248.

Harris, J. (1995). Where is the child's environment? A group socialization theory of development. *Psychological Bulletin, 102,* 458–489.

Hart, D. (1988). The adolescent self-concept in social context. In D. Lapsley & F. Power (Eds.), *Self, ego, and identity: Integrative approaches* (pp. 71–90). New York: Springer-Verlag.

Harter, S. (1999). *The construction of the self : A developmental perspective.* New York: Guilford Press.

Harter, S., & Monsour, A. (1992). Development analysis of conflict caused by opposing attributes in the adolescent self-portrait. *Developmental Psychology, 28,* 251–260.

Holland, J. L. (1985). *Making vocational choices: A theory of careers* (2nd ed.). Englewood Cliffs, NJ: Prentice Hall.

Humphrey, N. (1976). The social function of intellect. In P. Bateson & R. Hinde (Eds.), *Growing points in Ethology* (pp. 303–318). New York: Cambridge University Press.

Inghilleri, P. (1999). *From subjective experience to cultural change.* Cambridge, England: Cambridge University Press.

James, W. (1950). *The Principles of Psychology.* New York: Dover. (Original work published 1890)

Jaynes, J. (1976). *The origin of consciousness in the breakdown of the bicameral mind.* Boston: Houghton Mifflin.

John, O. (1990). The "Big Five" factor taxonomy: Dimensions of personality in the natural language and in questionnaires. In L. Pervin (Ed.), *Handbook of personality theory and research* (pp. 66–100). New York: Guilford Press.

Joiner, T. E., Jr. (2002). Depression in its interpersonal context. In I. H. Gotlib & C. L. Hammen (Eds.), *Handbook of depression* (pp. 295–313). New York: Guilford.

Jones, E. E., & Nisbett, R. E. (1972). The actor and the observer: Divergent perceptions of the causes of behavior. In E. Jones, D. Kanouse, H. Kelley, R. Nisbett, S. Valins, & B. Weiner (Eds.), *Attributions: Perceiving the causes of behavior* (pp. 79–94). Morristown, NJ: General Learning Press.

Jorgenson, D., & Papciak, A. (1980). The effects of communication, resource feedback, and identifiability on behavior in a simulated commons. *Journal of Experimental Social Psychology, 17,* 373–385.

Jourard, S. (1974). *Healthy personality.* New York: Macmillan.

Juarrero, A. (1999). *Dynamics in action: Intentional behavior as a complex system.* Cambridge, MA: MIT Press

Kagan, J. (1994). *Galen's prophecy.* New York: Basic Books.

Kahneman, D., Diener, E., & Schwartz, N. (Eds.). (1999). *Well-being: The foundations of hedonic psychology.* New York: Russell Sage.

Kasser, T. (2002). *The high price of materialism*. Cambridge, MA: MIT Press.

Kasser, T., & Ryan, R. M. (1993). A dark side of the American dream: Correlates of financial success as a central life aspiration. *Journal of Personality and Social Psychology, 65,* 410–422.

Kasser, T., & Ryan, R. M. (1996). Further examining the American dream: Differential correlates of intrinsic and extrinsic goals. *Personality and Social Psychology Bulletin, 22,* 80–87.

Kasser, T., & Ryan, R. M. (2001). Be careful what you wish for: Optimal functioning and the relative attainment of intrinsic and extrinsic goals. In P. Schmuck & K. M. Sheldon (Eds.), *Life goals and well-being: Towards a positive psychology of human striving* (pp. 116–131). Goettingen, Germany: Hogrefe & Huber.

Kasser, T., Ryan, R. M., Zax, M., & Sameroff, A. J. (1995). The relations of maternal and social environments to late adolescents' materialistic and prosocial values. *Developmental Psychology, 31,* 907–914.

Kasser, T., & Sheldon, K. M. (in press). Non-becoming, alienated becoming, and authentic becoming: A goal-based approach. In J. Greenberg & T. Pczyzynski (Eds.), *Handbook of experimental existential psychology.*

Kauffman, S. (1995). *At home in the universe: The search for laws of self-organization and complexity.* New York: Oxford University Press.

Kelley, H. H., & Stahelski, A. J. (1970). Social interaction basis of cooperators' and competitors' beliefs about others. *Journal of Personality & Social Psychology, 16,* 66–91.

Kendler, H. (1999). The role of value in the world of psychology. *American Psychologist, 54,* 828–835.

Kernis, M. H., & Paradise, A. W. (2002). Distinguishing between secure and fragile forms of high self-esteem. In E. L. Deci & R. M. Ryan (Eds.), *Handbook of self-determination research* (pp. 339–360). Rochester, NY: University of Rochester Press.

Keyes, C. L., Shmotkin, D., & Ryff, C.D. (2002). Optimizing well-being: The empirical encounter of two traditions. *Journal of Personality & Social Psychology, 82,* 1007–1022.

Kidder, A. (1940). Looking backwards. *Proceedings of the American Philosophical Society, 83,* 527–537.

Kihlstrom, J. F. (1997). Consciousness and me-ness. In J. Cohen & J. Schooler (Eds.), *Scientific approaches to consciousness. Carnegie Mellon Symposia on cognition* (pp. 451–468). Mahwah, NJ: Lawrence Erlbaum Associates.

Kincaid, H. (1997). *Individualism and the unity of science: Essays on reduction, explanation, and the special sciences.* Lanham, MD: Rowman & Littlefield.

Kiresuk, T., Smith, A., & Cardillo, J. (1994). *Goal attainment scaling: Applications, theory, and measurement.* Hillsdale, NJ: Lawrence Erlbaum Associates.

Kluckhohn, C., & Murray, H. A. (1953). Personality formation: The determinants. In C. Kluckhohn, H. Murray, & D. Schneider (Eds.), *Personality in nature, society, and culture* (pp. 53–67). New York: Alfred A. Knopf.

Komorita, S., & Parks, C. D. (1994). *Social dilemmas.* Madison, WI: Brown & Benchmark.

Komorita, S., & Parks, C. (1995). Interpersonal relations: Mixed-motive interaction. *Annual Review of Psychology, 46,* 183–207.

Kouba, L., & Muasher, J. (1985). Female circumcision in Africa: An overview. *African Studies Review, 28,* 95–110.

Kraines, D., & Kraines, V. (1995). Evolution of learning among Pavlov strategies in a competitive environment with noise. *Journal of Conflict Resolution, 39,* 439–466.

Krebs, D., Denton, K., & Higgins, N. (1988). On the evolution of self-knowledge and self-deception. In K. MacDonald (Ed.), *Sociobiological perspectives on human development* (pp. 103–139). New York: Springer-Verlag.

Kristoff, A. L. (1996). Person-organization fit: An integrative review of its conceptualizations, measurement, and implications. *Personnel Psychology, 49,* 1–49.

Kuhl, J. (1986). Motivation and information processing: A new look at decision making, dynamic change, and action control. In R. Sorrentino & E. Higgins (Eds.), *Handbook of motivation and cognition: Foundations of social behavior* (pp. 404–434). New York: Guilford Press.

Kuhl, J., & Kazen, M. (1994). Self-discrimination and memory: State orientation and false self-ascription of assigned activities. *Journal of Personality and Social Psychology, 66,* 1103–1115.

La Guardia, J. G., Ryan, R. M., Couchman, C. E., & Deci, E. L. (2000). Within-person variation in security of attachment: A self-determination theory perspective on attachment, need fulfillment, and well-being. *Journal of Personality & Social Psychology, 79,* 367–384.

Laing, R. D. (1969). *Self and others.* New York : Pantheon Books.

Lamiell, J. T. (1997). Individuals and the differences between them. In R. Hogan, J. Johnson, & S. Briggs (Eds.), *Handbook of personality psychology* (pp. 117–141). San Diego: Academic Press.

Lazarus, R. (2003). Does positive psychology have "legs"? *Psychological Inquiry, 14,* 93–109.

Leary, M. R., & Baumeister, R. F. (2000). The nature and function of self-esteem: Sociometer theory. *Advances in Experimental Social Psychology, 32,* 1–62.

Leung, K. (1997). Negotiation and reward allocations across cultures. In P.C. Earley & M. Erez (Eds.), *New perspectives on international industrial and organizational psychology* (pp. 640–675). San Francisco, CA: Lexington Press.

Liebrand, W. (1984). The effect of social motives, communication and group size on behavior in an N-person multi-stage mixed-motive game. *European Journal of Social Psychology, 14,* 239–264.

Little, B. R. (1993). Personal projects and the distributed self: Aspects of a conative Psychology. In J. Suls (Ed.), *The self in social perspective: Psychological Perspectives on the self* (Vol. 4, pp 157–185). Hillsdale, NJ: Lawrence Erlbaum Associates.

Little, B. R. (1996). Free traits, personal projects and idio-tapes: Three tiers for personality psychology. *Psychological Inquiry, 7,* 340–344.

Livingston, J. (1994). *Rogue primate: An exploration of human domestication.* Toronto: Key Porter.

Loehlin, J. (1992). *Genes and environment in personality development.* Newbury Park, CA: Sage.

Loevinger, J. (1997). Stages of personality development. In R. Hogan, J. Johnson, & S. Briggs (Eds.), *Handbook of personality psychology.* (pp. 199–208). San Diego, CA: Academic Press.

Lykken, D. (2000). *Happiness: The nature and nurture of joy and contentment.* New York: St. Martin's Griffin.

Lykken, D., & Tellegen, A. (1996). Happiness is a stochastic phenomenon. *Psychological Science, 7,* 186–189.

Lyubomirsky, S., Sheldon, K. M., & Schkade, D. (in press). Pursuing happiness: The Architecture of sustainable change. *Review of General Psychology.*

MacDonald, K. (1991). A perspective on Darwinian psychology: The importance of domain-general mechanisms, plasticity, and individual differences. *Ethology & Sociobiology, 12,* 449–480.

Malinowski, B. (1944). *A scientific theory of culture and other essays.* New York: Oxford University Press

Marcel, A. J. (1993). Slippage in the unity of consciousness. Experimental and theoretical studies of consciousness. *Ciba Foundation Symposium, 174,* 168–186.

Marcia, J. E. (2002). Identity and psychosocial development in adulthood. *Identity, 2,* 7–28.

Markus, H., Kitayama, S., & Heiman, R. (1996). Culture and basic psychological principles. In E. T. Higgins & A. W. Kruglanski (Eds.), *Social psychology: Handbook of basic principles* (pp. 857–913). New York: Guilford Press.

Markus, H., & Ruvolo, A. (1989). Possible selves: Personalized representations of goals. In L. Pervin (Ed.), *Goal concepts in personality and social psychology* (pp. 211–241). Hillsdale, NJ: Lawrence Erlbaum Associates.

Maslow, A. (1962). *Towards a psychology of being*. Princeton, NJ: Van Nostrand.

Maslow, A. (1971). *The farther reaches of human nature*. New York: Viking Press.

Masten, A. S. (2001, March). Ordinary magic: Resilience processes in development. *American Psychologist, 56*(3), 227–238.

Matsumoto, D. (2001). Introduction. In D. Matsumoto (Ed.), *The handbook of culture and psychology* (pp. 3–10). Oxford, UK: Oxford University Press.

McAdams, D. P. (1993). *The stories we live by: Personal myths and the making of the self*. New York: Guilford.

McAdams, D. P. (1995). What do we know when we know a person? *Journal of Personality, 63,* 365–396.

McAdams, D. P. (1996). Personality, modernity, and the storied self: A contemporary framework for studying persons. *Psychological Inquiry, 7,* 295–321.

McAdams, D. P. (1998). Ego, trait, identity. In P. M. Westenberg & A. Blasi (Eds.), *Personality development: Theoretical, empirical, and clinical investigations of Loevinger's conception of ego development* (pp. 27–38). Mahwah, NJ: Lawrence Erlbaum Associates.

McAdams, D. P. (2001). *The person: An integrated introduction to personality psychology*. Fort Worth, TX: Harcourt.

McAdams, D. P., & de St. Aubin, E. (1992). A theory of generativity and its assessment through self-report, behavioral acts, and narrative themes in autobiography. *Journal of Personality and Social Psychology, 62,* 1003–1015.

McAdams, D. P., Josselson, R., & Lieblich, A. (2001). (Eds.). *Turns in the road: Narrative studies of lives in transition*. Washington, DC: American Psychological Association.

McClelland, D., Atkinson, J., Clark, R., & Lowell, E. (1953). *The achievement motive*. New York: Appleton-Century-Crofts.

McClelland, D., Koestner, R., & Weinberger, J. (1989). How do self-attributed and implicit motives differ? *Psychological Review, 96,* 690–702.

McConnell, A. R., & Leibold, J. M. (2001). Relations among the Implicit Association Test, discriminatory behavior, and explicit measures of racial attitudes. *Journal of Experimental Social Psychology, 37,* 435–442.

McCrae, R. (2001). Trait psychology and culture: Exploring intercultural comparisons. *Journal of Personality, 69,* 819–846.

McCrae, R., & Costa, P. (1990). *Personality in adulthood*. New York: Guilford Press.

McCrae, R., & Costa, P. (1995). Toward a new generation of personality theories: Theoretical contexts for the five-factor model. In J. Wiggins (Ed.), *The five-factor model of personality* (pp 51–87). New York: Guilford Press.

McCrae, R. R., Costa, P. T. Jr., Ostendorf, F., Angleitner, A., Hrebickova, M., Avia, M. D., Sanz, J., Sanchez-Bernardos, M. L., Kusdil, M. E., Woodfield, R., Saunders, P. R., & Smith, P. B. (2000). Nature over nurture: Temperament, personality, and life span development. *Journal of Personality & Social Psychology, 78,* 173–186.

McGregor, I., McAdams, D. P., & Little, B. R. (2003). *Personal projects, life-stories, and well-being: The benefits of acting and being true to one's traits*. Unpublished manuscript.

McGue, M., Bacon, S., & Lykken, D. (1993). Personality stability and change in early adulthood: A behavioral genetic analysis. *Developmental Psychology, 29,* 96–109.

Mealey, L. (1995). The sociobiology of sociopathy: An integrated evolutionary model. *Behavioral & Brain Sciences, 18,* 523–599.

Michel, L., & Herbeck, D. (2001). *American terrorist: Timothy McVeigh and the Oklahoma City bombing.* New York: HarperCollins.

Midlarsky, E., & Kahana, E. (1994). *Altruism in later life.* Thousand Oaks, CA: Sage.

Mikulincer, M., Florian, V., & Hirschberger, G. (2003). The existential function of close relationships: Introducing death into the science of love. *Personality & Social Psychology Review, 7,* 20–40.

Mills, J., & Clark, M. (1982). Exchange and communal relationships. In L. Wheeler (Ed.), *Review of personality and social psychology* (Vol. 3, pp. 121–144). Beverly Hills, CA: Sage.

Mischel, W. (1968). *Personality and assessment.* New York: John Wiley & Sons.

Mischel, W., & Shoda, Y. (1998). Reconciling processing dynamics and personality dispositions. In J. Spence, J. Darley, & D. Foss (Eds.), *Annual Review of Psychology* (pp. 229–258). Palo Alto, CA: Annual Reviews.

Murdock, G. (1945). The common denominator of Culture. In R. Linton (Ed.), *The science of man in the world crisis* (pp. 124–142). New York: Columbia University Press.

Murray, H. (1938). *Explorations in personality.* New York: Oxford University Press.

Myers, D. G. (2000). The funds, friends, and faith of happy people. *American Psychologist, 55,* 56–67.

Nisbett, R. E., & Cohen, D. (1996). *Culture of honor: The psychology of violence in the South.* Boulder, CO: Westview Press.

Nissle, S., & Bschor, T. (2002). Winning the jackpot and depression: Money cannot buy happiness. *International Journal of Psychiatry in Clinical Practice, 6,* 183–186.

Norenzayan, A., & Nisbett, R. E. (2000). Culture and causal cognition. *Current Directions in Psychological Science, 9,* 132–135.

Nowak, A., Vallacher, R. R., Tesser, A., & Borkowski, W. (2000). Society of self: The emergence of collective properties in self-structure. *Psychological Review, 107,* 39–61.

Nozick, R. (1993). *The nature of rationality.* Princeton, NJ: Princeton University Press.

Oishi, S., & Diener, E. (2001). Goals, culture, and subjective well-being. *Personality & Social Psychology Bulletin, 27,* 1674–1682.

Oishi, S., Diener, E. F., Lucas, R. E., & Suh, E. M. (1999). Cross-cultural variations in predictors of life satisfaction: Perspectives from needs and values. *Personality & Social Psychology Bulletin, 25,* 980–990.

Oishi, S., Diener, E., Suh, E., & Lucas, R. E. (1999). Value as a moderator in subjective well-being. *Journal of Personality, 67,* 157–184.

Overton, W. F. (1976). The active organism in structuralism. *Human Development, 19,* 71–86.

Parks, C. D., & Vu, A. D. (1994). Social dilemma behavior of individuals from highly individualist and collectivist cultures. *Journal of Conflict Resolution, 38,* 708–718.

Perse, E. M. (2001). *Media effects and society.* Mahwah, NJ: Lawrence Erlbaum Associates.

Pervin, L. (1994). A critical analysis of current trait theory. *Psychological Inquiry, 5,* 103–113.

Pervin, L. (2003). *The science of personality.* New York: Oxford University Press.

Pervin, L., & John, O. (2001). *Personality: Theory and research.* New York: John Wiley & Sons.

Piaget, J. (1971). *Biology and knowledge; An essay on the relations between organic regulations and cognitive processes*. Chicago: University of Chicago Press.

Pinker, S. (2002). *The blank slate: The modern denial of human nature*. New York: Viking.

Plomin, R. (1995). Genetics and children's experiences in the family. *Journal of Child Psychology and Psychiatry, 36*, 33–68.

Popper, K. R. (1961). *The logic of scientific discovery*. New York: Scientific Editions.

Popper, K. R., & Eccles, J. C. (1977). *The self and its brain*. New York: Springer International.

Poundstone, W. (1992). *Prisoner's dilemma*. New York: Doubleday.

Prabhakaran, V., Narayanan, K., Zhao, Z., & Gabrieli, J. D. E. (2000). Integration of diverse information in working memory within the frontal lobe. *Nature Neuroscience, 3*, 85–90.

Pruitt, D., & Kimmel, M. (1977). Twenty years of experimental gaming: Critique, synthesis, and suggestions for the future. *Annual Review of Psychology, 28*, 363–393.

Putnam, R. D. (2000). *Bowling alone: The collapse and revival of American community*. New York: Simon & Schuster.

Rachlin, H. (2000). *Science of self-control*. Cambridge, MA: Harvard University Press.

Rapoport, A., & Chammah, A. M. (1965). *Prisoner's dilemma; A study in conflict and cooperation*. Ann Arbor: University of Michigan Press.

Read, S., & Miller, L. (1989). Inter-personalism: Toward a goal-based theory of persons in relationships. In L. Pervin (Ed.), *Goal concepts in personality and social psychology* (pp. 413–472). Hillsdale, NJ: Lawrence Erlbaum Associates.

Reeve, J. (1992). *Understanding motivation and emotion*. Fort Worth, TX: Holt, Rinehart & Winston.

Reis, H. T., Sheldon, K. M., Gable, S. L., Roscoe, R., & Ryan, R. (2000). Daily well being: The role of autonomy, competence, and relatedness. *Personality and Social Psychology Bulletin, 26*, 419–435.

Roberts, B. W., & Donahue, E. M. (1994). One personality, multiple selves: Integrating personality and social roles. *Journal of Personality, 62*, 199–218.

Robins, R. W., Fraley, R. C., Roberts, B. W., & Trzesniewski, K. H. (2001). A longitudinal study of personality change in young adulthood. *Journal of Personality, 69*, 617–640.

Robinson, M. D., Johnson, J. T., & Shields, S. A. (1995). On the advantages of modesty: The benefits of a balanced self-presentation. *Communication Research, 22*, 575–591.

Rogers, C. (1951). *Client-centered therapy: Its current practice, implications, and theory*. Boston: Houghton Mifflin.

Rogers, C. (1961). *On becoming a person: A therapist's view of psychotherapy*. Boston: Houghton Mifflin.

Rogers, C. R. (1964). Toward a modern approach to values: The valuing process in the mature person. *Journal of Abnormal & Social Psychology, 68*, 160–167.

Rose, S. (1997). *Lifelines: Biology beyond determinism*. New York: Oxford University Press.

Rose, S. P. R. (1998). *Lifelines: Biology beyond determinism*. Oxford, NY: Oxford University Press.

Rowe, D. (1999). Heredity. In V. Derlega, B. Winstead, & W. Jones (Eds.), *Personality: Contemporary theory and research* (2nd ed., pp. 66–100). Chicago: Nelson Hall.

Rowe, D. C. (2001). Do people make environments or do environments make people? In A. Damasio, R. Antonio, A. Harrington, J. Kagan, B. McEwen, H. Moss, & R. Shaikh (Eds.), *Unity of knowledge: The convergence of natural and human science* (pp. 62–74). New York: Annals of the New York Academy of Sciences.

Runyan, W. M. (1997). Studying lives: Psychobiography and the conceptual structure of personality psychology. In R. Hogan, J. Johnson, & S. Briggs (Eds.), *Handbook of personality psychology*. (pp. 41–69). San Diego: Academic Press.

Ryan, R. M. (1995). Psychological needs and the facilitation of integrative processes. *Journal of Personality, 63,* 397–427.

Ryan, R. M., & Connell, J. P. (1989). Perceived locus of causality and internalization: Examining reasons for acting in two domains. *Journal of Personality and Social Psychology, 57,* 749–761.

Ryan, R. M., & Deci, E. L. (1999). Approaching and avoiding self-determination: Comparing cybernetic and organismic paradigms of motivation. In R. Wyer (Ed.), *Perspectives on behavioral self-regulation: Advances in social cognition* (Vol. XII, pp. 193–215). Mahwah, NJ: Lawrence Erlbaum Associates.

Ryan, R. M., & Deci, E. L. (2000). On happiness and human potentials: A review of research on hedonic and eudaimonic well-being. *Annual Review of Psychology, 52,* 141–166.

Ryan, R. M., Sheldon, K. M., Kasser, T., & Deci, E. L. (1996). All goals are not created equal: The relation of goal content and regulatory styles to mental health. In J. A. Bargh & P. M. Gollwitzer (Eds.), *The psychology of action: Linking cognition and motivation to behavior* (pp. 7–26). New York: Guilford.

Ryan, R. M., & Stiller, J. (1991). The social contexts of internalization: Parent and teacher influences on autonomy, motivation, and learning. *Advances in Motivation and Achievement, 7,* 115–149.

Ryff, C. D., & Keyes, C. L. M. (1995). The structure of psychological well-being revisited. *Journal of Personality & Social Psychology, 69,* 719–727.

Ryff, C. D., & Singer, B. (1998). The contours of positive human health. *Psychological Inquiry, 9,* 1–28.

Sartre, J. P. (1965). *Being and nothingness; An essay in phenomenological ontology* (Trans. H. E. Barnes). New York: Citadel Press.

Scarr, S., & McCartney, K. (1983). How people make their own environments: A theory of genotype ® environment effects. *Child Development, 54,* 424–435.

Sedikides, C., & Skowronski, J. J. (1997). The symbolic self in evolutionary context. *Personality & Social Psychology Review, 1,* 80–102.

Sedikides, C., Gaertner, L., & Toguchi, Y. (2003). Pancultural self-enhancement. *Journal of Personality & Social Psychology, 84,* 60–79.

Seife, C. (2003). *Alpha and omega: The search for the beginning and end of the universe.* New York: Viking Press.

Seligman, M. E. P. (1990). *Learned optimism.* New York: A. A. Knopf.

Seligman, M. E. P. (2002). *Authentic happiness.* New York: Free Press.

Seligman, M. E. P., & Csikszentmihalyi, M. (2000). Positive psychology: An introduction. *American Psychologist, 55,* 5–14.

Shah, J. Y., & Kruglanski, A. W. (2000). Aspects of goal networks: Implications for self-regulation. In M. Boekaerts & P. Pintrichs (Eds.), *Handbook of self-regulation* (pp. 85–110). San Diego: Academic Press.

Sheldon, K. M. (1995). Creativity and self-determination in personality. *Creativity Research Journal, 8,* 61–72.

Sheldon, K. M. (1999). Conformity and creativity. In M. Runco & S. Pritzker (Eds.), *Encyclopedia of creativity* (pp. 341–346). San Diego: Academic Press.

Sheldon, K. M. (1999). Learning the lessons of tit-for-tat: Even competitors can get the message. *Journal of Personality and Social Psychology, 77,* 1245–1253.

Sheldon, K. M. (2001). The self-concordance model of healthy goal-striving: Implications for well-being and personality development. In P. Schmuck & K. Sheldon (Eds.), *Life goals and well-being: Towards a positive psychology of human striving* (pp. 17–35). Seattle, WA: Hogrefe & Huber.

Sheldon, K. M. (2002). The self-concordance model of healthy goal-striving: When personal goals correctly represent the person. In E. L. Deci & R. M. Ryan (Eds.), *Handbook of self-determination research* (pp. 65–86). Rochester, NY: University of Rochester Press.

Sheldon, K. M. (in press). Positive value change during college: Normative trends and individual differences. *Journal of Research in Personality.*

Sheldon, K. M., Arndt, J., & Houser-Marko, L. (2003). In search of the organismic valuing process: The human tendency to move towards beneficial goal choices. *Journal of Personality, 71,* 835–869.

Sheldon, K. M. & Elliot, A. J. (1998). Not all personal goals are personal: Comparing autonomous and controlled reasons as predictors of effort and attainment. *Personality and Social Psychology Bulletin, 24,* 546–557.

Sheldon, K. M., & Elliot, A. J. (1999). Goal striving, need-satisfaction, and longitudinal well-being: The Self-Concordance Model. *Journal of Personality and Social Psychology, 76,* 482–497.

Sheldon, K. M., Elliot, A. J., Kim, Y., & Kasser, T. (2001). What's satisfying about satisfying events? Comparing ten candidate psychological needs. *Journal of Personality and Social Psychology, 80,* 325–339.

Sheldon, K. M., Elliot, A. J., Ryan, R. M., Chirkov, V., Kim, Y., Wu, C., Demir, M., & Sun, Z. (2004). Self-concordance and subjective well-being in four cultures. *Journal of Cross-Cultural Psychology, 35,* 209–233.

Sheldon, K. M., & Emmons, R. A. (1995). Comparing differentiation and integration within personal goal systems. *Personality and Individual Differences, 18,* 39–46.

Sheldon, K. M. & Houser-Marko, L. (2001). Self-concordance, goal-attainment, and the pursuit of happiness: Can there be an upward spiral? *Journal of Personality and Social Psychology, 80,* 152–165.

Sheldon, K. M., Joiner, T., Pettit, J., & Williams, G. (2003). Reconciling humanistic ideals and scientific clinical practice. *Clinical Psychology: Science and practice, 10,* 302–315.

Sheldon, K. M., & Kasser, T. (1995). Coherence and congruence: Two aspects of personality integration. *Journal of Personality and Social Psychology, 68,* 531–543.

Sheldon, K. M., & Kasser, T. (1998). Pursuing personal goals: Skills enable progress, but not all progress is beneficial. *Personality and Social Psychology Bulletin, 24,* 1319–1331.

Sheldon, K. M. & Kasser, T. (2001). Getting older, getting better? Personal strivings and personality development across the life-course. *Developmental Psychology, 37,* 491–501.

Sheldon, K. M., Kasser, T., Houser-Marko, L., & Jones, T. (2004). *Owning one's actions: Chronological age, internalized motivation, and subjective well-being.* Unpublished manuscript.

Sheldon, K. M., Kasser, T., Smith, K., & Share, T. (2002). Personal goals and psychological growth: Testing an intervention to enhance goal-attainment and personality integration. *Journal of Personality, 70,* 5–31.

Sheldon, K. M., & King, L. K. (2001). Why positive psychology is necessary. *American Psychologist, 56,* 216–217.

Sheldon, K. M., & Lyubomirsky, S. (2004). *Achieving sustainable happiness: Change your actions, not your circumstances.* Unpublished manuscript.

Sheldon, K. M., & Lyubomirsky, S. (in press). Achieving sustainable new happiness: Prospects, practices, and prescriptions. In A. Linley & A. Joseph (Eds.), *Positive psychology in practice.* New York: John Wiley & Sons.

Sheldon, K. M., & McGregor, H. (2000). Extrinsic value orientation and the "tragedy of the commons." *Journal of Personality, 68,* 383–411.

Sheldon, K. M., Ryan, R. M., Deci, E. L., & Kasser, T. (2004). The independent effects of goal contents and motives on well-being: It's both what you pursue *and* why you pursue it. *Personality and Social Psychology Bulletin, 30,* 475–486.

Sheldon, K. M., Ryan, R. M., Rawsthorne, L., & Ilardi, B. (1997). "True" self and "trait" self: Cross-role variation in the Big Five traits and its relations with authenticity and well-being. *Journal of Personality and Social Psychology, 73,* 1380–1393.

Sheldon, K. M., Ryan, R. M., & Reis, H. R. (1996). What makes for a good day? Competence and autonomy in the day and in the person. *Personality and Social Psychology Bulletin, 22,* 1270–1279.

Sheldon, K. M. & Schmuck, P. (2001). Conclusion: Suggestions for healthy goal striving. In P. Schmuck & K. Sheldon (Eds.), *Life goals and well-being: Towards a positive psychology of human striving* (pp. 213–226). Seattle, WA: Hogrefe & Huber.

Sheldon, K. M., Schmuck, P., & Kasser, T. (2000). Is value-free science possible? (commentary). *American Psychologist, 10,* 1152–1153.

Sheldon, K. M., Sheldon, M. S., & Osbaldiston, R. (2000). Prosocial values and group-assortation within an N-person prisoner's dilemma. *Human Nature, 11,* 387–404.

Sheldon, K. M., & Vansteenkiste, M. (in press). Personal goals and time-travel: How are future places visited, and is it worth it? To appear in A. Strathman & J. Joireman (Eds.), *Understanding behavior in the context of time: Theory, research, and applications in social, personality, health, and environmental psychology.*

Sheldon, K. M., Williams, G., & Joiner, T. (2003). *Self-determination theory in the clinic: Motivating physical and mental health.* New Haven, CT: Yale University Press.

Sheldon, W. (1940). *The varieties of human physique: An introduction to constitutional psychology.* New York: Harper.

Shweder, R. (1975). How relevant is an individual difference theory of personality? *Journal of Personality, 43,* 455–484.

Shweder, R. (2001). A polytheistic conception of the sciences and the virtues of deep variety. In A. Damasio, A. Harrington, J. Kagan, B. McEwen, H. Moss, & R. Shaikh (Eds.) *Unity of knowledge : the convergence of natural and human science* (pp. 217–232). New York: New York Academy of Sciences.

Sigmund, K. (1993). *Games of life: Explorations in ecology, evolution, and behaviour.* New York : Oxford University Press.

Simpson, E. H. (1951). The interpretation of interaction in contingency tables. *Journal of the Royal Statistical Society, 13,* 238–241.

Skinner, B. F. (1948). *Walden two.* New York: Macmillan.

Skinner, B. F. (1971). *Beyond freedom and dignity.* New York: Knopf.

Smith, E. A. (2000). Three styles in the evolutionary analysis of human behavior. In L. Cronk, N. Chagnon, & W. Irons (Eds.), *Adaptation and human behavior: An anthropological perspective* (pp. 27–48). New York: Aldine de Gruyter.

Smith, T. W., & Williams, P. G. (1992). Personality and health: Advantages and limitations of the five-factor model. *Journal of Personality, 60,* 395–423.

Sober, E., & Wilson, D. S. (1998). *Unto others: The evolution and psychology of unselfish behavior.* Cambridge, MA: Harvard University Press.

Sperry, R. W. (1988). Psychology's mentalist paradigm and the religion/science tension. *American Psychologist, 43,* 607–613.

Sperry, R. W. (1993). The impact and promise of the cognitive revolution. *American Psychologist, 48,* 878–885.

Srivastava, A., Locke, E. A., & Bartol, K. M. (2001). Money and subjective well-being: It's not the money, it's the motive. *Journal of Personality and Social Psychology, 80,* 959–971.

Steele, C. M. (1999). The psychology of self-affirmation: Sustaining the integrity of the self. In R. Baumeister (Ed.), *The self in social psychology. Key readings in social psychology.* (pp. 372–390). Philadelphia: Psychology Press.

Sternberg, R., & Lubart, T. (1995). *Defying the crowd.* New York: Free Press.

Stuss, D. T., & Levine, B. (2002). Adult clinical neuropsychology: Lessons from studies of the frontal lobes. *Annual Review of Psychology, 53,* 401–433.

Sugimoto, N. (1998). Norms of apology in U.S. American and Japanese literature on matters and etiquette. *International Journal of Intercultural Relations, 22,* 251–276.

Suh, E., Diener, E., Oishi, S., & Triandis, H. C. (1998). The shifting basis of life satisfaction judgments across cultures: Emotions versus norms. *Journal of Personality & Social Psychology, 74,* 482–493.

Swann, W. B., Jr. (2000). Identity negotiation: Where two roads meet. In E. T. Higgins & A. Kruglanski (Eds.), *Motivational science: Social and personality perspectives. Key reading in social psychology* (pp. 285–305). Philadelphia: Psychology Press.

Swim, J. K., Cohen, L. L., & Hyers, L. L. (1998). Experiencing everyday prejudice and discrimination. In J. Swim & C. Stangor (Eds.), *Prejudice: The target's perspective.* (pp. 37–60). San Diego, CA: Academic Press.

Tarnas, R. (1991). *The passion of the Western mind: Understanding the ideas that have shaped our world view.* New York: Harmony Books.

Tesser, A., Martin, L. L., & Cornell, D. P. (1996). On the substitutability of self-protective mechanisms. In P. Gollwitzer & J. Bargh (Eds.), *The psychology of action: Linking cognition and motivation to behavior* (pp. 48–68). New York: Guilford.

Thomas, A., & Chess, S. (1977). *Temperament and development.* New York: Bruner/Mazel.

Tice, D. M., Bratslavsky, E., & Baumeister, R. F. (2001). Emotional distress regulation takes precedence over impulse control: If you feel bad, do it! *Journal of Personality & Social Psychology, 80,* 53–67.

Tooby, J., & Cosmides, L. (1990, March). On the universality of human nature and the uniqueness of the individual: The role of genetics and adaptation. *Journal of Personality, 58,* 17–67.

Tooby, J., & Cosmides, L. (1992). The psychological foundations of culture. In J. Barkow & L. Cosmides (Eds.), *The adapted mind: Evolutionary psychology and the generation of culture* (pp. 19–136). New York : Oxford University Press.

Triandis, H. (1972). *The analysis of subjective culture.* New York: Wiley.

Triandis, H. (1995). *Individualism and collectivism.* Boulder, CO: Westview Press.

Triandis, H. (2001). Individualism and collectivism: Past, present, and future. In D. Matsumoto (Ed.), *The handbook of culture and psychology* (pp. 35–50). Oxford, UK: Oxford University Press

Trivers, R. (1971). The evolution of reciprocal altruism. *Quarterly Review of Biology, 46,* 35–57.

Tylor, E. B. (1889). *Primitive culture: Researches into the development of mythology, philosophy, religion, language, art, and custom.* New York: Holt.

Vaillant, G. (1977). *Adaptation to life.* Boston: Little, Brown.

Vallacher, R., & Nowak, A. (Eds.). (1994). *Dynamical systems in social psychology.* San Diego: Academic Press.

Van Lange, P. A. M., De Bruin, E. M. N., Otten, W., & Joireman, J. A. (1997). Development of prosocial, individualistic, and competitive orientations: Theory and preliminary evidence. *Journal of Personality & Social Psychology, 73*, 733–746.

Waterman, A. S. (1993). Two conceptions of happiness: Contrasts of personal expressiveness (eudaimonia) and hedonic enjoyment. *Journal of Personality & Social Psychology, 64*(4), 678–691.

Watson, D., & Walker, L. (1996). The long-term stability and predictive validity of trait measures of affect. *Journal of Personality and Social Psychology, 70*, 567–577.

Wegner, D. M. (2002). *The illusion of conscious will.* Cambridge, MA: MIT Press.

Wegner, D. M., & Wheatley, T. (1999). Apparent mental causation: Sources of the experience of will. *American Psychologist, 54*, 480–492.

Weiner, B. (1992). *Human motivation: Metaphors, theories, and research.* Newbury Park, CA: Sage.

Wilensky, R. (1983). *Planning and understanding: A computational approach to human reasoning.* Reading, MA: Addison-Wesley.

Wilson, D. S. (2002). *Darwin's cathedral: Evolution, religion, and the nature of society.* Chicago: University of Chicago Press.

Wilson, D. S., & Sober, E. (1994). Re-introducing group-selection to the human behavioral sciences. *Behavioral and Brain Sciences, 17*, 585–654.

Wilson, D. S., Wilczynski, C., Wells, A., & Weiser, L. (2000). Gossip and other aspects of language as group-level adaptations. In C. Heyes & L. Huber (Eds.), *The evolution of cognition. Vienna series in theoretical biology* (pp. 347–365). Cambridge, MA: MIT Press.

Wilson, E. O. (1978). *On human nature.* Cambridge, MA: Harvard University Press.

Wilson, E. O. (1998). *Consilience: The unity of knowledge.* New York: Alfred A. Knopf.

Wilson, E. O. (2001). How to unify knowledge. In A. Damasio, R. Antonio, A. Harrington, J. Kagan, B. McEwen, H. Moss, & R. Shaikh (Eds.), *Unity of knowledge: The convergence of natural and human science* (pp. 12–17). New York: New York Academy of Sciences.

Wilson, T. D. (2002). *Strangers to ourselves: Discovering the adaptive unconscious.* Cambridge, MA: Belknap Press/Harvard University Press.

Wilson, T. D., Lindsey, S., & Schooler, T. (2000). A model of dual attitudes. *Psychological Review, 107*, 101–126.

Winnicott, D. W. (1957). *Mother and child: A primer of first relationships.* New York: Basic Books.

Wu, J., & Axelrod, R. (1995). How to cope with noise in the iterated prisoner's dilemma. *Journal of Conflict Resolution, 39*, 183–189.

Wynne-Edwards, V. (1962). *Animal dispersion in relation to social behavior.* Edinburgh: Oliver and Boyd.

Yalom, I. D. (1995). *The theory and practice of group psychotherapy.* New York: Basic Books.

Yamagishi, T. (1986). The provision of a sanctioning system as a public good. *Journal of Personality & Social Psychology, 51*, 110–116.

Zuckerman, M. (1991). *Psychobiology of personality.* Cambridge, England: Cambridge University Press.

Author Index

Note: a number followed by a *f* indicates a figure

A

Abramson, L. Y., 59
Alexander, R., 166, 167, 169, 175
Allik, J., 93
Allport, G., 21, 74, 75, 82, 125, 126, 128
Alpert, R., 4
Amabile, T. M., 172, 173
Angleitner, A., 90
Apter, M. J., 91, 186
Argyle, M., 104
Arndt, J., 64, 67, 104, 110, 135, 138, 198
Atkinson, J., 82
Atran, S., 170
Aunger, R., 170
Avia, M. D., 90
Axelrod, R., 57, 144, 147, 148, 149, 153, 156, 158, 188

B

Baard, P. 63
Baars, B., 120
Bacon, S., 7, 90
Baird, E., 112, 192
Banaji, M. R., 83
Bardone, A. M., 59
Bargh, J. A., 97, 118

Barlow, C., 16, 19, 24
Barndollar, K., 97
Bartol, K. M., 112, 192
Baumeister, R. F., 7, 71, 123, 128, 129, 135, 155, 193
Becker, E., 64
Benedict, R., 65
Bettencourt, B., 70, 160, 189
Biddle, B. J., 158, 159
Biel, A., 145
Bingham, P., 168, 175, 176
Blackmore, S., 170
Blasi, A., 117, 120, 121, 123, 126, 130, 197
Block, J., 10
Bond, M., 174
Borkowski, W., 118, 123, 126
Boyd, R., 170, 171, 176
Brandon, R. N., 41
Bratslavsky, E., 135
Brehm, J. W., 118
Brewer, M., 146
Brickman, P., 93
Briggs, S., 88
Brown, D. E., 15, 54, 55, 186
Brown, D. R., 63
Brown, J., 117
Bruins, J. J., 145
Brunstein, J., 107

221

Subject Index

Note: a number followed by a *f* indicates a figure

A

Action systems, *see also* Control-theory model of action
  environment and, 38–39
  future images in, 37, 97
  as holistic, 39
  negentropy in, 38–39, 42, 187
  regulation of, 136, 184f, 187
  self-images in, 37, 38
  as self-programmed, 42, 43
  source of goals in, 42
  top-down organization of, 17f, 23, 36f, 190–191
  vertical coherence, 47f, 196f, 99–100, 102, 190, 191, 195
Agreeableness, 87, 88, 89, 90, 91, 184f, 186
Allison scenario
  arousal regulation in, 186
  causal role of traits, 74, 76
  fundamental attribution error in, 74
  gene-environment influences in, 80, 85
  goal-setting in, 89, 195
  self-awareness in, 92
  trait profile of, 73–74, 84
  variations in trait behaviors in, 74, 88, 89

Alpert, Richard, 4
Altruism, *see also* Cooperation; Game theory; Groups; Reciprocal altruism
  aging and, 110
  charitable giving, 147, 148
  group selection and, 57, 60, 68, 147, 149–153, 168, 175–177
  reciprocal altruism theory, 147, 148, 151
  the selfish gene, 149
Ambivalence, 100–101
Anger, 17f, 23
Anthropology, 25, 30, 65–66, 165–166
Attachment style, 47, 83
Autonomy
  adaptive processes, 70
  behavior, 104
  creativity, 173
  culture, 70
  goals and, 104, 173
  intrinsic motivation, 173, 193
  need satisfaction of, 200
  personality, 173
  role internalization support, 161, 163, 184f, 185, 189
  in SDT (self-determination theory), 70, 173, 193, 200

action system functions in, 34, 35, 43
consilience in, 41, 42
criticisms of, 42
decision making in, 37–38
discrepancy reduction, 37
goals in, 42, 43, 98, 102, 187
as holistic, 39, 42, 48, 190
as mechanistic, 40–41
negative feedback loop, 37
personality model and, 48
reductionism and, 39, 40
self-images in, 36*f*, 37, 48
teleology of, 34, 39, 40, 42, 190
vertical coherence, 41, 201
Cooperation, *see also* Collectivism head-
    ings; Culture; Game theory
    cheater-detection mechanism, 56–57,
        58, 60, 68, 148, 149, 151,
        155
    coalition enforcement, 168, 176
    collectivism, 175
    competition, 156, 157, 176, 188
    defection and, 146–147, 148, 149, 153,
        154
    exploitation, 58, 87, 148, 153–154,
        155, 184*f*, 185, 188
    failure of, 157–158
    forgiveness and, 149, 151, 153, 184*f*,
        185, 188
    free riders and, 57, 147, 149, 153, 168,
        175, 176
    in groups, 60–61, 68, 71, 149–154*f*
    kin selection theory, 147
    life experiences and, 156, 157
    niceness, 149, 153, 184*f*, 185, 188
    prisoner's dilemma, 146–147, 153
    reciprocal altruism theory in, 147, 148,
        151
    relatedness, 193
    risks in, 147, 149, 151, 153
    selection for, 168–169
    the selfish gene, 149
    social brain hypothesis, 167, 168
    social loafing, 175
    in tit-for-tat strategy, 148–149,
        153–154, 157–158
Coping strategies, 64, 85
Cross-cultural theory, 118, 174
Cultural anthropologists
    on cognitive psychology, 165–166
    on cultural universals, 65–66
Cultural evolution

coalition enforcement, 168, 176
conformist transmission mechanism,
    171
genetic evolution, 166, 170
memetic evolution, 170
personal-level factors in, 173
social brain hypothesis, 166–167, 168
Cultural selection
    group selection and, 57, 60, 68, 147,
        149–153, 168, 175–177
    memetic evolution, 170
    psychological selection, 172
    social brain hypothesis and, 166–167,
        168
Culture, *see also* Genetics; Heritability
    autonomy in, 70
    behaviors in, 17*f*, 66–67
    Big Five model of personality and, 55,
        84
    biology and, 66
    conformist transmission theory, 171,
        172
    countercultural activity, 180–181, 184*f*,
        185, 189, 191, 199*f*
    cultural relativism, 15–16
    definitions of, 164–165, 167
    "fundamental attribution error," 17*f*, 29
    group minding in, 167, 171
    individual creativity in, 172
    intercultural diffusion, 181
    memes in, 169–170, 172, 180
    mental representations of, 165
    personal narratives, 131, 132, 135
    psychology and, 66
    racism, 15–16, 18, 22
    resistance to, 180–181
    self-choice, 17*f*, 29
    sociobiological reductionism, 170–171
    SSSM (standard social science model),
        15, 52, 56, 61–62, 165
    stability of, 17*f*, 23
    universals in, 55, 65–67, 70–71, 156,
        157
    violence in, 22, 29, 179–180
Cybernetic control theory, 10

D

Darwin, Charles, 56, 176
Death awareness, 134–135, 137
Defection